The Sport Star

Theory, Culture & Society

Theory, Culture & Society caters for the resurgence of interest in culture within contemporary social science and the humanities. Building on the heritage of classical social theory, the book series examines ways in which this tradition has been reshaped by a new generation of theorists. It also publishes theoretically informed analyses of everyday life, popular culture, and new intellectual movements.

EDITOR: Mike Featherstone, *Nottingham Trent University*

SERIES EDITORIAL BOARD
Roy Boyne, *University of Durham*
Mike Hepworth, *University of Aberdeen*
Scott Lash, *Goldsmiths College, University of London*
Roland Robertson, *University of Aberdeen*
Bryan S. Turner, *University of Singapore*

THE TCS CENTRE
The *Theory, Culture & Society* book series, the journals *Theory, Culture & Society* and Body & Society, and related conference, seminar and postgraduate programmes operate from the TCS Centre at Nottingham Trent University. For further details of the TCS Centre's activities please contact:

Centre Administrator
The TCS Centre, Room 175
Faculty of Humanities
Nottingham Trent University
Clifton Lane, Nottingham, NG11 8NS, UK
e-mail: tcs@ntu.ac.uk
web: http://tcs.ntu.ac.uk

Recent volumes include:

The Body and Social Theory
Chris Shilling

Religion, Realism and Social Theory
Phillip A. Mellor

The Body in Culture, Technology and Society
Chris Shilling

Globalization and Belonging
Mike Savage, Gaynor Bagnall, Brian Longhurst

The Sport Star

Modern Sport and the Cultural Economy of Sporting Celebrity

Barry Smart

SAGE Publications
London ● Thousand Oaks ● New Delhi

First published 2005

Published in association with Theory, Culture & Society,
Nattingham Trent University

SAGE Publications Ltd
1 Oliver's Yard
55 City Road
London EC1Y 1SP

SAGE Publications Inc.
2455 Teller Road
Thousand Oaks, California 91320

SAGE Publications India Pvt Ltd
B-42, Panchsheel Enclave
Post Box 4109
New Delhi 110 017

British Library Cataloguing in Publication data

A catalogue record for this book is
available from the British Library

ISBN 0 7619 4350 1
ISBN 0 7619 4351 X (pbk)

Library of Congress control number: 2004099484

Typeset by C&M Digital (P) Ltd., Chennai, India
Printed in India by Gopsons Papers Ltd, Noida

Contents

Acknowledgements

These go first to my late father who introduced me to the pleasure of both playing and watching sport and to my son George who has continued the family tradition by playing competitive sport and enthusiastically supporting Arsenal Football Club. Then to colleagues and postgraduate and undergraduate students at the Universities of Sheffield, Auckland, and Portsmouth respectively who provided me with valuable opportunities to discuss my work on sport and offered helpful comments and criticisms as it progressed. I greatly value my longstanding association with the journal *Theory, Culture & Society* and it is appropriate that my research on modern sport and the culture of celebrity should be published in the TCS book series.

Finally I would like to express my gratitude to Chris Rojek for his editorial support and encouragement with this project and to Kay Bridger, Mila Steele and Ian Antcliff for their assistance with the publication process.

1

Heroism, Fame and Celebrity in the World of Sport

The popularity of sport

Sport is now at the heart of contemporary culture and in the words of one commercially interested observer seems destined to 'define the culture of the world' (Phil Knight, founder and chairman of *Nike* corporation, cited in Katz 1994: 199). The importance of sport has long been recognised. Early in the twentieth century, Walter Camp, widely acknowledged to be the father of American football, is reputed to have described sport as '"the broad folk highway" of the nation' (Pope 1997: 3). Sport is recognised to be one of the key cultural institutions involved in the constitution of national identity. It is also of vital economic importance, sport-related economic activity in England being identified by Mass Observation in 1939 as 'the biggest English industry' and by the Henley Centre in 1985 as 'the sixth largest employment sector' (Mason 1989: 10; Kuper 2003: 147–148).

Sport is exceptionally popular around the world and sporting figures, sport teams and sport events are particularly prominent in the media. As one analyst has observed, sport is located in a 'deep area of the collective sensibility' (Eco 1987: 160), it is an activity whose popularity and appeal cuts across all manner of social and political divisions. High profile sporting figures are generally well known and popular across the social spectrum. Sportsmen and to a lesser extent sportswomen appear regularly on television, in magazines, and in the press, not solely because of their sporting prowess, but in addition because of their acquired fame, achieved 'star' quality and/or attributed 'celebrity' status.

The popularity and prominence of sporting figures is by no means a recent phenomenon. From the beginning of modern sport in the nineteenth century there have been numerous sporting heroes. A wide range of individuals by virtue of their skill, the quality of their technique and the manner of their performance in sporting competition have been accorded special recognition by both the public and the media (Huntington-Whitely 1999). Acknowledgement of the distinctiveness of individual players, of specific sportsmen and sportswomen, as well as of particular feats or performances, has been virtually synonymous with the emergence and development of modern sport. In 1865 in England a very young W. G. Grace (1848–1915) played cricket for the Gentlemen for the first time. In a subsequent series of matches against the Players beginning in 1871 he achieved totals of 217,

77, 112, 163, 158 and 70 in consecutive innings. Through his performances W. G. Grace transformed the game of cricket.

Reflecting on W. G. Grace's contribution to the game as a whole the historian C. L. R. James observes that the 'whole imposing structure and organisation of first-class cricket' can be traced to him. He was a very popular figure, crowds of people went to see him play, 'they cheered him on the field [and] they walked behind him in the street' (James 1969: 180). W. G. Grace held a special place in the lives of people in Victorian England, he was a great popular hero who received 'the spontaneous, unqualified … enthusiasm and goodwill of a whole community' (James 1969: 182). Recalling the celebrations that followed W. G. Grace's hundredth hundred, celebrations that exemplified the wider cultural significance of sport, James asks what other occasion could produce 'such enthusiasm, such an unforced sense of community, of the universal merged in an individual?' (1969: 182). W. G. Grace was not just a great cricket player he was also an historic figure, an individual who helped establish the game of cricket as a national institution in England. In short he was a British sporting hero (Holt 1999).

The achievement of popularity through sporting prowess was not peculiar to cricket or confined to W. G. Grace as the comments of an observer of late-nineteenth-century 'football mania' in England reveal. Charles Edwardes writing in 1892 describes how professional football players in the North of England became 'the objects of adoration' in their neighbourhoods. Supporters regularly went to train stations to see their teams leave for away matches as well as to welcome them back on their return. They expressed their adoration by being ready to 'cheer them with affectionate heartiness, or condole with them and solace them with as much beer as … their trainer will allow them to accommodate' (Edwardes 1992: 8). At the close of the nineteenth century, professional footballers were already better known than local MPs, their photographs were displayed in shops, and it was said that 'they cannot move in their native streets without receiving ovations enough to turn the head of a Prime Minister' (1992: 8). Even at this relatively early stage in the development of the professional game it was recognised that professional footballers were becoming 'marketable goods', that their wages would rise 'much higher than they are at present' (1992: 9) and that there would be increasing scope for agents to act as mediators between players and club committees.

There are many other examples of individual sports men and women receiving wide public acclaim for their performances in sports competition. In American sport in the 1920s a number of individuals came to the fore. 'Babe' Ruth (1895–1948) was enthusiastically acclaimed for his baseball feats, Red Grange (1904–1991), an American footballer, was hailed as the 'Galloping Ghost of the Grid-iron', and Jack Dempsey (1895–1983) acquired a heroic status for his fighting skills in the boxing ring (Rader 1983a). In Europe and America a young French female tennis player, Suzanne Lenglen (1899–1938), became a celebrated figure, but not only for ability expressed on the court, which allowed her to dominate the

Wimbledon tournament from 1919 to 1926. She was reputed to hit the ball very hard, 'like a man', and was regarded as very fit. It was also alleged that she was 'high-strung, hot-tempered and imperial in manner' and that she led a 'racy private life' (Bouchier and Findling 1983: 230–231). But there was something else, an early trace of the baggage associated with appearance that subsequently many women in sport have had to carry with them. Suzanne Lenglen was considered to be the first female tennis player to wear a tennis costume that was not full in length and her clothing has been described as 'colorful and sensual' (Bouchier and Findling 1983). Being French, wearing a skirt that ended just below the knee, and achieving success in tennis by playing the game in a manner that set her apart from most other women of the time ensured that she would be a well-known, if controversial figure (Inglis 1977; Cashmore 2000).

Heroism in sport

In a number of respects another tennis player of the era, the American Helen Wills (1905–98), represents a comparable figure to Suzanne Lenglen. Wills based her game on hard serves and powerful ground strokes. Her preference was to practice by playing against male players. Her reputation and stature soared when at the age of seventeen she won her first US women's singles title (1923) and began to be regarded by sport writers as the 'great American hope', the one who might 'dethrone Suzanne Lenglen' (Bouchier and Findling (1983: 230). In 1926 Lenglen played Wills in a winter tennis tournament held on the French Riviera. In the match Lenglen won 6–3, 8–6 and then later in the year turned professional leaving Wills to become the 'unchallenged champion' of the women's game for a number of years (1927–33). Helen Wills has been described as an 'authentic American sports heroine', an individual who was not only a winner but a player with style, someone who came to prominence in an era in which organised sports were coming to the fore in America (Bouchier and Findling 1983: 233).

In the period following the First World War there was an unusually high level of hero-worship in America. It has been suggested that this reflected not only the celebrity-fabricating impact of the new media of popular culture (film, radio and mass-circulation magazines) but also the responses of people seeking escape from the forms of disillusionment and disorganisation that followed the end of the war. American soldiers returning from the First World War were disillusioned with the people and culture of Europe and there was a marked increase in nationalistic fervour. Heroic figures, seemingly representing simpler virtues, provided solace for a people whose faith had been shaken by the passage of events and whose lives had been disturbed by rapid economic and technological changes. In this period organised sport became a significant cultural phenomenon. During the First World War increased emphasis was placed on the military benefits of sport. There was also a significant growth in college sports and in the aftermath of the war there was a marked increase in leisure activities and the pursuit of pleasure. These changes coupled with a commensurate expansion of sport journalism led inexorably to unprecedented attention being devoted to sport personalities. This was the context in which Helen Wills came to prominence as a cultural hero and leading sporting figures as a whole grew in stature and cultural significance.

Between 1923 and 1938 Helen Wills won eight Wimbledon singles and three doubles titles, seven US National singles and four doubles championships, as well as four French National tournaments, plus numerous other less prestigious tournament titles, as well as gold medals for singles and doubles at the 1924 Olympics. On court Wills dressed modestly, played a 'power game', displayed intense concentration, and appeared impassive and imperturbable, hence her nickname, 'Little Miss Poker Face'. Off court she was described as 'pleasant, articulate and interested in the world around her' and as 'unostentatious' (Bouchier and Findling 1983). In the 1920s tennis was the most international of organised sports and the successes achieved by Wills were major events in America. By 1938, when she retired, Wills' fame had begun to decline, her 'star qualities had faded' and she became a forgotten hero (Bouchier and Findling 1983: 239).

In discussions of heroism in sport and the respects in which sport may replenish the moral spirit, without which community risks becoming merely a hollow abstraction, the contribution of American golfer Bobby Jones (1902–71), 'the immortal amateur', is frequently acknowledged to be of significance (Ford 1977: 51; Porter 1983). In an obituary broadcast in one of his *Letters from America* in 1972 Alistair Cooke remarked that 'the twenties were the last decade when the idea of style was essential to the conception of a sporting hero' (quoted in Inglis 1977: 83). For Cooke 'style' was exemplified by the 'effortless grace' of the golfer Bobby Jones who won the British and American Open Championships as well as the British and American Amateur tournaments in the same year (1930) and then retired from tournament play. Cooke comments that long before his 'Grand Slam' achievement Bobby Jones was well known in America and Britain, not simply for his golfing ability but for the way in which he conducted himself. Describing Jones as an easy-going and modest individual, who had 'great grace and ... remained an amateur' throughout his career, Cooke adds that he was one of the few sporting heroes who became 'famous even to people who knew and cared little about golf' (quoted in Inglis 1977: 84–85).

Bobby Jones was certainly a famous figure and his fame has endured. However, while Jones's achievements on the golf course and his reputation for 'unfailing sportsmanship' are legendary, Cooke's celebration of Jones's sporting style and prowess omits any mention of the fact that Jones was also 'known for being a racist' (Billings 2000: 418). It is now acknowledged that until relatively recently overt racism has been a prominent feature of golf in America (Sinnette 1998). Indeed from 1934 to 1961 the constitution of the Professional Golfers Association 'explicitly limited that organization's membership to "Professional golfers of the Caucasian race"' (Owen 2001: 179).

It took the emergence of golfing phenomenon Tiger Woods and in particular a *Nike* advertising campaign in 1996 that deliberately emphasised the issue of race to draw public attention to the history of discrimination in the sport (Goldman and Papson 1998; Sinnette 1998; Rosaforte 2002).

There is a strong sense in Alastair Cooke's remarks about Bobby Jones that sport, for a time at least, has constituted a repository of concepts and ideas 'which have been central to our morality' (Inglis 1977: 85). Sport has been accorded a special moral quality, has been credited with a potential capacity for nurturing 'the natural impulses of generosity, elation, heroism, grace, [and] decorum' (Inglis 1977: 35). However the impression has also been conveyed that the influences to which sport and sporting figures became increasingly subject in the course of the twentieth century eroded, if they did not undermine completely, the moral value of sport and the prospect of genuine sporting 'heroism' (Hoch 1972). Certainly the mythology of the sporting hero exemplified by Neville Cardus's narratives on early-twentieth-century cricket and the heroic feats of aristocratic gentlemen and yeoman peasants seem to have little relevance to the professional, media-savvy world of contemporary sport. The 'casual' heroism considered to be exemplified by Bobby Jones and his achievement of the Grand Slam are described by Alistair Cooke as unlikely to be repeated 'because today golf … has turned into a money-making industry and the smart young amateurs go at it like navvies' (quoted in Inglis 1977: 84).

Questioning whether there can be any place for 'effortless grace' in a world of sport that has been radically transformed by increasing professionalism, heightened competition and a dramatic rise in the level of direct and indirect financial reward is justified. Contemporary sportsmen and sportswomen do need to apply themselves to their increasingly competitive sporting endeavours with diligence, maximum effort and unremitting discipline. While there may still be elegance and beauty of movement or expression in sport, as competition has increased in intensity there has been a marked reduction in goodwill shown towards opponents. Displays of propriety and consideration for others are now more the exception than the rule. With increasing professionalism and growing commercialism sport has indeed become more serious (Huizinga 1949). It has become an industry, a business, and sportsmen and sportswomen are in consequence required to be more businesslike in their approach to preparation, practice and performance. Making money is now an important part of sport and professional participants have to work hard at their games because it is their job to do so.

However, the idea that epic sporting achievements are unlikely to be repeated is very controversial and in respect of golf, as well as a number of other popular sports such as basketball, football and tennis, contemporary evidence suggests the contrary may well be the case. Certainly there are a good many analysts who consider the feats in 2000/2001 of the American professional golfer Tiger Woods to be 'heroic' and more than comparable to the achievements of Bobby Jones in 1930. Winning the US Open, the US

Amateur, the British Open and the British Amateur tournaments in 1930 Bobby Jones achieved the 'Grand Slam', golf's 'Impregnable Quadrilateral' (Rosaforte 2002: 167). In 2001 Woods became the first ever to hold all four professional major championships at the same time. Woods won the PGA, as well as the US and British Open Championships in 2000 and while still holding these he won the Masters tournament in 2001, achieving what has been called the 'Tiger Slam'. Comparison of the achievements of the two players is made difficult by the fact that the four major golf championships won by Jones in 1930 are 'not the same four that are considered to be the majors today' (Owen 2001: 197). Nevertheless, comparisons have been made and *Sports Illustrated* has described Tiger Woods's feat as 'the greatest stretch of dominance in golf history' (Rosaforte 2002: 369).

Making comparisons over time between competitors from different eras, who are in many respects playing a different game, if developments in technique, technology and terrain, not to mention increased pressure of competition are taken into account, has been described as a potentially 'treacherous' yet 'irresistible' practice (Owen 2001). Is it appropriate to make comparisons that cannot effectively take historical and cultural differences into account? How would Bobby Jones have fared in match play with Tiger Woods? As one analyst has noted,

> Equipment evolves, playing conditions change, and the ambitions and expectations of the players themselves cannot be extricated from the times in which they live. In Jones's day, no golfer made a living from tournament purses; all the great players, whether amateurs ... or professionals ... necessarily spent most of their time and energy doing something else – going to school and practising law in Jones's case. (Owen 2001: 197)

Had Jones been born later he might, as Owen suggests, have applied himself exclusively to the game and reached even greater heights, then again he might have 'been overwhelmed by the depth of talent in the modern professional tour and given up' (Owen 2001: 197). We will never know.

Recognition of the different historical and cultural circumstances in which sporting figures performed and the impossibility of determining the effect of differences on performances has not brought an end to comparisons. To the contrary the growing cultural prominence of sport has led to a proliferation of comparative narratives on sporting performances and sporting heroes. Undoubtedly an important part of the appeal of sport, a significant part of its cultural popularity, is that it licenses nostalgic narratives recalling heroes of the past and outstanding performances. Sport is a powerful source of vivid images and compelling narratives about heroes and heroic deeds that provide a 'scrapbook of memories that define a life' (Inglis 1977: 2) and constitute a history that contributes to our sense community. If heroes are 'the products of their period' (Holt and Mangan 1996: 5), the narratives on heroic sporting figures are no less products of their time.

Undoubtedly a great deal has changed in the world of sport as professionalism, commerce, sponsorship and the increasing prominence of the media, and television in particular, have made a significant impact on sporting figures and events. The ways in which sport is played, and its social and cultural status and significance have been dramatically transformed. The profile of sport has been raised considerably. Sport is now an increasingly prominent feature on the news agenda. No longer confined to the back pages of the press, sport-related stories appear throughout newspapers and in special inserts and magazines devoted entirely to the subject and associated issues. On radio and television sport occupies a prominent, in some instances pivotal position in programming schedules. Sport is now a business and in many respects it is almost indistinguishable from show business. Sport has become an integral part of the entertainment industry and high profile sporting figures have acquired fame and are accorded the status of stars and celebrities.

On fame and its acquisition

The state of being widely known was very different before the twentieth century and the development of mass circulation means of communication. The advent of mass circulation newspapers followed by radio and then, perhaps most significantly, television had a major impact on the acquisition and attribution of fame. Before the 'graphic revolution', that is the 'ability to make, preserve, transmit and disseminate precise images' (Boorstin 1963: 24), to become well known it was generally necessary to have demonstrated greatness in deed or action. With the development of mechanical means of image production and dissemination fame began to be manufactured as the media fabricated 'well-knownness'. The 'electronic revolution' (McLuhan 1973) and the development of television in particular led to a marked increase in the speed of image production and dissemination and to the emergence of a new kind of eminence, 'celebrity'. Where do heroes now stand? What has become of the hero in an age of celebrity? Does the rise of the celebrity signify the demise of the hero?

The capacity to make and present vivid images of events developed rapidly from the late nineteenth century. The ability to make and transmit news and images of greater precision and with increasing rapidity gathered momentum following the development of dry-plate photography in the 1870s, roll film in 1884, radio transmission from 1900 and the commercial development of television from the 1940s (Boorstin 1963). The development of television in the decades following the Second World War led to communications media being 'restructured and reorganised in a system' (Castells 1996: 330) at the cultural epicentre of which was television. In America in 1947 there were around 14,000 sets; in 1948, 172,000; and by 1950, 4 million. By 1954 there were 32 million sets and before the end of that decade 90 per cent of American homes had a television (Gamson 1992: 20 n8). Now it is a question of how many televisions each household possesses.

With the development and growing influence of television a culture of 'entertainment' has become increasingly prominent. The predominant assumption is that whatever the programme, whatever the content, if it is on television 'it is there for our amusement and pleasure' (Postman 1985: 87). Increasingly television sets the agenda and influences the terms in which events and processes, 'from politics to business, including sport and art' (Castells 1996: 336), are communicated within contemporary society. The impact of the information technology revolution on media and communications has further enhanced the capacity to deliver vivid images of individuals and events in real-time around the globe. Satellite and digital television, computer technology and the Internet have developed and considerably extended the capacity to make, transmit and disseminate images. Sports and sporting teams now have their own websites and there are a growing number of sites related to individual sportsmen and sportswomen.

Considering the impact of a quantitatively increased and qualitatively enhanced media capacity to manufacture and disseminate images Boorstin remarks that 'Two centuries ago when a great man appeared, people looked for God's purpose in him; *today we look for his ... agent*' (1963: 55, emphasis added). In the past fame, or being famous, tended to be associated with greatness, but this no longer may be the case. Actions and deeds may continue to be so regarded, but now fame may be acquired in other ways. There is no shortage of well-known individuals, of figures who are perceived, and who would claim, to be famous, for whom 'greatness' seems to be an entirely absent quality. Fame may still reside in greatness of deed or achievement, but it has also become a product or creation of media representation. In a culture dominated by media-image dissemination,

> The household names, the famous men who populate our consciousness are with few exceptions not heroes at all, but an artificial product ... We can fabricate fame, we can at will ... make a man or woman well known; but we cannot make him great. We can make a celebrity, but we can never make a hero. (Boorstin 1963: 58)

The implication is that celebrity-worship may be mistaken for hero-worship and that in so far as this is the case we risk 'depriving ourselves of all real models' (Boorstin 1963: 58).

The media construct celebrity individuals and effectively place them on a pedestal in the course of attempting to accord them something akin to heroic status. After an indeterminate period, in which such celebrity individuals tend to be excessively feted, it is frequently the case that the media machine turns its attention to reports on the shortcomings and misdemeanours of the very same celebrities. In short, the celebrity as role model is both made and undone by press and television coverage. These newly elevated individuals, in whom greatness is a noticeably absent quality, have been described as 'marketable human models – modern "heroes" – ... mass-produced to satisfy the market' (Boorstin 1963: 58). Such figures, while achieving the status of 'nationally advertised brand', are argued to represent 'a new category of human emptiness', they are at best little more than hollow heroes (Boorstin 1963: 58).

The diversity of media available to people and the proliferation of narratives outlining the acts and achievements of individuals means that accounts of exceptional endeavours and of potential claims to greatness have to vie for attention with a plethora of competing texts. Exposed to a range of communications media we are continually confronted by representations of numerous individuals, their names and their faces, as well as the actions and events with which they are reported to be associated. In consequence the potentially truly exceptional figure is inclined to get lost in a sea of mediocrity, to be obscured from view by the deluge of celebrity images and narratives to which routinely we find ourselves exposed.

Sport represents one of the most significant remaining institutional sites for popular cultural recognition and acclaim of exceptional performance and prowess, if not the most prominent context in which the deeds of participants continue to retain authenticity. In the case of sport it is evident that it is not so much that there are no more heroes, but that historic heroic figures and their later modern equivalents are now in the shadow of a new and far more vivid species, the celebrity.

Celebrity

As the twentieth century unfolded, a new kind of eminence known as 'celebrity' emerged. In a critical study of the process of celebrity formation Chris Rojek (2001) argues that the emergence of celebrity is a consequence of three inter-connected historical processes:

1   the democratisation of society
2   the decline of organised religion
3   the commodification of everyday life

There has been a relative shift of emphasis from the reverence and deference shown to traditional establishment institutional figures (court society, monarchy and aristocracy) to a public display of interest in, identification with and expression of awe towards a new species, 'celebrities'. The quality of being 'sacred' is no longer confined to organised religion and in a secular society reverence and awe are 'attached to mass-media celebrities who become objects of cult worship' (Rojek 2001: 53). Lastly, the formation of a culture of celebrity is closely articulated with the development of a culture of commodity consumption.

The implication is that we both consume celebrities and are reconstituted as subjects of consumption by them. Celebrities are commodities to which consumers are drawn as they engage in the process of commodity consumption. Consumers are encouraged in various ways to identify with celebrities and the images and life-styles with which they are associated in press, magazine and television reports and advertising. A graphic illustration is provided by *Gatorade's* advertising campaign featuring the American basketball legend Michael Jordan, which exhorted the consumer to 'Be like Mike' by drinking their sport beverage.

Sport stars are increasingly being employed to endorse, help promote and market consumer commodities. For example, American golfer Tiger Woods has been a spokesperson for the *American Express* brand and has appeared in commercials for the Japanese company *Asahi's* canned coffee drink, *Wonda*. Woods has also featured in promotional campaigns for everything from breakfast cereals (*Wheaties*) and cars (*Buick*) to watches (*TAGHeuer*) and laser eye surgery (*TLC Laser Eye Centers*). English footballer David Beckham has a range of commercial commitments including modelling *Police* sunglasses, designing clothing for the *adidas 'DB'* range and appearing in commercials for the soft drink manufacturer *Pepsi* and razor company *Gillette*. The highly successful American tennis player Venus Williams is contracted to promote *Reebok* clothing and sports goods. Less successful on the court, Russian tennis star Anna Kournikova has been very much a winner off of it by being awarded very lucrative commercial contracts with a variety of companies, including *adidas, Berlei, Yonex, Omega* and *Lycos*.

'Michael Jordan', not the biological being, but the social and cultural signifier that has become a brand, most clearly exemplifies the way in which within sport 'celebrity culture is irrevocably bound up with commodity culture' (Rojek 2001: 14). Without doubt Jordan has demonstrated extraordinary skill as a basketball player and his exceptional performances not only transformed the game of basketball but in addition 'catapulted Nike to branded heaven' (Klein 2001: 52). In turn, however, Jordan gained enormously from being associated with *Nike* and not simply in financial terms. In 1984 *Nike* put all their advertising resources into one basket and made Jordan their 'signature athlete'. The rest, as the saying goes, is history. Reflecting a few years later on the success of the association Jordan commented that what 'Nike has done ... is to turn me into a dream' (quoted in Halberstam 2001: 183). The various *Nike* advertising campaigns from the 1985 'Jordan Flight' commercials onwards contributed significantly to the process by which Jordan was transformed from a major basketball talent into a global superstar, celebrity figure and commercial brand (Goldman and Papson 1998). Comparable commercial contracts and portfolios of product endorsements have in a broadly comparable manner contributed to the elevation of a number of other sporting figures, including Tiger Woods, David Beckham and Anna Kournikova, each of whom now has the status of global superstar.

The world of advertising illustrates clearly the inter-relationship between celebrity culture and commodity culture. Advertising demonstrates the respects in which celebrity culture might be regarded as a 'tool of commodification' (Rojek 2001: 187). But the process of product endorsement by celebrities in advertising campaigns not only 'uses celebrities; it helps to make them' and as a well-known name becomes better known celebrity status is enhanced (Boorstin 1963: 68). In the case of sporting figures it is in good part their participation in endorsement activities and advertising that extends their profiles beyond a specific sporting field and leads them to become identified as celebrities. It leads to them becoming famous beyond their respective fields of play, well known even to those who know little or nothing, and care even less, about sport and their specific sporting abilities.

Celebrity originally referred to a condition; its roots are in the Latin terms *celebritas* meaning 'multitude' or 'fame' and *celeber* which means 'frequented', 'populous', or 'famous' (Boorstin 1963: 66). Celebrity now refers to a person, someone who is known for being well known. The process of being well known for something or another is now dependent upon media representation. In short celebrity status is a direct product of media coverage and the elevation to public attention it provides. As a result a celebrity might be described as 'a person who is known by people whom he does not know', or even as 'a name which, once made by news, now makes news by itself' (Rein et al. 1997: 14). Without doubt celebrity is subject to management and is recognised to be in many significant respects a product of a complex industry. What has been termed the 'celebrity industry' includes a multiplicity of individuals who are responsible for negotiating on behalf of clients (agents, personnel managers, promoters), handling publicity (public relations firms), managing media profile and image, as well as legal and business aspects and 'tools-of-the-trade' and 'non-tool' endorsements (Rein et al. 1997).

If some individuals are in some respects 'naturals', already possessing, or appearing to possess qualities that audiences find appealing and of value, then high public visibility or celebrity may come without much effort. However, for many individuals such visibility has to be actively sought or worked for through strategic marketing. It has been suggested that celebrity is increasingly 'fabricated on purpose to satisfy our exaggerated expectations of human greatness' (Boorstin 1963: 67), but whether it is to meet people's exaggerated expectations of greatness, or it is to be accounted for in other ways, celebrity is very much subject to production.

Idols of production and consumption

In the course of the twentieth century an historical process of transformation took place which led to a relative shift of emphasis away from 'celebration' of political, business and professional subjects and towards the increasing prominence of figures from the fields of entertainment and sport. At the close of the twentieth century celebrities were being drawn primarily from film, television and popular music, but increasingly also from sport. The relative shift of emphasis marked a significant change in social and cultural priorities away from the world of production and towards the dream-world of consumption (Lowenthal 1961). The growing prominence of the entertainment industry, the steadily increasing popularity of sport and the accelerating development of communications media coincided with a gradual decline of manufacturing industry and a steady growth of diverse service industries.

In a series of analyses of popular culture conducted in the 1940s Leo Lowenthal identified a growing fascination with and interest in 'individuals' and described the increasing number of biographical articles in various publications as constituting a 'kind of mass gossip' (1961: 110). A significant change was found in the period 1901–41 in both the frequency with which biographies were appearing in publications and in the professions of the subjects of such biographical features. By 1941 there were almost four times as many biographical features as there were at the beginning of the century. In the first two decades of the twentieth century it was political figures that predominated and there was a roughly 'equal distribution of business and professional men, on the one hand, and of entertainers on the other' (Lowenthal 1961: 111). At the same time there was not a 'single hero from the world of sports' (Lowenthal 1961: 110–111) and relatively few from the sphere of popular entertainment. By the end of the period under consideration there had been a significant reduction in biographical features on figures from politics, business and other related professions and a marked increase in the number of biographies of individuals from entertainment in general and sporting fields in particular. Whereas the heroes of the past were 'idols of production' the new emerging heroes were in contrast 'idols of consumption' (Lowenthal 1961: 115). The individuals who were increasingly attracting attention in biographical features were 'active in the consumers' world', they were drawn from the sphere of leisure and represented 'the heroes of the world of entertainment and sport' (Lowenthal 1961: 115).

The 'idols of the masses' in the 1940s were increasingly being drawn not from politics or production but from different spheres of consumption and figures from sport were coming 'close to the top of favorite selections' (Lowenthal 1961: 115). A detailed content analysis of the period 1940–41 revealed a significant number of sport biographies in the publications studied. These included biographical features on baseball managers, coaches, umpires, players and pitchers; boxers (e.g. Jack Johnson); tennis players (e.g. Bill Tilden); a football coach and a football player; a golfer (Bobby Jones); a hockey coach; a ski champion; a softball player; and a sailor. With the exception of two features, one on a tennis player (Helen Bernhard) and another on a sailor (D'Arcy Grant) the biographies were exclusively of sportsmen (Lowenthal 1961). Evidence of an under-representation of female sport figures has continued to be a notable feature of narratives on sport. As confirmed by analyses of feature articles in *Sports Illustrated* (Lumpkin and Williams 1991), ESPN's list of the top 100 athletes of the twentieth century (Billings 2000) and sport reporting in the press and on television (Eastman and Billings 2000; Kennedy 2001) qualitative and quantitative gender differences remain a prominent feature of sport.

The Golden Age of American Sport

The growing prominence of sporting figures in America first became apparent during the 1920s, the so-called 'Golden Age of American Sport'. In virtually every field of American sport there seemed to be heroic figures. The near simultaneous emergence of 'transcendent performers ... in almost every field' has subsequently been acknowledged to be quite exceptional (Danzig and Brandewein 1948: xi). What was it about the 1920s that led to sporting figures receiving what were at the time quite exceptional levels of public acclaim?

Two explanations of the emergence of 'magic names' across a range of popular sports that included baseball (Babe Ruth), boxing (Jack Dempsey), football (Red Grange), golf (Bobby Jones) and tennis (Bill Tilden) have been offered. One explanation is that 'cultural intermediaries' (Bourdieu 1984) were largely responsible for creating larger-than-life images of the feats and achievements of sporting figures. It has been suggested that in this period the same promotional skills that were employed to market consumer goods began to be employed to 'sell' sporting figures to the public. Professional pitch men, journalists and radio broadcasters 'created images of athletes which often overwhelmed the athlete's actual achievements' (Rader 1983a: 11). In short the level of public acclaim was deemed to be a product of something more than the quality of sporting performance alone. However, the cultural prominence accorded to sporting figures in the 1920s cannot be attributed solely to the promotional and representational skills of cultural intermediaries. On the contrary, the American public played a very significant part in the creation of heroic sporting figures who,

> served a compensatory cultural function. They assisted the public in compensating for the passing of the traditional dream of success, the erosion of Victorian values and feelings of individual powerlessness. (Rader 1983a: 11)

With the development of a more formal bureaucratically structured society life appeared more complicated, the paths to success more difficult to discern and more problematic to negotiate. It was in this context that 'the need for heroes who leaped to fame and fortune outside the rules of the system seemed to grow' (Rader 1983a: 11) and film stars and sport heroes began to achieve a prominent cultural position.

The emergence of a popular culture of compensation was exemplified not only by the high profile of the sport hero in the 1920s, but also by the prominence of other popular cultural figures from the worlds of film and entertainment, examples include Charlie Chaplin, Douglas Fairbanks and Rudolph Valentino, actors who portrayed 'heroic' characters in various films. Figures from the world of entertainment, from the film industry and Hollywood in particular, as well as show business, have tended to predominate in accounts of fame, celebrity and stardom. This predominance is reflected in analyses of the social phenomenon of 'stars' (Dyer 1992) and the culture of celebrity (Gitlin 1998; Rojek 2001). The emphasis in such analyses has tended to fall disproportionately upon those who have achieved fame through appearances on screen or stage, rather than through performances on the pitch or in the stadium. However, increasing popular cultural appeal and media visibility, along with growing commercial value to corporations around the world, has made sport stars an important focus of contemporary analytic reflection (Andrews and Jackson 2001; Whannel 2002).

Making sense of celebrity and stardom

It has been argued that celebrity is distinguished by image or trademark rather than achievement – 'the hero was a big man; the celebrity is a big name' (Boorstin 1963: 70). Whereas heroes emerge with the passage of time, through a process of gestation in which their feats have to withstand the test of time, celebrity is forever 'now', by definition contemporary. Celebrity is forged through media attention, through the cultivation and projection of image. Celebrity needs the oxygen of publicity. It needs to be continually demonstrated, if not regenerated, by remaining in the public eye. Heroes may be temporarily forgotten, but they can and do endure in the collective psyche that is the memory of a people. Heroes can be recalled. The heroic quality of their feats can be remembered. In contrast the celebrity is destined to disappear and to be 'quickly replaced' (Boorstin 1963: 75).

Celebrity is superficial, trivial, bereft of distinction, in short insubstantial. When reference is made to celebrities the emphasis tends to be placed on 'their marital relations and sexual habits, on their tastes in ... drinking, dress, sports cars, and interior decoration ... [in a] desperate effort to distinguish among the indistinguishable' (Boorstin 1963: 74). The cultural preoccupation with celebrity not only tends to overshadow heroism but to colonise and transform it. Heroes and their achievements are subject to a culture of celebrity that emphasises image, dissolves distance and forges familiarity. Such processes tend to diminish the aura associated with heroic figures and heroic performances.

Reflecting on the fate of the hero in mid-twentieth-century America Boorstin remarked that,

> We have our Hall of fame for Great Americans, our Agricultural Hall of Fame, our Baseball Hall of Fame, our Rose Bowl Hall of Fame. We strain to reassure ourselves that we admire the admirable and honour the meritorious. But in the very act of straining we confuse and distract ourselves ... Despite our best intentions, our contrivance to provide substitute heroes finally produces nothing but celebrities. (1963: 84)

The clear implication of such remarks is that in the modern media age the only hero is the unsung hero, anonymity serving to protect the hero from 'the flashy ephemeral celebrity life' (Boorstin 1963: 85).

In the world of entertainment, especially in respect of music, film and television, celebrities are frequently described as 'stars'. Culture industries work continually to nurture and enhance the institution of stardom, capitalising on 'the star power that binds fans to their celebrities' (Gitlin 1998: 81). A star system was well established by the 1920s and was largely bound up with the commercial world of film. The initial stimulus for the development of a star system lay with a public that had grown tired of the anonymity of actors. Audiences 'demanded that their idols should be named ... made into celebrities ... with a definable publicizable personality' (Boorstin 1963: 162). This was made possible by innovations in the use of film as a medium, in particular close-ups that allowed a focus on the face, a magnification of emotion and establishment of intimacy between performers and audience. The close-up provided a means of 'establishing a performer's "unique" personality' (Walker 1970: 21). From the 1920s film stars became a vital part of the film industry, often carrying a film and frequently determining box office appeal. As stars were singled out and recognised to be vital to a film's success they received increasingly high salaries and these attracted additional publicity. This was the period in which a fully-fledged consumer culture began to develop (Gamson 1992). High salaries made extravagant life-styles possible and these in turn attracted media attention and further publicity. An escalating spiral of publicity raised the individual actor or actress to star status.

The star system quickly extended well beyond the film industry to encompass the world of entertainment as a whole. As well as a growing number of stars from stage and screen, authors became celebrities as their books were accorded 'best-seller' status. In turn figures from the worlds of music, painting and sculpture began to be transformed into stars. One field after another became subject to the star system. But discussions of fame, celebrity and stardom have continued to be focused disproportionately on film and entertainment (Morin 1960; Boorstin 1963; Monaco 1978; Dyer 1992). If considered at all sport and sporting figures have been at the periphery of discussion of the character and significance of the culture of celebrity and the star system in contemporary society. To a substantial degree this reflects the relatively marginal place accorded to sport in contemporary social and cultural inquiry, which is paradoxical, and analytically unacceptable, given the increasingly prominent, if not central, position occupied by sport in popular culture and everyday social life.[1]

Sport: image, media and authenticity

The contemporary world is preoccupied with image, 'the language of images is everywhere' (Boorstin 1963: 188). An image is synthetic, in the sense that it is deliberately contrived. It is important that it is credible, that people believe in it, particularly in so far as in a consumer society images are designed to stimulate or promote consumer behaviour. To be effective an image needs to be *vivid* and simplified. Also to a degree it needs to be open-ended or ambiguous to allow it both to be believed in by as wide a range of people as possible and to be open to re-negotiation or development in an indeterminate future (Boorstin 1963: 190–199).

Images now abound, from corporation to commodity to consumer subject, a concern with the right 'image' is prevalent. This is particularly evident in respect of sport and sporting figures. Increasingly corporations have sought to associate themselves with the imagery of sport through endorsement and sponsorship deals. Images of high profile sportsmen and sportswomen are employed to promote the corporation as a brand as well as particular product lines. In turn sportsmen and sportswomen have become increasingly aware of their 'image' value and the respects in which the right brand and product associations may enhance their image and magnify its value to potential future corporate clients.

It is now commonplace for leading sport figures not only to have agents who look after their commercial transactions but also for their 'image' to be handled by public relations companies. The new hyper-commercial reality of sport really began to take shape in the mid-1980s. It was in this era that American basketball legend Michael Jordan's agent David Falk changed 'the nature of sports representation' by turning an individual player in a team sport into a 'commercial superstar' (Halberstam 2001: 139–140). Initially the Jordan image served to promote the *Nike* brand as a whole, as well as particular lines of *Nike* sports goods, but with time 'Jordan' became a brand, if not a 'superbrand', in his own right.

The Real Madrid and England midfielder David Beckham's commercial career offers another good example of image management. SFX Sports Group (Europe) and the Outside Organisation represented Beckham for a substantial part of his career. When his contract with his former club Manchester United was being re-negotiated in 2002 SFX succeeded in obtaining recognition of the commercial merchandising value of Beckham's 'global image' to the club. The Outside Organisation had responsibility for taking care of Beckham's media-generated public profile, trying to ensure that he retained control of his 'public image' (Cashmore 2002). Unauthorised use of Beckham's image by *easyJet* in 2003 led SFX to threaten litigation unless the advertising copy concerned was withdrawn and the airline paid £10,000 to the NSPCC children's charity (Fresco 2003). A further example of image management is provided by the International Management Group (IMG) which has successfully represented the American golfer Tiger Woods, ensuring that the right image is presented to the world. Under IMG's tutelage Tiger Woods is recognised to have become 'more than just an athlete' and to have 'crossed over into the realm of icon' (Rosaforte 2001: 44).

From its complex development from folk recreational roots modern sport has made a significant contribution to 'collective sensibility', to the cohesiveness of community life. It has been very much the 'idiom of the people' (Inglis 1977), genuinely expressive of popular feelings and interests. The powerful and vivid imagery of sporting events and outstanding sport performers is firmly etched on people's memories. Sport has provided the possibility of fulfilling images 'which replenish the body and the spirit', but increasingly such images have become more and more highly mediated (Inglis 1977: 35). It is primarily through media narratives that sport performers become known as public figures and have qualities of 'personality' attributed to them. Personality or image has been described as 'the strange configuration of qualities which makes a public figure, what in the popular imagination, he [she] is' (Inglis 1977: 95). The sporting figure is only known through their public image and that is formed from 'materials that person chooses either to make available or else involuntarily betrays to that public and its publicly accredited image-makers' (Inglis 1977: 129). Modern sport as a whole, including the profiles of individual athletes and players, has been transformed by the impact of processes of commercialisation and media amplification into a spectacle, into 'a social relation among people mediated by images' (Debord 1973: 4).

From the 1920s cinema newsreel footage served to bring to life press reports of sporting figures and their performances through the development of powerful and vivid sport imagery. Subsequent media developments in radio commentary, the tabloid press, specialist magazines, television coverage (itself radically transformed by satellite technology and digitalisation), as well as the growth of internet websites, have transformed further the representation of sporting figures. With the emergence of mass communications, sporting figures became public figures and as communications media have developed the profile of the sporting figure has been raised and extended, if not radically transformed. The sporting hero has become the sport star and increasingly the celebrity. Sporting figures have long been revered within, and in the past were very much members of, the communities they represented on the sport field (Mason 1996; Lanfranchi and Wahl 1996). From initially being primarily local and/or regional figures a significant number of sportsmen and subsequently sportswomen have become national public figures and in some instances international, if not global figures. For example, it has been said of the American heavyweight boxer Muhammad Ali that he became the most recognised face on the planet (Remnick 2000). Michael Jordan has been recognised as 'the greatest basketball player of all time', but also as the 'most famous American in the world, more famous in many distant parts of the globe than the President of the United States or any movie or rock star' (Halberstam 2001: 7). In turn golfer Tiger Woods has been described as a 'world figure … a world celebrity' (Owen 2001: 63).

High incomes and associated extravagant lifestyles plus the media attention they attract, have transported prominent and successful sporting figures onto another plain, an astral plain that testifies to the growing Americanisation of sport culture. Sport stars appear in many respects now to be comparable to celebrities from the worlds of film, television and popular music, although the extent and the durability of their appeal may be greater. In terms of global popularity or appeal there are now few, if any, other professions that can begin to compare to sport.

In an 'age of contrivance' in which daily life is exposed to and influenced by media images and a culture of celebrity, interest in activities and events that are not contrived, that exemplify spontaneity, remains strong, if it has not grown in intensity (Boorstin 1963: 255). A significant example is provided by the continuing public passion for sport, which has been described as 'one expression of our desperate hunger for the spontaneous, for the non-pseudo event … [for] *uncorrupted authenticity*' (Boorstin 1963: 255, emphasis added). Since the 1960s a series of economic and cultural processes have transformed the world of sport. An extension of professionalism to encompass virtually all sports, increasing commercialism exemplified by the rapid growth of sponsorship, and a dramatic increase in media involvement with sport, in particular through the medium of television in all its forms, have had a powerful impact. To what extent have these transformations affected the 'authenticity' of sport? What have the consequences been for high profile sportsmen and sportswomen?

The contemporary sport star is the product of a complex process of historical development that has involved the emergence of modern formally organised and commercially focused professional sports from traditional recreational folk games, a growth in media interest and a dramatic rise in the value of commercial sponsorship and endorsement contracts. The identification of individual players and a focus on the attributes and performances of particular individuals has become an increasingly prominent feature of contemporary sport. The identification of some sporting figures as outstanding and their associated elevation to star status became a significant feature of modern sports from the moment they began to attract spectators and the interest of the media. It is to the broad social and historical processes that have shaped the development of modern sport and provided the cultural and economic context in which sport stars have become consumer cultural icons and celebrity figures that the following discussion is directed.

Note

1 A number of exceptions are worthy of note. In his broad analysis of the emergence and development of celebrity and its connection with the commodification of everyday life Chris Rojek briefly acknowledges the 'pre-eminence enjoyed by sport celebrities' (2001: 37), their social and cultural impact, as well as the difficulty particular individuals have had coping with the pressures of sport stardom (2001: 81). More substantial analyses of sport stars and sporting celebrity are provided in a number of other recent texts (Wenner 1998; Andrews and Jackson 2001; Whannel 2002).

2

The Development of Modern Sport in Britain and America

The folk roots of popular sport

Competitive playful activities or pastimes with characteristics comparable to what are now universally described as sport have a long and complex history. Social and historical analysts have noted how physically competitive and playful activities can be found in virtually all cultures throughout human history (Huizinga 1949; Mandell 1984). Thrilling, competitive, physically challenging and risky activities were a prominent feature of the ancient civilisations of Greece and Rome and there is evidence of comparable activities in early Egyptian civilisation as well as in the ancient cultures of South Asia (Cashmore 2000). However, it is in Western Europe, especially Britain and to be more precise England, in the course of the development of a modern industrial capitalist and increasingly urban form of social life from the nineteenth century onwards that the foundations of modern sport really lie (Mason 1989; Birley 1995). An early twentieth century German observer of modern social life Agnes Stiven described England as 'the cradle and loving "mother" of sport' and proceeded to note how the culture of sport migrated with relatively 'few changes from one country to another' (cited in Elias 1986: 126). The keen interest in games of various kinds in Britain during the fifteenth and sixteenth centuries received expression in the appearance of early forms of golf, cricket and real tennis. But it was not until the second part of the nineteenth century that modern forms of sport with formal and elaborate systems of rules and national governing bodies began to be established in England and, in turn, in America (Guttmann 1978; Rader 1983b).

Football

Most forms of popular modern sport have their roots in a variety of folk games and traditional recreational activities. There are early records of ball games resembling folk forms of football in China, ancient Greece and Rome, but it is the accounts of various forms of folk 'fotebal' in England between 800 and 1800 that have been central to the construction of association football's (soccer's) genealogy. The union and league codes of rugby football derive from the same folk games and the American variant of 'grid-iron' football also has its roots in pre-modern manifestations of these English games (Dunning and Sheard 1979; Rooney and Davidson 1995). Traditionally folk football games were played on feast and saint's days, as well as after weddings. The eve of Lent was a particularly popular time for games between rival villages, with many taking place on Shrove Tuesday. The games were rough, riotous even, and they were played according to simple unwritten rules. Indeed it would be fair to say that such activities were largely without rules, save for a minimal shared understanding of the unmarked and ill-defined terrain across which the game would be played and the objective or end to which activity was to be directed. Games would not be limited to open spaces but would run through towns and villages. Each game or match had its own particular idiosyncratic customs and goals.

At Derby thousands of people from the parishes of Saint Peter and All Saints, along with other members of the borough and those drawn to the event from the countryside, participated in a fiercely contested game that might last a day or two and that bordered on a feud. It is from this fiercely fought ritual event in Derby that the description of comparably competitive modern football matches between such local rivals as Arsenal and Tottenham Hotspur, Liverpool and Everton, or Glasgow Rangers and Celtic as 'local-derbies' is derived. In the nineteenth century the game at Derby might involve anywhere between five hundred and a thousand people on each team. The objective of the respective teams was to get the ball to their opponent's goal. For the team from the parish of Saint Peter that was the gate of a nursery ground about a mile outside of Derby in the direction of London. For All Saints it was the wheel of a watermill about a mile to the west of Derby. It is not clear whether the player who brought the game to a close by reaching the goal was accorded the status of 'local hero', but it was customary for the individual concerned to receive the honour of starting the game the following year (Malcolmson 1973; Dunning and Sheard 1979; Bowden 1995).

There are extensive records of other comparable versions of folk football matches taking place during holidays at various places around the country, including Alnwick, Sedgefield, Ashbourne, Nuneaton, Twickenham, Teddington, Dorking, Richmond, Kingston-upon-Thames, Hampton and Thames Ditton (Malcolmson 1973: 37). It is from such 'half game, half free-for-all' activities that modern forms of football were to develop in England and America in the late nineteenth century (Guttmann 1978: 127; Rader 1983b).

Golf

Golf is another game with a long history. Stick and ball games were played across Europe during the Middle Ages and some have seen an affinity between the modern game of golf and a 'medieval Dutch game called "Kolve", a sort of individual hockey played on ice' (Lowerson 1989: 188). The Romans played a game called *paganica* that involved a bent stick and a ball made of feathers and it might be argued that this is the source of golf.

The precise origins of the modern game remain a matter of dispute (Browning 1955). However, the home of golf is rightly considered to be Scotland, records show that a version of the game has been played there since at least the fifteenth century. The game was clearly popular and in 1457 the Scottish Parliament of King James II issued a decree to ban both 'Futeball and Golfe', in the case of the latter because it interfered with the practice of archery, a military necessity at the time (Ford 1977). The people ignored the decree and the game grew in popularity. Early in the sixteenth century James IV of Scotland took up the game and his granddaughter Mary, later to become Queen of Scots, introduced the game into France where she received her education. Mary was accompanied on the golf links by 'cadets', that is young gentlemen who were preparing for commissions in the army. It is from 'cadet' that the term 'caddy' or 'caddie', subsequently adopted in Scotland and England to describe an attendant who carries golf clubs, is derived. It is worth adding that while the caddie became for a long time an integral part of the game the introduction in the twentieth century of golf carts and later electronically powered golf buggies rendered them largely redundant save for the professional game.

Without doubt it is in Scotland that clear traces of the early development of what would become the modern game of golf are to be found. It is from the natural sites or settings of Scotland on which golf began to be played that the formative architecture and vocabulary of the contemporary golf course can be traced. Early 'folk' forms of golf were played along the coast in Scotland on undulating sandy ground or links, ground on which grass grew, shaped by coastal winds that created dunes and depressions. In places gorse would grow, in others the grazing of sheep and the nests and holes of small animals would create various hazards. This was the environment in which golf and golf courses began to evolve. It is in response to the challenges posed by the linksland setting that the strategies, equipment and rules of the game developed along with the basic features of the course on which it was to be played:

> The 'playable swards' became 'fairways'. Bordering areas of high grass, heather or gorse became known as 'rough'. Holes ... located in relatively level areas with good grass covers ... were to evolve into 'greens'. And scars that exposed the underlying sand were later to be termed 'sand traps or bunkers'. (Adams 1995: 238)

The early game was played with wooden handmade clubs and a leather-covered ball that was stuffed with feathers, the 'feathery'. As the game grew in popularity and its appeal extended around the world so the implements employed were subject to a process of transformation that has shown no sign of slowing down (Adams 1995; Kirsch 1998).

From the middle of the eighteenth century, courses that had evolved naturally began to be subject to human intervention, modification and improvement. No longer were the location and number of holes determined in an impromptu manner. With the establishment of the Honourable Company of Edinburgh golfers in 1744 and more significantly the founding in 1754 of the St. Andrews Society of Golfers (which in 1834 became the Royal and Ancient Golf Club of St. Andrews) there was a formalisation of standards, rules and etiquette (Lowerson 1989). This led in 1764 to the standardisation of a round of the Old Course at St. Andrews as consisting of eighteen holes and this has subsequently become the standard through-out the world. Before the establishment of the eighteen-hole standard com-petitive play was based on the number of holes won and lost and this has subsequently become known as 'match play', providing analysts with further confirmation of golf's 'Scottish heritage' (Adams 1995).

The game began to be played in England at Blackheath at the beginning of the seventeenth century by the Scottish court of James I (James VI of Scotland). The next significant sign of the game's growth was the formation of the Royal Blackheath Club in 1766 by a number of Scots living in London. As with other contemporary sports it was during the nineteenth century that the development of the game accelerated as its popularity grew both at home and abroad, with Scottish exiles particularly important to the development of the game in England. Scottish exile clubs at Manchester, Blackheath and Wimbledon were particularly influential and in the 1860s professionals from St. Andrews were invited by the North Devon and Hoylake clubs to help determine the layout of their courses (Lowerson 1989; Birley 1995). A not dissimilar pattern was to be repeated in the United States of America.

Introduced by immigrants from Scotland and further exemplifying the process of 'acculturation or cultural borrowing in the world of sport' (Kirsch 1999: 330) golf became popular in America from around the 1890s. The Scottish influence is evident from the identity of two key figures regarded as 'founding fathers' of American golf. John Reid from Dunfermline, along with a few friends, formed the St. Andrews Golf Club of Yonkers, New York, in November 1888 and Charles B. McDonald a second-generation Scottish-American helped to set up the Chicago Golf Club. McDonald went on to 'distinguish himself as a prominent player [and] golf course architect' (Kirsch 1999: 331). From its folk roots in Scotland the game of golf was car-ried to the New World where it in turn would over time be transformed, effectively 'Americanised', by the development of such distinctive features as country clubs and clubhouses and new types of courses and equipment (Lowerson 1989; Adams 1995).

Tennis

Just as modern football and golf can be traced back to their early folk roots, so it is possible to find early forms of what would become the modern game of lawn tennis. It has been suggested that lawn tennis developed from the ancient game of 'real' or 'royal' tennis in fourteenth-century France. The game has been described as class exclusive, 'an aristocratic and regal passion', one that in 1388 and again in 1410 was forbidden to the lower orders, to 'servants and laborers' (Guttmann 1978: 30). In 1535 Henry VIII is reported to have introduced a class restriction on the playing of the game by limiting it to 'noblemen and property owners' (Guttmann 1978). Such class distinction, in respect of who might and who might not engage in a particular pastime, in some respects at least seems to anticipate a much later distinction between different class categories of participants in modern forms of sport identified as 'amateur' and 'professional'.[1]

However, such an account of the origins of tennis has been contested. A detailed and wide-ranging cultural history of the development of tennis effectively challenges the notion that the game was the preserve of kings and princes in the Middle Ages (Gillmeister 1998). Examination of historical material on 'knightly tournaments' and the early ball games of 'commoners' leads Gillmeister to conclude that they fulfilled the same purpose. The medieval knightly tournament and games like folk football are depicted as events in which a positive impression can be made through a demonstration of skill and courage. Both types of event are held to be commonly associated with wedding ceremonies serving to 'hammer the marriage contract into the memories of those concerned' (Gillmeister 1998: 6). The medieval tournament is described as constituting something like a continuation of warfare and a range of evidence is provided to support the view that early ball games may be similarly regarded (see Figure 1 outlining the pedigree of competitive ball games). In particular it is argued that inventors of ball games drew inspiration from the simulation of warfare exemplified by the medieval *tournament* and for support reference is made to early images of folk football in which the goals to be 'defended' and 'attacked' appear to resemble medieval city or castle gates. Such a view might be regarded as offering historical support for George Orwell's familiar description of sport as 'mimic warfare' or 'war minus the shooting' (1992 [1945]: 38–39).

The reference to folk football is not incidental for it is suggested that 'tennis is in fact an offshoot of football' (Gillmeister 1998: 9). The argument is that it was monks who developed the game of tennis in the cloisters of their monasteries when they were prohibited by church authorities from participating in the riotous assembly that folk football too readily became. In support of the notion that tennis might be regarded as a distant cousin of football reference might be made to other folk ball games, like *parkspel*, in which the ball hit with the palm of the hand may also be kicked when and where necessary (Gillmeister 1998: 10). Additional signs of the common roots of football and tennis are explored through a detailed discussion of the language of games. For example, the large family of early tennis-like games and the varieties of folk football divide their terrain into an upward and downward section. Such a distinction is found in the Saterlandic version of the game, the late seventeenth century 'German ball-house game', as well as in comparable ball games found in Tuscany and Colombia. In turn,

> In the football game of La Mayenne and Ille-et-Villaine in the Canton de Melle, France the terms *haut* and *bas* are used, and in the British Isles the traditional

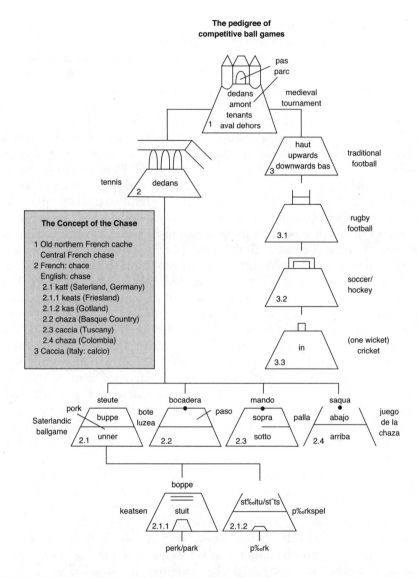

The pedigree of competitive ball games

The Concept of the Chase

1 Old northern French cache
   Central French chase
2 French: chace
   English: chase
   2.1 katt (Saterland, Germany)
   2.1.1 keats (Friesland)
   2.1.2 kas (Gotland)
   2.2 chaza (Basque Country)
   2.3 caccia (Tuscany)
   2.4 chaza (Colombia)
3 Caccia (Italy: calcio)

Figure 1.1 *Tree diagram documenting the survival of tournament expressions in various ball games. (Source: Gillmeister, 1998: 94)*

Shrovetide football in Ashbourne in Derbyshire, as well as the games of Workington and Kirkwall, show a strikingly similar usage. In Workington, the terms are *up'ards* and *down'ards* or *Uppies* and *Downies*, in Kirkwall *Uppies* and *Doonies;* or *Up-the-Gates* and *Down-the-Gates* respectively. (Gillmeister 1998: 96)

The frequent assumption that tennis was monopolised by kings and princes led in some quarters to the game being designated 'Royal tennis'. In turn, 'Royal tennis' has frequently been equated with the notion of 'Real tennis'.

There were tennis playing aristocrats but cultural history shows the game was not their exclusive property. Historical records reveal that from early in the fifteenth century there were a good many other people – clergymen, monks, young people – playing 'tenys' in the cloisters of medieval monasteries. Moreover 'Real tennis' has a much later provenance than is implied by the association with 'Royal tennis'. The term 'Real tennis' first appeared in the 1870s when the followers of the traditional game of tennis sought to maintain a distinctive identity for their game in the face of the growing popularity of a new version designated 'lawn tennis' (Gillmeister 1998: 28).

Medieval sources suggest that tennis 'had its home in the seclusion of the cloisters' (Gillmeister 1998: 34). It was within the monastery that the children of the aristocracy received their education and it was there also that they learnt of tennis. On returning to their homes they wanted to be able to continue playing. This led the aristocracy to develop private courts based on the architectural features of the original monastic setting.

As I have indicated there are different historical accounts of the early development of tennis. Tracing the origins of tennis reveals disagreements over definitions of the game and the range of other ball games that might be included in 'the tennis family' (Ryan 1995). For example, Ryan argues that the game seems to have begun in France in the eleventh century in open fields 'where handballers squared off on opposite sides of a mound' (1995: 144). Another analysis of the roots of the game identifies a twelfth-century French game 'paume' in which players hit a small ball by hand over a net. This game is said to have evolved into *'le jeu de paume'*, a tennis-like game involving the use of a racket, itself reputed to be a sixteenth-century invention.[2] From the eleventh century the cloisters of monasteries, later courtyards of castles, and then later still quadrangles of universities and town squares provided the setting for walled versions of the game (Ryan 1995). These walled versions effectively anticipated the indoor courts that began to increase in number by the fifteenth century under the patronage of the royal households of France and England.

Ryan argues that tennis began to decline in popularity in France after 1600 and that England subsequently 'became the bastion' of the game (1995: 145). By the late eighteenth century the popularity of versions of tennis was such that the indigenous game of cricket was considered to be under threat (Walker 1989). In England tennis became very much an aristocratic game played by the 'propertied, the patrician and the highborn', a game largely confined to 'exclusive country houses, private clubs, and the inane or quirky faddists of Cambridge and Oxford' (Ryan 1995: 145). Until that is, the emergence in 1874 of what has been described as a 'mongrel alternative' with a 'more plebeian appeal' developed by Major Walter Clopton Wingfield who introduced the game of 'sphairistike or lawn tennis' (Ryan 1995: 145; Gillmeister 1998: 174–175).

Wingfield's introduction of a version of tennis that could be played, once again, in the open air rather than within covered courts proved to be popular with over a thousand boxed sets of equipment being sold in the first year.

Lawn tennis began to displace croquet, literally so, by using the carefully prepared and trimmed lawns that had been necessary for the smooth running of croquet bowls (Gillmeister 1998). The publicity associated with Wingfield's success attracted the development of other forms of lawn tennis and in response the Marylebone Cricket Club, which had also been concerned about the addition of tennis courts to cricket clubs, moved in 1875 to establish a universally accepted set of rules. The new rules were greeted with criticism and these in turn were amended in 1877. In this year the All England Croquet Club in the vicinity of Wimbledon, 'where tennis had been played for some time', decided to call itself the All England Croquet and Lawn Tennis Club in an attempt to become the dominant influence in the game (Gillmeister 1998: 188; Ryan 1995). The club announced a grand tournament and set up a commission to reconsider the rules. Gillmeister remarks that,

> The three commissioners ... achieved something truly remarkable. When the first ball at a Wimbledon tournament was served on Monday, 9 July 1877, they had laid down rules which have been allowed to stand until the present day, and with hardly any exception. (1998: 188)

The advertisement for the first championship meeting was placed in *The Field* of 9 June 1877 and it informed readers that the event was 'open to all amateurs' (Walker 1989: 259). There were 22 entries in 1877, two years later the figure had risen to 45. The inaugural Ladies' Singles Championship held at Wimbledon in 1884 attracted 13 entries.

It is with the drawing up of a common code in 1877 that the popular modern game of tennis emerged. Attendance at the All England Wimbledon championship grew from just over 2,000 in the early 1880s to 3,500 by 1885. In 1882, in acknowledgement of the fast growing popularity of lawn tennis, the All England Club had switched the order of the games identified in its title and became the All England Lawn Tennis and Croquet Club.

In America it was initially within cricket clubs towards the end of the nineteenth century that lawn tennis first achieved popularity as a socially exclusive summer sport for the wealthy (Rader 1983b). Subsequently the game became an established part of summer sport in the elite clubs. When the game was first played in America has been a matter of dispute. It has been suggested that the inaugural match, a *private* affair between Fred Sears and James Dwight, took place in 1874 in Nahant, Newport. The first recorded *public* sign of the game at a sport club occurred when Mary Outerbridge obtained permission to set up a net, using Wingfield's sphairistike set, at Staten Island Cricket and Baseball Club (Gillmeister 1998: 209). The precise date is a matter of some dispute, some sources cite 1874 (Rader 1983b; Ryan 1995), another 1875 (Gillmeister 1998), the central issue being precisely when Mary Outerbridge arrived back from Bermuda where she is reported to have acquired a set of Wingfield's tennis equipment. It was one of Mary's brothers who had the idea to hold a national championship on the club grounds in 1880. Particular idiosyncrasies at the event concerning net height, scoring method and ball type – one third of the size of the type generally used in England – led to calls for a governing body to establish common rules and regulations. In May 1881 the inaugural meeting of the United States Lawn Tennis Association (USLTA) duly took place with the 36 delegates present agreeing to follow the rules of the All England Club for a period of one year (Gillmeister 1998). It was also agreed to hold an official championship, the first United States Championships, in August 1881 at the Newport Casino, Rhode Island, the current site of the International Tennis Hall of Fame.

American football and baseball

The connection between early folk games and popular modern sports can be demonstrated by examining other distinctive sporting activities that developed in the New World. The sports of American football and baseball offer additional good examples for they reflect to a substantial degree the folk roots of the migrants who took their recreational activities and pastimes with them when they travelled to the New World. American football has its roots in the forms of folk football from which association football (soccer) and rugby football subsequently developed in England. Various forms of folk football were carried to America as 'part of British immigrants' cultural cargo' (Rooney and Davidson 1995: 211–212). As was the case in England, schools and colleges played a pivotal role in the formalisation and development of the particular version of the game of football that ultimately emerged in America. From 1869, when a game took place between Princeton and Rutgers that is described as 'more like soccer than rugby', through various phases of rule change and rule development, American football began to take shape (Guttmann 1978: 128; see also Oriard 1993). In 1876 Princeton, Columbia, Harvard and Yale sought to overcome the problem of local variations in rules by formulating an agreed code. They established the Intercollegiate Football Association and with Harvard and Yale exerting the greater influence, the rules of play agreed, initially at least, 'did not vary substantially from the Rugby Union code' (Oriard 1993: 26). In the following decades a series of innovations led to the gradual emergence of a game that was by 1912 'recognizably [American] football in the modern sense' (Guttmann 1978: 128; see also Oriard 1993: 27).[3]

In a comparable manner baseball has its roots in stick-and-ball games brought to the American colonies by Europeans in the seventeenth century. Most of the popular stick-and-ball games originated in England and two in particular were prominent. Cricket was played by a number of people in north-eastern cities such as Boston, New York and Philadelphia (Rader 1983b). But it is the English game of rounders that was played throughout America, in both urban and rural communities, that is generally identified as the folk source of baseball (Neilson 1995; Pope 1997). Popular legend has it that the game of baseball was the invention of General Abner Doubleday in Cooperstown, New York, in 1839. However, there is little to substantiate this view, although the legend undoubtedly accounts for the fact that the Baseball Hall of Fame Museum was opened in Cooperstown in 1939 to celebrate 'baseball's mythological centennial' (Levine 1985: 112–115).

An explanation of the quite literal invention of a distinctive American origin for baseball lies in the need to free the game from a close association with British culture. As Pope remarks, 'the invented tradition of baseball as a distinctively American game was inspired in large measure by transatlantic rivalry, and by a more general effort to differentiate American culture from anything that hinted at the old-world motherland' (1997: 71). By creating an American origin for the game a claim could be advanced that baseball truly exemplified American values and character (Levine 1985).[4] Notwithstanding the persuasiveness of the mythology, powerfully reinforced by the 1939 centennial celebrations, the establishment of a Hall of Fame, and US Government commemorative stamps, that has led baseball to acquire a unique place in American culture, historical evidence confirms the influence of British cultural cargo. There is now a wealth of evidence that indicates baseball derived from 'simple, informal folk games played mostly by boys on empty lots or village greens', subsequently evolving into a 'formally organized sport of young gentlemen, and then within a few decades, into a spectator-centered sport' (Rader 1983b). As ever the mythology is more colourful. It is understandable that the story of a minor heroic Gettysburg figure, a former Major General in the US army, drawing a diagram of a diamond and outlining rules of the game behind a Cooperstown tailor's shop, should have been so eagerly embraced. But the indigenous creation story, while popular and useful in promoting a sense of American identity, has been shown to be unfounded (Rader 1983b; Levine 1985; Pope 1997).

Precisely when *organised* baseball began is difficult to determine as there are differing accounts of early formative events. One account suggests that the first organised baseball club was established by a group of New York men in 1842. Their games were played on a regular basis at '27th Street and 4th Avenue in Manhattan' (Rader 1983b: 108). The team was encouraged to become more organised by Alexander Cartwright who suggested they 'form a socially exclusive club and secure a permanent playing site' (Rader 1983b: 108). In 1845 the group became known as the Knickerbocker Base Ball Club or New York's Knickerbockers. The club developed a set of twenty rules in 1845 and these are regarded as the first 'recognizably modern rules' for playing the game (Guttmann 1978; Rader 1983b). Another related account draws attention to evidence of games similar to modern baseball being played throughout the New York City area during the 1840s. A report in the *New York Morning News* refers to '"a friendly match of the time-honored game of Base" that was played on October 21, 1845, at the Elysian Fields, "between eight members of the New York Ball Club and the same number of players from Brooklyn"' (Pope 1997: 60). One possible implication of this report is that the rules generally attributed to Cartwright and the Knickerbockers were already established practice by 1845.

The first official modern baseball game is reported to have taken place on 19 June 1846 between the Knickerbockers and the New York Club, subsequently to become Hoboken. During the 1850s the game spread throughout New York and beyond, particularly so during the American Civil War (1861–65) when Union soldiers from the New York area played the game as they moved across country from state to state. Reflecting on baseball's rapid development in the late 1850s Henry Chadwick, described as the 'dean of baseball publicists' (Rader 1983b: 111), observed that the game was more compatible with the American way of life than cricket. Chadwick remarked that 'Americans do not care to dawdle over a sleep-inspiring game all through the heat of a June or July day … What they do they want to do in a hurry' (cited in Pope 1997: 60–61). Baseball's appeal continued to grow throughout the remainder of the nineteenth century, assisted by the introduction of a daily sports page and sports sections in the popular press in the 1880s and 1890s respectively, and it duly established itself as the national game (Levine 1985; Pope 1997).

It has been suggested that baseball, specifically *professional* major league baseball, 'shaped the way that most Americans have played and thought about sport' (Pope 1997: 59). The formation in 1876 of a National League led to the introduction of particular structures and procedures that set the pattern for the subsequent development of commercialised sport – 'league structure; territorial franchise monopolies; annual championship tournaments; the "reserve clause"; assignment of game officials; and revenue sharing' (Pope 1997: 59). Major league baseball's professional structure and the subsequent relationships that developed with sporting goods companies and consumers established the foundations on which the American professional sports industry developed throughout the twentieth century (Pope 1997).

For the most part modern sports can be traced back to folk roots. However, there are exceptions, an important example being the modern sport of basketball which developed in America in 1891 (see Chapter 5). Without doubt contemporary sports such as football and rugby, golf and tennis developed from folk roots through a complex process of modernisation. These modern forms of sport emerged and developed along with other key institutional forms of modern life and to that extent what is now known and loved as sport clearly constitutes a corollary of modernity.

Modernity and the development of sport

A number of analysts have noted the respects in which the development of sport is closely connected with the modern project (Hargreaves 1986; Oriard 1993; Whannel 2002). In Europe from the seventeenth century onwards, traditional forms of social and cultural life became subject to transformation as ideas and beliefs, and ways of behaving and producing things, as well as forms of recreation and play, were exposed to emerging new forms of social, cultural, economic and political life (Smart 1992).

A series of developments in respect of key institutions during the course of the eighteenth and nineteenth centuries ultimately led to the emergence of a new social formation, modernity. It is to key institutional features of modern forms of life such as science, industrialism, capitalism, government and administration, and a culture of individualism, that brief consideration will be given to illustrate the respects in which sport has been closely articulated with the development of modernity (Giddens 1990a).

Scientific rationality

Modern scientific investigation of social and natural phenomena has not only generated a rational understanding of the order of things but, in turn, has opened up the potential for intervention to regulate and redesign socio-cultural and natural forms of life (Bauman 1987). A conception of the 'instrumental value' of scientific knowledge constitutes an intrinsic feature of modern life as a whole and of the practice of modern sport in particular.

Innovation and development in pursuit of improvement are an integral part of modern sport. Scientifically based innovations are directed towards quantitative and qualitative improvements in the performances of individuals and teams. In the case of organisations increasingly necessary enhancements of capital revenue-generating capacity are now at the forefront of the 'rationalist project' of modern professional sport (Whannel 2002). Sport landscapes – courses, courts and stadiums – are continually subject to modification, to refinement and to improvement, if not redesign, as a consequence of innovations made possible by developments in various scientific fields (Raitz 1995). In turn the performances of sport participants are subjected to continual scientific surveillance and re-engineering. Scientifically based programmes of physical development and training, changes in diet and playing techniques, as well as innovations in organisation and equipment are now a prominent feature of sport.

More controversially the performances of participants have also become subject to re-engineering through recourse to scientific developments in respect of performance-enhancing drugs. The use of substances to improve performance grew as modern professional forms of sport developed in the course of the twentieth century. From the use of ether and caffeine by cyclists in the late nineteenth century through to the mid-twentieth-century identification of the benefits of anabolic steroids for increasing weight and strength, there was a growing recognition of the potential advantages medical science might offer to athletes. At this stage there were no restrictions on pharmaceutical supplements and 'strength-reliant performers, like field-eventers and football players [from the National Football League] started using steroids' and it became 'commonplace for cyclists, skiers and an assortment of other athletes' to use drugs (Cashmore 2000: 192).

Although drug-testing has become an increasingly prominent part of sport since the late 1960s there is a substantial body of evidence that points to the continuing use of prohibited substances by athletes and players in a number of sporting fields (Hoch 1972; Hoberman 1992; Yesalis and Cowart 1998). As coaches, sportsmen and sportswomen have sought to improve performance there has been a growing medicalisation of the culture of sport. Notwithstanding the introduction of lists of prohibited substances, drug-testing regimes, and the imposition of sanctions on those found to be in contravention of regulations, drug use remains a problematic feature of contemporary sport – a potential threat to its authenticity.

As modern sport has developed there has been increasing recourse to a 'scientific approach to talent identification and development' and a growth in forms of scientific specialisation 'both on and off the field of play physio-therapists, psychologists and dieticians etc.' (Houlihan 2003: 347). The equipment used in sport is itself now subject to continual refinement and modification. The scientific development of new technologies has led to new materials and new designs being employed in training and play. A comparable calculating scientific approach is evident in respect of the increasingly vital capital revenue-generating aspects of sport. Financial management, promotion and marketing, merchandising, and the activities of numerous sponsors and agents are now central to, if not at the forefront of what has become the sport *business*.

There is now a discursive formation of 'sport science' that is closely associated with the institution of sport, which has as its central objective not simply the study of sport but also enhancement or improvement of performance not only of players, but also managers and organisations in the field. As sub-fields within sport science, sport psychology, sport medicine and sport nutrition are each committed to the same end. The objective is to maximise potential, to achieve more, to improve on existing times, distances, weights, heights, scores and points totals and to enhance the aesthetic aspects of performance while reducing the wear and tear on the body and other stresses and strains experienced in competitive sporting endeavours. If once the game was all that mattered and taking part was the essence of sport, now it is achievements, winning and the breaking of records that are accorded priority, along with attracting spectators and the interest of television companies and commercial sponsors. The prospect and pursuit of improvement is a central part of modern sport (Guttman 1978). Sport competitors and teams aim to progress both in terms of playing and commercial success and in the pursuit of improvement they have turned increasingly to science.

The process of transformation from pre-modern, disorganised and disorderly recreational activities to formalised modern sports has been described as an evolution from 'primitive physicality' to 'reason and order' (Oriard 1993: 42). Consider for example the case of American football. Walter Camp, widely regarded as the founding figure, described the game's history as involving a movement away from the 'nondescript running and kicking' associated with the English game of rugby towards a more 'scientific contest' (cited in Oriard 1993: 42). American football, as developed under Camp's influence, exemplified a modern corporate form of organisation and shared many of the features of Frederick Taylor's approach to scientific management. Camp's version of 'scientific management' has close parallels with Taylor's key principles. Taylor emphasised that science should be employed to optimise the performance of individual tasks, to determine training and development requirements, co-ordination and co-operation, and division of labour and responsibility in the work process. Camp in a comparable manner brought scientific planning to,

> the devising of plays; the training of players for the positions that suit them; the cooperation of coach, captain, and quarter-back with the rest of the players so as to ensure common purpose; and the distribution of responsibilities according to position and ability. (Oriard 1993: 43)

It is evident that Taylor and Camp shared a common view of the value of science for specifying tasks or activities and then co-ordinating or organising them to optimise outcomes in the workplace or on the playing field.

The increasing turn to science and the reduction of the element of chance that became a feature of late-nineteenth-century American football as it sought to differentiate itself from the English game of rugby led to concerns about the incursion of professionalism in an amateur sport. The introduction of the scrimmage for the rugby scrum in 1880 and the emphasis placed on strategy, science and winning led to an increased emphasis on coaching and to a professional approach to play. The prominence of instrumental values exemplified by the emphasis placed on coaching, teamwork, discipline, training and commitment ran counter to the amateur ethos and led to a debate about where the sport was heading.

Basically there were two opposing views. These were articulated by various contributors, including Walter Camp 'the voice of scientific football' in *Harper's Weekly* and Caspar Whitney 'the voice of gentlemanly "sport for sport's sake"' in the pages of *Harper's Weekly* until 1890 and then in *Outing*, a monthly magazine devoted to amateur sport (Oriard 1993: 146). Camp promoted football as a game based on teamwork, coaching and science, a game with clear affinities with other forms of work in an industrial society in so far as it necessitated a 'division of labour … well-defined classes of workers … clock-work play and machine-like efficiency' (Oriard 1993: 150).

The counter-narrative on football developed by Whitney argued that the American game had become too subject to the scientific and managerial worldview, to the detriment of the amateur spirit and sporting ethos of 'fair play'. Scientific football was criticised for promoting violence and brutality, but most of all for introducing 'unprincipled professionalism' into an amateur game. Where Whitney's conception of the game reflected the values of an English aristocratic approach to sport and constituted a counter-force to the social and economic world, Camp sought to promote the distinctive virtues of American football, to emphasise its congruence with 'an emerging corporate, bureaucratic industrial order' and to portray sport, and football in particular, as a 'training ground for success in corporate industrial America' (Oriard 1993: 156, 159).

Industrial capitalism

Transformations in manufacturing associated with the deployment of inanimate sources of power and the introduction of machines into the production process in England from the mid-eighteenth century had a profound impact on most, if not all, aspects of people's ways of life (Giddens 1990a). Associated changes in what was being produced and how things were being produced are generally considered to exemplify the emergence of a new form of life identified as 'industrialism'. What is known as 'the industrial revolution' (circa 1750–1850 in England) was fuelled by the prior accumulation of capital and is closely articulated with another key institutional feature of modernity, namely capitalism. Industrialism is also associated with the movement of populations from rural locations, where people worked on the land, to towns and cities, where they worked predominantly within the environment of the factory. In brief, industrialism is associated with urbanisation and, in turn, a 'related process of embourgeoisement' that had a significant impact on the class structure and class relations (Dunning and Sheard 1979: 178).

The application of scientific and practical knowledge to manufacture led to a considerable growth in levels of productivity and increasing specialisation led to further transformations in the nature and practice of work. The emergence of industrialism directly and indirectly affected not only the workplace but also other significant aspects of everyday life including 'transportation, communication, and domestic life' (Giddens 1990a: 56) and, subsequently, recreation and play (Malcolmson 1973; Bailey 1978; Hargreaves 1986). In addition, as industrialism increased productivity, in the sense of both the range and quantity of goods available, it contributed to the conditions necessary for the growth of consumerism.

The development of modern industrial productive practices in England and America took place in a context that was powerfully shaped by prevailing social and economic relationships. The economic system of production in which industrialism developed was capitalist, 'a system of commodity production' (Giddens 1990a: 55) where the principal objective is capital accumulation achieved through production of goods and services, their distribution, sale and consumption. Capitalism is an economic system that continually works to expand the market for its products. Its objective is to find new markets for current product and service ranges and to generate new as-yet-unimagined products and services for existing markets. To that end all aspects of human endeavour are potentially subject to commodification, to being identified as a potential focus of capitalist economic activity and as a potential source of capital accumulation.

The impact of industrialism and capitalism on traditional forms of recreation and play has been immeasurable (Hargreaves 1986). With the development of industrial capitalism traditional ways of life to which the majority of people were accustomed became subject to disruption and transformation. Where people lived, how they lived, what they did to earn a livelihood, as well as the recreational activities in which they engaged, and when and where they did so, were substantially affected by the formation of industrial capitalism (Hoch 1972; Bailey 1978; Holt 1989). With the movement to congested urban environments in towns and cities and a separation of work and home life following the growth of employment in the more disciplined environments of the factory and the workshop, spatial and temporal aspects of social life became subject to increased specification and greater regulation.

The social meaning and experience of space was transformed with the increasing density of population in urban environments. A comparable transformation of the social meaning and experience of time followed inexorably from the 'calculating' rationality and new forms of organisation intrinsic to the new industrial order. The rational specification of and restriction on space and the necessity to order life, literally to 'keep time' and later to 'time budget', through a rational calculation of duration, undermined and displaced the seemingly more 'natural' sense of space and temporal rhythm associated with traditional or pre-modern forms of sociality. The potential for disorder and destruction associated with, at best loosely structured, folk games and popular recreational activities proved unacceptable in confined urban spaces and incompatible with the promotion of the 'civilising' virtues of self-restraint, rational conduct and consideration for others (Elias 1986).

Popular recreational activities became increasingly subject to containment and curtailment in the face of the administrative regulation and police powers of the modern state and the arduous and disciplined character of the long working week (Bailey 1978; Coakley 2001). This was a period in which the popular pastimes of the people were disappearing and the space and time in which 'leisure' might be enjoyed was being subject to the constraints of waged work, reductions of open space, and legislative restriction. Furthermore, with the growth of a new middle class interested in the potential 'self-improvement' value of new forms of recreational activity, traditional pastimes began to encounter competition from emerging 'rational' forms of recreation (Bailey 1978).

In England and America from the mid-nineteenth century, traditional recreational activities and pastimes were being steadily displaced by the emergence of embryonic modern sports. This was a period in which bodies of agreed rules concerning how particular games should be played were being formulated in a number of institutional contexts (Dunning and Sheard 1979; Rader 1983b). Governing bodies in various sporting fields were beginning to emerge and competitions and tournaments were increasing in frequency as the development of the railways made travel easier and contributed significantly to the growing popularity of 'national' games such as cricket and association football in England and baseball in America.

A number of important developments in respect of sport were beginning to take place in the latter part of the nineteenth century. A particular development is worthy of note at this point. A significant social and cultural distinction was beginning to be drawn between different categories of sport participation in relation to social class membership (Hargreaves 1986). The distinction in question was between participants accorded, what was recognised in the nineteenth century and in a number of sports for much of the twentieth century, to be an elevated status of 'amateur' and those designated, generally in a derogatory manner, as 'professional'. At issue in this distinction, at least in initial formulations, are the social origins of sport participants, specifically their social class roots. The distinction served as a signifier of social differences and as the basis on which the prevailing social class hierarchy could be replicated within the institution of modern sport (Guttmann 1978; Hargreaves 1986; Pope 1997).

The generation of a social class-based distinction between 'amateur' and 'professional' also served to draw attention to the wider intrusion of the cash-nexus in sport. The distinction signified the increasing importance of two other related developments, namely the growth of organised 'professionalism' in sport and the fact that sport was gradually becoming 'commodified'. As the popularity of modern sports increased and they attracted spectators willing to pay for the pleasure of watching matches, competitions and contests, modern sports became a potential source of revenue and began to be recognised as such. An increasing number of participants were beginning to be paid to play, initially as compensation for earnings lost through absence from work, but as sport became professionalised it became a form of employment for players who became professionals and received a wage. Increasing professionalisation and commodification would in due course dramatically transform sport in England and America.

National and international governing bodies

The growth of rational bureaucratic organisational forms has been a corollary of the development of modern forms of life. Rational bureaucratic organisation receives its fullest development in the administrative form of the modern state, a form of life that constitutes a distinctive institutional feature of modernity (Weber 1970). The modern state is a complex organisational form. It employs a variety of techniques (formalisation, standardisation, and legislation) to systematically order and regulate the actions of agents within its jurisdiction. It was at the 'threshold of modernity' that a series of political technologies began to be directed at 'living conditions [and] the whole space of existence' (Foucault 1979: 143–144). The emergence of the modern state brought into being a reorganisation or re-ordering of all aspects of social life, including recreation. Re-ordering was particularly apparent in the processes of transformation to which the domain of popular recreation was subject in the course of the nineteenth century as institutional forms of modern sport developed.

During the nineteenth century popular recreational activities and games became increasingly subject to rational regulation and transformation through processes of formalisation. Longstanding folk games that had been played according to local custom and tradition began to be transformed. Regional, national and later international governing bodies were established to introduce and administer rules and codes of conduct that served to discipline sport and determine consistency in respect of ways of playing the various games. Modern sports became rationalised as rules and standards of play specified the permitted patterns and behavioural and spatial parameters within which competitive activity could take place. Rules and standards apply irrespective of the idiosyncrasies of time and place and their universal application makes competition possible between individuals and teams, notwithstanding the existence of continuing national, regional and local cultural differences.

As well as being charged with the responsibility of ensuring that rules of competition are universally applied, governing bodies have served as the organisational forum in which agreed modifications and innovations in respect of rules and standards of play can be implemented. They have also played a critical role in determining not merely the terms on which players may compete but who may and may not be included in official competitions and tournaments. For example, in England and America at the close of the nineteenth century, governing bodies in the field of athletics excluded particular classes of persons from membership of clubs and competition on the grounds that they did not meet the criteria necessary to be accorded the status 'amateur'. Also in America in the first half of the twentieth century governing bodies in a number of sports, including baseball, bowling, cycling, football and golf excluded players on the grounds of race and this led to forms of segregation in sport which persisted until after the end of the Second World War when a 'slow process of desegregation' began to gradually redress the situation (Rader 1983b).

National governing bodies brought order and coherence to competitive sport within the territorial boundaries of the nation state. They introduced and regulated local, regional and national competitions and in turn promoted the prospect of international sport.[5] International governing bodies served to order international competition and constituted an early organisational sign of the processes of economic and cultural globalisation to which modern sport became increasingly subject in the course of the twentieth century. In Britain national governing bodies were established in a number of sporting fields in the course of the nineteenth century. Examples of these include:

Royal and Ancient Golf Club of St. Andrews	1834
Football Association	1863
Rugby Football Union	1871
Amateur Athletic Association	1880
Amateur Boxing Association	1881
Lawn Tennis Association	1888
Rugby League	1895

In America a comparable series of sports organisations emerged to govern the playing of various games in the period in question. These included:

National Association of Amateur Athletes of America	1868
Rowing Association of American Colleges	1870
Baseball National League	1876
The United States Lawn Tennis Association	1881
Amateur Athletic Association	1888
United States Golf Association	1894
National Football League	1902

As international sporting exchanges and competitions began to increase towards the close of the nineteenth century and into the twentieth century a number of international organisations emerged. These included the following:

International Football Association Board	1886
International Rugby Football Board	1886
International Olympic Committee	1894
Federation Internationale de Football Association	1904
International Amateur Athletic Association	1912
International Lawn Tennis Federation	1913
International Amateur Athletic Federation	1913
Federation Internationale de Basketball Amateur	1932

The internationalisation of sport demonstrated by the formation of international organisations and the development of international competitions exemplifies the globalising character of modernity. As the twentieth century developed sport became an increasingly significant institutional feature of the process of globalisation. Sport served to intensify social relations and contribute, through media coverage and marketing of events, stars and celebrities, to a global diffusion of particular cultural forms (Whitson 1998; Houlihan 2003). Events such as the Olympic Games and the World Cup have become truly global in scale and appeal, as in turn have the profiles of popular sporting celebrities, including contemporary figures like Michael Jordan, Tiger Woods, David Beckham and Anna Kournikova. In so far as globalisation is a process bringing about an 'overall movement towards "one world"' (Giddens 1990a: 66) sport constitutes an institutional dimension whose economic and cultural impact would appear to be unparalleled.

Culture of individualism

The autonomy of the individual, the right to decide things for oneself and to live as one thinks fit, is central to the notion of modern individualism. Individualism developed out of 'the struggle against monarchical and aristocratic authority that seemed arbitrary and oppressive to citizens prepared to assert the right to govern themselves' (Bellah et al. 1996: 142). The heroic individual, the person that stands out from the crowd by virtue of an achieved or ascribed quality, has become a prominent and popular figure in contemporary culture.

A culture of individualism has been argued to be a corollary of 'the capitalist imaginary of the unlimited expansion of production and consumption' (Castoriadis 1997: 347). The notion of the individual as an autonomous or self-constituting subject seeking personal development, fulfilment, identity affirmation and/or status enhancement through the exercise of self-interest is closely articulated with capitalist modes of production and consumption (Harvey 1989). Whereas early in the twentieth century it was idols of production that were feted and accorded heroic status, as the century progressed and a mass consumer society developed it was individuals from the worlds of sport and entertainment, individuals associated with the sphere of consumption, that were elevated in status. Increasingly the outstanding individuals, the names, the celebrities, came 'from the sphere of consumption and organized leisure time' (Lowenthal 1961: 121).

A culture of individualism places emphasis on personal effort, achievement, toughness and strength and it 'adulates winners while showing contempt for losers' (Bellah et al. 1996: viii). The institution of modern sport is a culturally significant repository of these values, an institutional setting in which such values are continually re-affirmed and accorded popular acclaim. From its inception the competitive character of modern sport has led to emphasis being placed upon individuals giving of their best, being strong and brave in pursuit of sporting achievements. Whether in respect of team or individual sports the efforts or contributions of talented and/or charismatic individuals have attracted attention. Individuals are identified and celebrated, feted, for the quality and significance of their contributions to the game(s) in which they are involved, whether they are participating in individual or team sports.

Throughout the history of modern sport in Western societies individuals have been identified as heroes, as stars, and to that extent a contrast between 'individualistic' sports and 'co-operative' or team sports is analytically unproductive (Guttmann 1978). For while there may be important differences between 'individualistic' and 'team' sports in respect of cultural significance, popularity, participation rates, media representation and so on, both of these categories of modern sport, certainly in England and America, have been constituted within and powerfully shaped by a culture of individualism.

In modern Western societies individualism has been a prominent and significant feature of all sport, including team sports. The attributes and achievements of individual players and their thoughts and feelings about their performances have become an important focus of reflection and analysis, particularly in the media. Individual players or performers are promoted through the media as personalities, their achievements are dramatised and their contributions on the field of play are turned into a spectacle. It is as a consequence of the increasing incidence of social relations being mediated by images that analysts have made reference to the spectacular character of contemporary social life and, in turn, have drawn attention to the growing prominence of 'the celebrity' as a manifestation of 'spectacular representation' and as a 'star of consumption' (Debord 1973: 60; see also Rojek 2001).

The history of sport in modern Western societies provides numerous examples of the significance of a cult of the individual. In Victorian England the feats of W. G. Grace, a major celebrity and not just in the team game of cricket, became the stuff of legend. Grace is credited with transforming the game of cricket, with contributing to its modernisation, and he remains an historic national figure. In America 'Babe' Ruth occupies a comparable cultural position. In the 1920s Ruth's aptitude at baseball led him to be regarded as 'the country's pre-eminent athletic hero' (Rader 1983b: 182) and to be credited with revolutionising the national game. Ruth signed a professional baseball contract in 1914 with the Baltimore Orioles moving later in the same year to the Boston Red Sox and then in 1920 on to the New York Yankees. Initially hired as a left-handed pitcher Ruth's reputation in baseball was made as an outstanding hitter whose feats have been equalled by few others in the history of the game. Unrivalled playing success led to lucrative commercial opportunities for baseball's outstanding individual, so many that a business agent was required to handle matters. There were ghost-written newspaper and magazine columns, a vaudeville tour and endorsements of a wide range of products, including 'hunting and fishing equipment, ... men's wear, alligator shoes, baseball gear and sporty automobiles' (Rader 1983b: 181), as well as fees for appearing at banquets, grand openings and celebrity golf tournaments.

The growth of new communications media (radio, film, newsreels), the competitive character of sport journalism, and the development of advertising in the opening decades of the twentieth century have been identified as creating the appropriate economic and cultural context for the first modern sport agent to emerge. Christy Walsh, a former sport journalist, became Ruth's agent and proceeded to turn him into 'a one-man conglomerate, SportsWorld's first great commodity' (Lipsyte and Levine 1995: 109). In a series of observations on Ruth's wider social and cultural significance it has been remarked that he was

> completely in tune with the new attitudes towards leisure and consumption fostered by the new urban markets for consumer goods, aided and abetted by a communications revolution heralded by the radio, and a new aggressive advertising industry that persuaded – no demanded – that Americans live big with their new free time and disposable income. (Lipsyte and Levine 1995: 107)

Ruth's rise represents a realisation of the mythic rhetoric that followed the loss of the frontier with the colonisation of the American West. From lowly stock and lacking in etiquette and social graces the hedonistic Ruth's career served as a powerful demonstration that the American dream might be realised, that any individual, however humble or modest their origins, could make it if they tried hard enough. The notion that sport can be an avenue for social mobility for the disadvantaged remained strong throughout the twentieth century and continues today to be upheld, although not without its critics (Horne et al. 1999; Cashmore 2000; Coakley 2001).

In the same era in another team sport, the American football player 'Red' Grange's phenomenal talent and virtuous life-style led him to become an 'idol of the nation's youth' (Rader 1983b: 185) and to be accorded heroic status. In 1925 Grange exposed the myth of college athletes playing football merely for the fun of it by turning professional and if his reputation was initially tarnished it was not to the detriment of his subsequent career. The record crowds Grange drew to the professional game and the publicity he attracted led in turn to a number of commercial endorsement opportunities. Among the commodities endorsed by Grange were 'sweaters, shoes, caps, a Red Grange football doll, and soft drinks' and there was a brand of 'Red Grange Chocolates' and a film contract (Rader 1983b: 185–186). In the 1920s America was moving away from 'Victorian morality and the Protestant work ethic toward a new mentality that encouraged immediate gratification' (Lipsyte and Levine 1995: 106). Both Ruth and Grange exemplified that emerging new mentality, a consumer ethos that was becoming a prominent part of social life and an increasingly significant feature of sport in particular.

By the end of the twentieth century modern sport in England and America had been transformed by the impact of commercialisation and media representation and had become a spectacle. Growing media interest and coverage, especially in respect of television and developments associated with that particular technological form (satellite, cable and digital transmissions) coupled with an exponential increase in sponsorship of sport events and the awarding of lucrative endorsement contracts to players, have dramatically transformed sport. A corollary of the processes of transformation to which sport has been subject has been an increasing focus on individuals, their characteristics and performances.[6]

Within team sports individuals are now prominent. Names are displayed on team shirts to distinguish and identify individuals. Individual matches and whole seasons are reviewed and evaluated in order to determine best performance by an individual in various positions and categories. Players are interviewed to obtain their views on a game or on a controversial pattern of play. Whether reference is made to 'individualistic' sports or to 'team' sports it is individual athletes or players, the stars, that are increasingly at the forefront of media discussion and public attention.

Notes

1 As modern forms of sport developed in the latter part of the nineteenth century in England governing bodies of various sports prohibited anyone who had been 'by trade or employment for wages, a mechanic, artisan or laborer' (Guttmann 1978: 30). The Amateur Athletic Club formed in 1866, to become the Amateur Athletic Association in 1880, and the Amateur Rowing Association and Bicycling Union emphasised that only the 'gentleman-amateur' could be a member. The rationale was that a physically strenuous form of work might provide an unfair competitive advantage (Horne et al. 1999).

2 http://britishtennis.com/newtotennis/history The issue of the introduction of the racket into tennis and the origin of the term is addressed by Gillmeister (1998) who notes a number of historical references to rackets being used in matches in England and Germany in the course of the sixteenth century.

3 Two simple rule innovations are recognised to have created the break with Rugby Union and created a distinctive American version of football (Oriard 1993: 26). The first, adopted on 12 October 1880 by the Intercollegiate Football Association, states:

A scrimmage takes place when the holder of the ball, being in the field of play, puts it down on the ground in front of him and puts it in play with his foot. The man who first receives the ball from the snap-back shall be called the quarter-back, and shall not then rush forward with the ball under penalty of foul.

The second, approved two years later, states:

If on three consecutive fairs and downs a team shall not have advanced the ball five yards or lost ten, they must give up the ball to the other side at the spot where the fourth down was made. Consecutive means without leaving the hands of the side holding it. (Oriard 1993: 26)

As Alan Guttman confirms,

From 1880 the ball was 'hiked' out by the center from a static line of scrimmage. By 1882, the eleven positions of single-platoon football were established and the 'first down' was invented – three tries for five yards. In 1906 came the forward pass ... By World War I football was a thoroughly specialized, rationalized, bureaucratically organized example of modern sports'. (1978: 128–9)

4 A. G. Spalding, the father of baseball, described the sport as an exemplification of 'American Courage, Confidence, Combativeness; American Dash, Discipline, Determinism American Energy, Eagerness, Enthusiasm; American Pluck, Persistency, Performance; American Spirit, Sagacity, Success; American Vim, Vigor, Virility' (Pope 1997: 72).

5 However there are notable exceptions, particularly involving England, where a national governing body proved, for a time at least, to be obstructive to the development of international competition. The Football Association joined FIFA in 1905 but left the organisation in 1920. It left because of a series of 'disputes over contact with Germany and its allies after World War I, ... the nature of amateurism and ... admission of the Football Association of the Irish Free State in 1923' (Sugden and Tomlinson 1998: 18). In consequence the England international team did not enter the World Cup tournaments in Uruguay (1930), Italy (1934) and France (1938). For a considerable time the FA's relationship with FIFA was influenced by its view that 'world football was too weak to be bothered with' (Sugden and Tomlinson 1998: 10). This view served to prevent the English national team and a number of club sides from participating in a variety of prestigious international tournaments.

6 A note of caution is in order. A culture of individualism is a significant feature of modern Western sport. However, there are other cultures where modern sports are played and where interesting and important differences have been noted. In his intriguing study of the experiences of fading American baseball stars opting to end their careers in the Japanese league playing *besoboru* for a final lucrative contract Robert Whiting (1989) notes the difficulty American players experienced in trying to come to terms with the different culture of Japanese baseball. Whiting argues that it is 'the concept and practice of group harmony or *wa* ... [that] most dramatically differentiates Japanese baseball from the American game' (1989: 70). For athletes accustomed to a culture of individualism, where individual players and star-performers are regularly singled out for special attention and treatment, the requirement to subordinate if not sacrifice self-interest and individual initiative to enhance 'team spirit' has proven difficult, if not impossible in some cases, to cope with.

3

The Professionalisation of Modern Sport

A common thread running through the developmental processes to which different forms of modern sport have been exposed, virtually from their inception in England and to a substantial degree in America, is a distinction between amateur and professional orientations, which itself has been closely associated with social class membership.

Secure in status in a pre-industrial, predominantly agrarian English society the aristocracy and gentry had not only tolerated, but to a great extent had acted as patrons of popular folk games and events. In some instances the eighteenth-century aristocracy and gentry participated in games alongside those of inferior social status. This was particularly evident in games of cricket when men with good cricket ability would be employed on the estates or in the houses of members of the aristocracy and gentry (Ford 1977; Dunning and Sheard 1979). In this way men with cricket skills effectively began to earn a living from their ability to play the game well, but this early manifestation of professionalism was regarded as 'neither morally nor socially suspect' (Dunning and Sheard 1979: 177).

With the development of industrialisation the dominance of the landed classes (the aristocracy and the gentry) began to be eroded by the growth of an industrial bourgeoisie. As the dominance of the landed classes was undermined by the rise of a new 'bourgeois' class of industrial entrepreneurs, merchants and factory owners, members of the aristocracy and gentry began to experience 'status insecurity'. In the last quarter of the nineteenth century in England rising class tensions and growing status insecurity lead to the social construction of rigid distinctions between different categories of sport participant designated as either 'amateur' or 'professional' (Whannel 1983). In due course the traditional social pattern, where the classes had mixed freely on the sport field, was replaced by a 'more class-exclusive pattern' (Dunning and Sheard 1979: 178).

While a comparable distinction between amateur and professional began to be employed in America towards the close of the century it was in practice more ambiguous in its application (Pope 1997). In America the amateur code was not rooted in a 'body of established customs or the sponsorship of an inherited aristocracy' (Rader 1983b: 59) as was the case in England. Rather the amateur ethos was adopted by an emerging entrepreneurial class that sought to add the cultural capital that 'gentleman amateur' signified to the economic capital it had already acquired through commerce and industry. While athletic clubs acknowledged the amateur ethos and the need for fair play, in practice the code was interpreted fairly loosely as wealthier clubs sought to gain advantage over rivals by attracting the best athletes by offering 'more generous expense and travelling allowances and superior facilities' (Rader 1983b: 60).

Amateurism in America in the closing decades of the nineteenth century, playing simply for the love of the game, was recognised to have derived from England. The issue of amateurism in the American context inevitably called to mind the quintessentially English figure of the gentleman-amateur. Initially sport clubs had appeared to be disinterested in drawing distinctions between amateur and professional and wagers on competitions between club members were commonplace. However fearing the prospect of 'an invasion by "professional" athletes and athletes with "inferior" social credentials – working class, ethnics and blacks – the clubs gradually placed strictures on participants at their meets' (Rader 1983b: 58). As in the English context, amateurism was invoked to promote class and status differentiation. But the deployment of a distinction between amateur and professional also reflected important transformations in the way sports were beginning to be played and the cultural and economic significance that they were beginning to assume.

Central to the distinction between the amateur and the professional are differences in the terms on which those involved in particular sporting endeavours approach and participate in their games. Intrinsic to the development of modern sport is a process of transformation that led to recreational activities and pastimes becoming formally organised, rule governed and regulated, as well as more competitive and serious. The increasing seriousness of recreational activities and pastimes that were being steadily transformed into modern sports in part reflects the respects in which sport events with the popular cultural appeal to attract spectators were being recognised as having a commercial potential. Increasing competitiveness and seriousness, along with the prospect of revenue raised from spectators at the gate being used for paying players, fuelled debates about the status of participants. It led to distinctions being drawn between those 'amateurs' for whom play was a diversion, quite literally a pastime, where the merit of the activity was largely intrinsic, and those 'professionals' for whom play was increasingly a source of financial reward or compensation. Broadly, the development of modern sport has coincided with an 'inexorable erosion of "amateur" attitudes, values and structures' and a 'correlative replacement by attitudes, values and structures which are "professional"' (Dunning and Sheard 1979: 9–10). In turn, the growth of competitiveness, seriousness and professionalism in respect of the ways in which games have come to be played in modern societies has been identified as detrimental, as representing a loss of the 'play spirit' (Huizinga 1949) or as signifying a 'degradation' of sport (Lasch 1991).

During the greater part of the nineteenth century in America there was a significant degree of commercialisation associated with racing, running, pedestrianism and prize-fighting. Until the 1870s even within prestigious American colleges such as Yale, Harvard and Dartmouth sporting competitions tended to be commercialised. Entrepreneurs would help organise events and expensive prizes 'worth twice an average laborer's annual income' would be awarded to the victors (Pope 1997: 21). In the 1860s Harvard took part in regattas in Boston where purses of $500 were at stake and both Harvard and Yale played leading professional baseball teams on a relatively regular basis between 1866 and 1874 (Pope 1997). It was in the course of the 1870s that an 'amateur ethos' made its way across the Atlantic and began to have an impact within elite American colleges. The ethos articulated most clearly by the Amateur Athletic Club in London, that gentlemen amateurs ought to compete among themselves and not with professionals and other socially inferior individuals, began to be promoted on American campuses. Although many professional features had become an important part of American college sport the merits of amateurism were increasingly espoused. The figure of the English gentleman was held up as the model for college sport and off campus the amateur ethos began to be championed by athletic clubs (New York Athletic Club) and sport journals (*Spirit of the Times*) culminating in 1888 in 'the NYAC, along with the Amateur Club of the Schuylkill Navy and 15 other clubs' founding the Amateur Athletic Union (Pope 1997: 24).

Although there was criticism of professionalism as the amateur ethos was promoted on college campuses, in the media, as well as in debates in the wider society, particular aspects of the professional model continued to be a feature of amateur sport. For example, Yale had an athletic budget which was effectively managed by the 'unofficial' football coach, Walter Camp, and 'student managers of football, baseball, track and rowing' (Pope 1997: 25). It was usually substantially in surplus and was drawn on to pay a salary to both an athletic trainer and later the 'unofficial' football coach. In the ten year period 1893–1903 the athletic budget doubled 'equalling the combined salaries of 30 professors, and nearly equalling the incomes of the law, divinity, and medical schools combined' (Pope 1997: 25).

The dilemma colleges faced was the certain prospect of missing out on sporting success, status and prestige if the amateur ethos was followed to the letter and the virtual certainty that they would lose social esteem if they openly embraced professionalism. The solution adopted was to resort to subterfuge. The unwritten rule became to openly acclaim and promote the amateur ethos while quietly practising forms of professionalism. In consequence 'amateurism was harder to define in America, where class lines were less distinct and more fluid than in the mother country' (Pope 1997: 25).

The precise historical point and manner in which a distinction of amateur and professional statuses became an issue has varied from sport to sport. Responses to the existence or perceived threat of professionalism have also varied between sports. In late nineteenth century America summer baseball began to be seen as a particularly contentious sport, if not a test-case for the possibility of distinguishing effectively between amateur and professional statuses. A proportion of the more athletically gifted children of wealthy Americans at eastern colleges, which had extolled the virtues of the amateur ethos would spend their summers playing baseball on what was in effect a semi-professional basis. Players were accommodated in the finest hotels or by 'the best of [local] society', provided with cash payments and had all their expenses covered (Pope 1997: 26). Although there were attempts to discourage the practice, the rules and guidelines that were drafted proved to be ineffective as proof of payments to players always proved elusive. For example, players took to playing under assumed names or claimed to be in receipt of payment for a 'phantom job like waiter or casino attendant' (Pope 1997: 26).

There were other inconsistencies that contributed to the ambiguous character of the amateur professional distinction in America. Students were advised that they should not participate in sports competition for prize money yet athletes were allowed to 'accept endorsement money from tobacco companies … [and] keep the entire proceeds from the sale of programs at games' (Pope 1997: 26–27). In England in the period in question no college athlete would have entertained the idea of turning professional, it would simply have been unthinkable. By contrast in America the emphasis was increasingly on achievement and merit rather than ascription and heredity, and wealthy young men at prestigious colleges showed no inhibitions about selling their skills in the developing 'sports marketplace' (Pope 1997: 27).

Football and rugby in England

In the case of association football (soccer) professionalisation began to have an impact from the late 1870s as working-class teams from the north of England began to attract paying spectators from local communities. In 1882 the Football Association had forbidden payment to players other than in respect of expenses and compensation for lost wages. However, football clubs in the north of England continued to pay players as well as offer financial incentives to sign players from outside of their community. The threatened breakaway establishment of a north of England centred 'British Football Association' ultimately forced the FA in July 1885 to 'compromise and legalize professionalism under "stringent conditions"' (Dunning and Sheard 1979: 186; Giulianotti 1999: 5). In 1888 a professional football league was established with twelve founding members – Accrington, Aston Villa, Blackburn Rovers, Bolton Wanderers, Burnley, Derby County, Everton, Notts County, Preston North End, Stoke, West Bromwich Albion and Wolverhampton Wanderers (Dunning and Sheard 1979; Horne et al. 1999; Giulianotti 1999).

In respect of rugby, professionalism did not become a particularly significant issue until the 1890s. But when it did become an issue it led in 1895 to a split between an amateur version of the game, the 'Rugby Union' code, and a professional version of the game, the 'Rugby League' code. The different responses to professionalism in football and rugby were a consequence of wider social differences. To begin with there were evident social status differences between the respective establishments in the two sports. The governing members of the football establishment had attended more socially prestigious public schools than their rugby equivalents, indeed a 'proportion of the former had titles' (Dunning and Sheard 1979: 189). Also in football fewer professional clubs had an active role in the regional administration of the game than was the case in rugby, where in the Yorkshire and Lancashire Unions professional clubs were directly represented and influential. In consequence the football establishment were more likely to have been,

> secure in identity and status, and therefore, less likely than their counterparts in the RFU to have perceived the working-class as a threat ... And although they did not like professionalism, they had no wish to stamp it out or to drive its proponents out of the Association fold. On the contrary, they were confident in their ability to control it. (Dunning and Sheard 1979: 189)

Professionalism became a critical issue in football in the 1880s, a period of 'relatively harmonious class relations' (Dunning and Sheard 1979: 191). When professionalism became a prominent issue in rugby some ten years later social class relations were becoming more difficult. The class structure of British society was being transformed by the rise of an industrial bourgeois class. Wealth was no longer the monopoly of the aristocracy, but through investment in industry the aristocracy and gentry were able to 'keep a foothold in the ruling class' (Dunning and Sheard 1979: 191). The working classes through trades unions and associated forms of political representation were beginning to appreciate their potential power. It was changes of this order in the structure of late nineteenth century British society that 'led Rugby to be the only sport in Britain to undergo a total amateur-professional split' with the formation of the Rugby Union (amateur) and Rugby League (professional) codes (Dunning and Sheard 1979: 191; see also Collins 1998). The amateur-professional split remained a feature of the game of rugby until late in the twentieth century when in 1995 the Rugby Football Union recognised the need to abandon the sham that amateurism had become and openly embrace professionalism.

American football

In the case of American football the first instance of professionalism is reported to have been a payment of $500 to former Yale All-American guard William 'Pudge' Heffelfinger by the Allegheny Athletic Association in 1892 to persuade him to play against Pittsburgh Athletic Club. In 1893 the first known professional contract in American football was signed. The first completely professional team played in 1896, but only for an abbreviated two-game season. Then in 1897 Latrobe Athletic Association went through a full season using only professionals and in 1902 the first attempt was made to stage a professional National Football League (NFL website: http://ww2.nfl.com/history/chronology/1869-1910.html).

In contrast to the college game of football which had 'upper-status, old-stock American' roots, the professional game was initially 'ethnic, Catholic and working class' (Rader 1983b: 251). However, as with summer baseball, college players and ex-college players employing an alias would turn out for teams offering the most money and would sometimes play for several different teams during the course of a season. Such practices, along with associated concerns about players gambling on the outcome of matches and fears over game fixing, did considerable harm to the public image of the game. To improve the status and financial prospects of football Joseph Carr proposed that professional teams form an association and in 1920 the American Professional Football Association was duly established. In 1922 it became the National Football League (NFL) (Rader 1983b).

Throughout the 1920s and 1930s professional football teams struggled to attract support, yet college football continued to be popular. Whereas the latter could bask in its 'amateur' status, no matter how ambiguous it might have been, and could draw on a 'built-in constituency', pro football was regarded as 'ungentlemanly' and had to try to appeal to a non-college audience that had no familiarity with the game (Rader 1983b: 252). To make matters worse the press confined their reporting to the college game and generally did not cover professional matches. In addition the relatively low costs involved in running a team (the average payment for players per game was $100 and franchises were low) led to the emergence of small town franchises. In the 1920s turnover was high as teams pulled out then later chose to re-enter the league. The NFL suffered further because it was generally unable to attract a large enough number of the top college players, for whom a career in business, or a more established profession, promised better financial rewards. However, in the 1930s following a number of rule changes the popularity of pro football increased significantly and began to threaten the superior status enjoyed by the college game.[1]

A sequence of inter-related events played an important part in significantly transforming the fortunes of professional football. In 1959 two millionaire Texans, unable to obtain franchises in the NFL, formed their own rival league the American Football League (AFL) with eight teams. To reduce early financial losses the league sold their national television rights to ABC in 1960. The NFL duly followed suit in 1961 signing with CBS and this led to a Justice Department lawsuit over the issue of the elimination of competition between franchises. The outcome was that the leagues were found to have engaged in a practice that constituted 'undue restraint' of trade. In response the professional leagues turned to Congress which quickly passed the Sports Broadcasting Act of 1961.

The Act represented an especially important landmark for the NFL. The Act allowed professional clubs 'to negotiate as a single economic unit the sale of national broadcasting rights' and along with the rising popularity of the game it produced a rapid increase in the value of television contracts (Rader 1983b: 256). Contracts with broadcasting organisations eager to transmit live coverage of professional football took off in 1962 when NFL Commissioner Pete Rozelle negotiated an annual contract with CBS worth $4.5 million. By 1987 NFL pro football was receiving $430 million for television transmission of eighty-one regular-season games (Eastman and Meyer 1989).

The successful relationship that American professional football established with television is one that other sports would subsequently seek to emulate as they attempted to increase their popularity and revenue. The advent of television coverage after the Second World War proved to be positively beneficial to the NFL. Televised coverage of football provided 'a new source of lucrative income for pro teams' as well as offering a showcase for potential new fans (Rader 1983b: 253). Television coverage of pro football stimulated the popularity of the game by revealing aspects of the play that were not evident from the grandstand, allowing fans to develop a better understanding and appreciation of 'the intricacies of the sport' (Rader 1983b: 255).

Baseball: America's national pastime

Baseball occupies a special place in American culture and rivals football in status as *the* national game. If football better reflects 'the sexual, racial and organizational priorities of American social structure' (Real 1975: 38), baseball remains a significant national pastime. Baseball began to turn professional. in the mid-nineteenth century. Professional baseball has been described as a 'by-product' of the American Civil War (Neilson 1995). In a discussion of the early years of its development into a professional game Neilson notes how prior to the Civil War an aristocratic notion of gentlemanly amateurism prevailed in the 'Atlantic South' and that professionalism was strictly forbidden. The experience of the war led to cultural exchanges across social class and regional boundaries, one unintended consequence of which was that 'the game was germinated, codified, standardized and then carried back to farms, towns and cities from the Atlantic to the western frontier' (Neilson 1995: 32).

In the aftermath of the Civil War a number of factors combined to provide the social, economic and cultural conditions conducive to the emergence of a professional form of baseball. Widespread familiarity with the game meant that there was a popular foundation on which to draw for support and more importantly from which paying spectators might be attracted. Industrialisation across a victorious North was associated with urbanisation and a concentration of population. Add to these factors the growth of a 'commercial ethic' and an 'appetite for mass entertainments' (Neilson 1995: 32) and the conditions were present for professional baseball to emerge and to begin to secure a place for itself within 'national consciousness'.

Professional baseball developed in cities that were 'marked by both a new splendour … and a spreading industrial squalor' (Neilson 1995: 32). Baseball parks were built on the periphery of developing industrial cities and tended to be located close to the factories and tenement buildings in which their customers, the spectators or fans, worked and lived. The steady growth of a mass industrial consumer-oriented society along with an associated separation of urban life into quite distinct spheres of work and non-work activity created the social, economic and cultural conditions in which organised forms of recreation and amusement, including spectator sports like baseball, could develop.

In 1858 spectators 'were charged 50 cents admission to watch a three-game championship series between teams from New York and Brooklyn' (Cashmore 2000: 307). The first completely enclosed baseball park, the Union Grounds, Brooklyn, New York was finished in 1862. In 1868 the Cincinnati Red Stockings, a team that had been actively recruiting salaried ballplayers for some time, refurbished their playing field and provided their manager, Harry Wright the son of an English professional cricketer, with $15,000 to sign the best players in the country. In 1869 the Cincinnati Red Stockings became the first openly professional team 'on which all players received salaries for a season's play' and other professional clubs soon followed in cities across the north-east and mid-west of America (Rader 1983b; Levine 1985: 10).

In 1871 ten clubs formed the National Association of Professional Base Ball Players (NAPBBP) and expressed 'their intention to operate openly as professionals' (Levine 1985: 14). Poor financial returns and inadequate organisation led the league to collapse after five seasons. By this time baseball had begun to acquire a bad reputation,

> Uneven competition, collapsing franchises, numerous instances of gambling and game throwing, and rowdy, drunken behavior by ball-players had rapidly diminished baseball's status as a 'gentleman's game' and marked the professional version as a poor investment and as questionable fare for reputable people to enjoy. (Levine 1985: 23)

It was in this context that the figure of Albert Goodwill Spalding has been described as the 'messiah' or 'father of American baseball', a status shared with Henry Chadwick a sportswriter on the *New York Clipper* (Levine 1985: xi; McChesney 1989: 51). Spalding, hired as pitcher, captain and manager of the Chicago White Stockings for the 1876 season, was one of a small group led by William A. Hulbert the president of the club who helped to draft a constitution and gather support for a new league. The new National League of Professional Baseball Clubs formed in 1876 introduced a number of changes to the game. Owners now had complete control of 'management, regulations and the resolution of disputes' and measures were introduced to improve the image of the game (Sunday games and betting at ball parks were no longer permitted) (Rader 1983b: 115).

The league acted quickly in response to unacceptable player conduct (for example, taking bribes from gamblers and threatening umpires) and when 'the Philadelphia and New York teams failed to take their final road tours of the 1876 season' they were expelled (Rader 1983b: 115). The Cincinnati club received similar treatment in 1880 for continuing to sell beer and play on Sundays. In 1881, along with five other excluded clubs, Cincinnati formed the American Association of Base Ball Clubs, described by critics as the 'Beer Ball League' or the 'beer and whiskey league' because four of the club owners owned breweries (Levine 1985: 51). A combination of low admission fees, the selling of alcohol and Sunday games proved popular and league players began to join the new organisation. Fearing the impact of the new association's practices on league standards and the possibility that league players might break contracts to join association clubs, the National League sought to achieve an agreement with the new organisation. Before the 1883 season the National League and the American Association signed a National Agreement. The agreement established exclusive territorial rights and recorded the parties' consent to abstain from competitive bidding for contracted players of other teams. If a player was on a club 'reserve list' no other club was entitled to open contract negotiations. However players on the list could be sold on to other clubs. In addition both organisations recognised 'the existence of the Northwestern League as a minor league' (Levine 1985: 52).

The wider industrial unrest that was a feature of American social life in the 1880s and 1890s received expression in professional baseball. Enforcement of a strict code of conduct, the reserve list and league salary limits, coupled with evidence of the growing prosperity of major league baseball led in 1885 to the foundation of what was in effect a player's union, the Brotherhood of Professional Base Ball Players. John Montgomery Ward, lawyer, star player and founder of the organisation, presented the league with an ultimatum – 'abandon the salary ceiling system and stop selling players' (Rader 1983b: 117) or the players would establish their own league. Club owners refused to discuss the reserve rule – the 'fugitive slave law' as Ward described it – or the issue of salary ceilings and in consequence the 1890 season saw the establishment of a Player's League (Levine 1985: 58).

What was called the 'Brotherhood War', the battle for the control of professional baseball, 'dramatized various concerns that defined the emergence of an industrial society' (Levine 1985: 58). The Player's League won the support of entrepreneurs who wanted to challenge those already in control of professional baseball. While seeking to obtain an appropriate level of return on their capital investment the entrepreneurs funding the new league suspended the reserve rule, offered 'three-year contracts at salaries equal to 1888 figures' and agreed to share club profits with players (Levine 1985: 60). The Player's League was successful in attracting good players from major league clubs and it attracted more fans to its games than the National League. For example, in 'mid-May the Chicago *Tribune* reported that sixty-six Brotherhood games had attracted 183,560 patrons, while seventy-one National League contests had drawn only 117,050' (Levine 1985: 61).

The National League policy of deliberately scheduling games on the same day in the same city as the Player's League reduced levels of attendance and financial returns in both leagues. However, with its greater financial resources the National League was better placed to cope with losses than the financial backers of the Player's League that it described as 'subversive' and 'undemocratic' (Levine 1985). The prospect of future losses along with threats and payments made by the National League induced backers of the Player's League to agree to 'unconditional surrender' and so the 'experiment in co-operative-capitalistic baseball ended in failure after one season' (Rader 1983b: 119; Levine 1985: 63–4).

From the closing decade of the nineteenth century to the beginning of the 1920s both professional baseball and college football confronted an organisational challenge, namely how to achieve an appropriate degree of order and stability. In football it was a matter of establishing governing bodies at regional and national levels to ensure fair competition, preserve the game's amateur status and enhance its appeal. In baseball it was a matter of how to preserve the freedom of franchise holders to run their clubs as they saw fit, while preventing clubs competing for players and rival leagues being established, as well as placing limitations on the number of big league teams.

In 1891 in the wake of the 'Brotherhood War' the American Association collapsed and the National League increased its membership from eight to twelve teams (Levine 1985). However, the new format proved to be unpopular with fans and unprofitable for the owners and in 1899 the latter moved to restore the league to eight clubs (Boston, Brooklyn, Chicago, Cincinnati, New York, Philadelphia, Pittsburgh, and St. Louis). In 1901 the president of the minor Western League encouraged the establishment of baseball franchises in the four cities abandoned by the National League and claimed major league status for a newly constituted American League. In 1903 a National Agreement between the rival leagues established a National Commission to oversee what became known as 'Organized Baseball' (Rader 1983b). However, 'Organized Baseball' suffered further bouts of disruption with the formation of another player's union, the Base Ball Player's Fraternity in 1912 and the establishment of a third major league, the Federal League, which ran from 1912–1915.

From paid athlete to sporting celebrity

Key features of the opening decades of the century were a rise in attendance at games and a growth in club profits that led to players demanding better salaries. Rader reports that 'as many as ten superstars received salaries of $10,000 or more by 1910' (1983b: 125). Attendance in the big league doubled between 1903 and 1908 while minor league baseball circuits increased by more than a factor of three in the period 1903–1913. By 1913 more than 300 cities had pro baseball teams and the game had 'gained social respectability', a status exemplified from 1909 by the practice of the President starting each season by ceremonially pitching the first ball (Rader 1983b: 127).

In an analysis of the early development of the sport it has been noted that 'Professional baseball created a new category of workers in American life, the paid athlete-specialist' (Neilson 1995: 34). Initially their status was comparable to that of actors and other travelling players. Typically players were drawn from the locality with which the baseball team was associated and for the most part they were the sons of immigrants, boys from the farm or the town. But this was destined to change with the 'massification' of American society. The establishment of a popular press, increased mobility through the development of new rail technologies, new forms of economic life ('oligopolistic corporate structures and strategies') together with 'mas-sification of habits of consumption through homogenization of production and advertising' (Neilson 1995: 36), created a context in which professional baseball could flourish.

As major league baseball grew rapidly in popularity in the early twentieth century players were no longer likely to be local boys, increasingly they were being drawn from across the nation and were becoming a 'quasi-professional class' (Neilson 1995: 37). The new professional baseball players were effectively,

> among the first examples of a *new human type*, the '*celebrity*', the object of con-stant curiosity, adoration, envy and scorn. Though most, in the early years, drew modest salaries and had little security, *they were, by virtue of such unremitting scrutiny, beginning to be set apart from, and above, other men.* (Neilson 1995: 37 emphasis added)

The growth of a mass popular culture and a relative shift of emphasis from production to consumption was exemplified by an increasing 'enthu-siasm for sports and spectacle' and an associated emergence of new idols who began to displace the 'republican model of the hero-citizen' and its affirmation of the virtues of the gentleman amateur (Neilson 1995: 37; Lowenthal 1961).

Amateurism and professionalism in golf

Initially golf's appeal was as an amateur game with the emphasis placed upon aesthetics and style rather than efficiency (Lowerson 1989). In the late nineteenth century in England golf was an exclusive game. To play golf con-siderable resources of time and money were required, as was membership of an exclusive social institution, the golf club. Golfers required appropriate equipment, the hire of a caddie and frequently would need to 'make use of the professional's services as a teacher or playing partner' (Birley 1995: 103). By virtue of the costs and time involved golf was largely out of reach of the working man and in the event that that would not serve to guarantee social exclusivity, clubs developed discriminatory rules to keep the lower orders out, or resorted to blackballing 'undesirables' (Ford 1977; Birley 1995).

Although there was no explicit class discrimination in golf comparable to the Amateur Athletic Club's (AAC) 1866/1887 exclusion of anyone but 'gentlemen amateurs' from a range of sports (Horne et al. 1999), the golf professional was not treated as an equal. The AAC excluded a wide category of people from membership and participation in events under their control. Namely anyone who had participated in 'open competition', or for money, or with professionals, or who had 'taught or assisted in the pursuit of athletic exercises as a means of livelihood, or is a mechanic, artisan or labourer' (Bailey 1978: 131). In contrast in golf it was 'perfectly acceptable to play regularly against a professional', although the latter tended to be treated like a 'superior domestic employee' (Lowerson 1989: 196). But while playing with professionals was accepted, forms of social discrimination nevertheless continued to be practised. For example, while club professionals were excluded from amateur-only tournaments, those of a higher social standing, for example paid golf club secretaries and those who derived their living from golf journalism and writing golf books, were allowed to play. Such variations in treatment associated with differences in status and employment gave rise to increasing anxieties among professionals and led, in due course, to the formation of the Professional Golfers' Association in 1902 (Birley 1995).

While club members were content to play against a professional, mixing socially with the artisan class was another matter. Golf clubs tended to be socially exclusive institutions for 'people with plenty of money but no particular skill or competitive ambition' (Birley 1995: 109). There was a relative scarcity of clubs interested in extending the social range of their membership. In response, towards the end of the nineteenth century there were signs of an emerging movement to found artisan clubs, motivated more by the need to head off local opposition to the use of common land for golf course development than by any concerns about equality. It was a slow process, one limited by 'availability of space and of clubs which could attract a more popular membership' (Lowerson 1989: 201). Where artisan members were permitted to play it was generally when other members 'of the right sort' did not wish to and while they frequently benefited from a reduced membership fee it was usually in exchange for helping to maintain courses and buildings. It was really only following the formation of the Artisan Golfer's Association in 1921 that artisan clubs became a 'source of great English players, as well as club pros' (Lowerson 1989: 197).

The first Open Championship had been inaugurated at Prestwick in Scotland in 1860 where it continued to be held for ten years. It was then shared with the Royal and Ancient and the Honourable Company from Edinburgh until 1893 when English clubs were admitted (Lowerson 1989). The early years of the Open tournament were dominated by Scottish professionals, their monopoly finally being broken in 1890 by 'one of the new-style full-time English amateurs, John Ball, of Royal Liverpool' (Birley 1995: 108). Notwithstanding Ball's success the Open continued to be dominated by professionals, the significant difference being that increasingly it was the new English professionals that were to dominate with J. H. Taylor and Harry Vardon being particularly successful.

Like the game itself, the history of the golf 'professional' starts in Scotland. In the nineteenth century the golf professional was someone who would be employed to perform a number of necessary golf related tasks. From tending the greens, making, repairing and carrying golf clubs, to playing with and instructing members, the golf professional was a man of many parts. In 1888 the *Golfing Annual* referred to most professionals as 'greenkeepers' and one celebrated individual is reported as having the title 'Greenkeeper, Club-maker and Professional' (Birley 1995: 106). Professionals frequently had other manual trades that they would combine with golf playing. At the time the professional was thought to be 'a "feckless", reckless creature' whose interests extended no further than golf and whisky, but there were notable exceptions. Willie Park the Open Champion of 1887 and 1889 was 'the first professional to put his name to a book of instruction and also one of the first golf architects much in demand for designing and supervising the construction of new courses' (Birley 1995: 107).

As the nineteenth century drew to a close social and economic changes were rapidly transforming the game of golf and the position of the golf pro-fessional. Golf was becoming increasingly popular both in England and America and as it did so opportunities for golf professionals grew. If the growth of workshop manufacture of golf clubs was reducing some of the demand in the lower price ranges there nevertheless remained a buoyant demand for first-rate hand-made clubs. For example, James Braid, even before his five Open successes, was appointed to the lucrative position of club maker for the *Army and Navy* stores (Birley 1995). The market for good quality equipment was growing rapidly, especially in America. There was an increasing demand for professionals 'eager to capitalize on the sudden boom in the demand for their sporting expertise in North America' (Kirsch 1999: 331). Harry Vardon was able to make lucrative tours of America, where he won the US Open in 1900, and J. H. Taylor established a reputa-tion as a fine golf architect. Growing interest in the game promoted by rising press and public interest in events like the Open led to increased club memberships and related benefits in the form of greater demand for teach-ing as well as for equipment, from which less celebrated lower level golf professionals also benefited.

The growing popularity of golf, an increase in professionals entering the Open and other tournaments, and a rise in the value of prizes, contributed to the emergence of 'the super-player whose link with a club often became nominal' (Lowerson 1989: 198), causing concern to be expressed about 'professional entrepreneurism'. There was increasing tension between on the one hand professionals eager to participate in the growing number of tournaments and on the other club members and secretaries who did not welcome their increasing absence. Tensions between tournament players and the rest increased with the introduction of a new ball, the Haskell.

The original golf ball was hand-made of leather and stuffed with feath-ers, hence its designation the 'feathery'. From the mid-nineteenth century the feathery was replaced by the 'guttie', a considerably cheaper moulded ball made from Malay gum extracted from a 'percha tree'. Then in 1898 Coburn Haskell from Cleveland and Bertram Work of the Goodrich Rubber Company 'developed the rubber-wound ball' that would be known as the 'Haskell' (Birley 1995: 196–7; Kirsch 1999: 333). The new ball invented and produced in America flew further and was easier to control. It was felt that it made golf an easier game. The reaction of professionals in England was initially resistant. Professionals felt threatened on two counts. One of the sources of income for club professionals was 'making and re-moulding gutties' and this would disappear with the adoption of the new rubber-cored ball. No less important was the fear that the new ball would reduce the skill required to play the game and thereby narrow the gap between amateur and professional (Birley 1995; Kirsch 1999). However, resistance to the new ball was undermined in 1902 when Sandy Herd used it in the Open Championship and won the tournament. By the end of 1903 the new ball had been 'grudgingly accepted' (Kirsch 1999).

Women's golf

The Haskell is also believed to have had a significant impact on women's golf in so far as it made the game more pleasurable and did not require as much strength to hit (Ford 1977). Although golf clubs were regarded as a male preserve 'ladies golf clubs' had been established at St. Andrews and at North Devon 'as early as the 1860s' (Birley 1995: 111). The game had distinct advantages for women interested in participating in recreational activity as it was not athletically demanding and could be played while conforming to the restrictive dress conventions of the age. Also the handicapping system was conducive to the development of mixed golf and this in turn stimulated interest in the segregated form of the game and contributed to the founding of more clubs for women (Birley 1995).

Although initially confined to small putting greens women moved to establish clubs where they were permitted to play off shortened tees at times that would not disturb male members (Lowerson 1989; Birley 1995). By the 1890s in the Stirling region of Scotland 13 of the 31 active golf clubs had 'a significant number of lady members' (Birley 1995: 111). Failure to gain admission to an established male club in 1892 led women to form the Brighton and Hove Ladies Golf Club. Then in 1893 20 Ladies Clubs established the Ladies Golf Union and in the same year an amateur championship.

The Haskell not only made golf an easier game to play, it also made it an even more popular one among both men and women. This in turn increased the interest of the press and equipment makers in the professional game and prepared the way for commercial sponsorship, leading in 1903 to the *News of the World* sponsoring the PGA World Match Play championship the prize money for which, £200, 'was more than twice that of the Open' (Lowerson 1989: 205; Birley 1995: 197). Media interest, sponsorship and the impact of innovations in manufacture and design of equipment have subsequently played a significant role in the development of the game and, in turn, have substantially raised the profile and earning potential of the golf professional.

Professional tournament golf

While professionalism may have been a feature of golf in America from its inception, professional tournament golf only began to develop a culturally significant profile in the 1920s. It was in this period that American players of the stature of Walter Hagen, Gene Sarazen and the amateur Bobby Jones began to excel and to usher in 'the age of modern tournament golf' (Adams 1995: 248). In the aftermath of the First World War American golfers achieved international mastery in both professional and amateur golf. Americans seemed more ready to respond positively to innovations in equipment design. They had been much quicker to adopt the new and superior tubular steel-shafted club that superseded the hickory shaft. Furthermore, whereas they welcomed innovations such as the Schenectady putter (with a shaft in the centre of a mallet-shaped head), in 1910 the Royal and Ancient Golf Club of St. Andrews banned it. The United States Golf Association refused to accept the ruling and the implied notion that equipment should be standardised (Kirsch 1999).

Reflecting on the different responses to professionalism on each side of the Atlantic Lowerson remarks that,

> The British still wallowed in a widespread ambivalence to professionals, who were ... regarded as little more than the talented servant of amateurs. When the American, Walter Hagen, was runner-up in the 1923 British Open he refused to attend the award ceremony in a clubhouse that had been banned to professionals during the week of play. (1989: 202)

Walter Hagen (1892–1969) has been described as an historic figure, the person who made professional golf a 'socially respectable occupation in America' (Rader 1983b: 227). From humble origins Hagen started out as a caddy but his 'pleasing personality, sartorial elegance and ... impeccable manners' coupled with his success as a full-time golf professional is argued to have helped to dismantle social barriers in America and Europe (Rader 1983b: 228).

While prize money was a source of income for golf professionals like Hagen the values at stake in tournaments were relatively meagre. For example $500 was the prize for the winner of the annual Professional Golfer's Association tournament. The bulk of Hagen's income from golf, estimated to be between $30,000 and $50,000 per year, came from exhibition tours and product endorsements for golf equipment. Like other high profile sportsmen who came to the fore in the same era Hagen 'embodied the new consumer ethic' (Rader 1983b: 229). A lover of fine food and fashion the unorthodox and hedonistic Hagen became a popular golfing figure.

Although professionalism in some shape or form had been a longstanding feature of American society, by the beginning of the twentieth century the tenets of amateurism, albeit fraught with contradictions, had become a mark of social distinction (Pope 1997). It was in this context that a highly successful golfing contemporary of Hagen's, the amateur Bobby Jones, acquired the status of a 'truly national, even international, golfing celebrity' (Rader 1983b: 229). Jones was recognised to be a golfing prodigy from the age of nine when he won a junior championship against an opponent who was seven years older. He competed in the US Amateur tournament at fourteen years of age and won the US Open in 1923. From that date through to 1930 he won 'thirteen national titles – five United States amateurs, four United States Opens, three British Opens and one British amateur', finishing his career with the historic Grand Slam of 1930 after which he retired (Rader 1983b: 230). Although Jones played as an amateur, attended college and began to practice law while competing in tournaments, on retirement, just like a professional, he sought to take advantage of the profile and image he had acquired through his golfing prowess. Jones became involved in a range of businesses and income generating opportunities that included radio shows about golf, instructional films, product endorsements for a line of golf equipment produced by Spalding, as well as helping with the design and development of the Augusta National golf course.

Racial discrimination in golf

The idea that Hagen's prowess as a golfer and endearing personality broke down the social barriers that had been a feature of golf is contentious in at least one important respect. While Hagen's unwillingness to tolerate the exclusion of professionals from clubhouses is commendable and evidence of the success of his responses and those of other professionals to remedy matters is indisputable, other too often unacknowledged barriers remained firmly in place. In particular, Hagen's experiences in America and England of the amateur ethos and its discriminatory social consequences for professionals would no doubt have struck a chord with African-Americans in the United States who were routinely prevented, through racial discrimination, from participating in a range of professional sports. While during the period of slavery there had been black boxers and jockeys competing for their masters, by the late 1880s they had been largely excluded from mainstream sport in America (Captain 1991). For example, black players were not allowed to compete in major league baseball from the mid-1880s to the mid-1940s when Jackie Robinson broke the 'color-line' in organised baseball by signing for the Montreal Royals, a minor league team (Lipsyte and Levine 1995). Robinson subsequently became the first black player in major league baseball since the 1880s when he moved to the Brooklyn Dodgers in 1947.

Initially in golf the signs were relatively promising with John Shippen, a black player, and Oscar Bunn, an American Indian, participating in the second United States Open held in 1896 at Shinnecock Golf Club (Owen 2001). Notwithstanding protests by English and Scottish professionals Shippen and Bunn were permitted to play. Shippen tied for fifth place in the tournament and collected ten dollars in prize money and by so doing became 'the first African-American to earn money as a contestant in a US Open' (Sinnette 1998: 19). Shippen went on to play in four more Opens (1899, 1900, 1902 and 1913) and he acted as a head professional at a number of clubs, but this represented 'the high-water mark of enlightened race relations in American golf for many decades to come' (Owen 2001: 179).

At the beginning of the twentieth century golf continued to be popular with the social elite and it was becoming increasingly appealing to a growing business and professional class that was keen to enjoy the exclusive privileges and status associated with the private country club. The country club, an American social institution, provided a way for rich Americans to ostentatiously 'display the wealth they had acquired in the age of industrialization' (Sinnette 1998: 59). Golf quickly became an important activity in such clubs. Indeed the game of golf has been described as 'the most potent of all sports' in promoting the spread of country clubs (Rader 1983b: 66). As the game grew in popularity in the opening decades of the twentieth century so did the status conscious institution of the country club. Within 15 years around 40 country clubs had golf courses (Sinnette 1998). As the country clubs increased in number they remained highly exclusive and continued to be 'bastions of racial and social discrimination' (Adams 1995: 257). In the 'golden age' of American sport, the 1920s, the barriers to black players were virtually insurmountable and 'only by "passing" for white could someone of African descent join a country club' (Sinnette 1998: 59).

Until 1928 no African-American had become a member of the Professional Golfer's Association but in that year 'a very light skinned' Dewey Brown joined. In 1934, without explanation or warning, the PGA withdrew his eligibility, the suggestion being that the organisation had been unaware of his racial identity when granting membership (Sinnette 1998: 31). The low point in the history of American golf was finally reached in 1943 when in the context of increasing legal challenges to racially discriminatory practices in golf the Professional Golfer's Association (PGA) modified its constitution to restrict membership to those of the 'Caucasian race'. It would take until 1961 for the clause to be deleted from the PGA's constitution and then only after legal pressure from the California Attorney General.

Tennis

Historically, like golf and polo, tennis has tended to be a sport confined largely to men and women in the higher social strata. From the late nineteenth century tennis developed in the refined environment of the socially exclusive (country) club. The tennis club became an essential part of an exclusive social landscape that placed emphasis on the virtues of the gentleman-amateur and simultaneously treated the professional as a socially inferior species.

In England 'society' magazines promoted the virtues of the game as a pleasant diversion for weekend house parties and in America the game was also keenly pursued (Walker 1989). Although the All England Club had first acknowledged the growing popularity of lawn tennis in 1877, by the time the United States Lawn Tennis Association (USLTA) was formed in 1881 there was still no governing body for tennis in England. An attempt was made to establish such a body in 1883 but club secretaries voted against the idea. It was not until 1888 that a national governing body, the Lawn Tennis Association (LTA), was established. The fact that there was already an American LTA in existence did not disturb the founders who 'showed little interest in what was going on outside their own country' (Gillmeister 1998: 191). Affiliation of clubs to the LTA grew from more than 250 in 1900, to 1,620 in 1925, close to 2,500 by 1930 and reached 3,220 in 1938 (Walker 1989).

Professionalism manifested itself in tennis in a number of different ways. One respect in which professionalism appeared in tennis is comparable to the emergence of the professional in the early history of golf. From the end of the nineteenth century tennis clubs had employed grounds-men or court attendants who were also able to offer professional instruction for a 'nominal charge' per set. Independently of club membership the cost of professional instruction lay in the region of 'half a guinea per hour plus expenses' (Walker 1989: 257). The presence of professionals in the club environment served to exemplify the game's possibilities, it revealed other ways of playing the game, including an array of potential strokes and tactics that opened new horizons for club members only accustomed to playing social tennis. It has been suggested that the 'faster and more aggressive game played by professionals' began to permeate club play and contributed to a lowering of the age profile of tennis club members in the early decades of the twentieth century (Walker 1989: 251). The implication is that a once leisurely game played by a predominantly middle-aged male membership was steadily being transformed by the increasing presence of the professional into a faster, more competitive, more serious game that appealed to a younger membership.

Notwithstanding the centrality of an 'amateur ethos' to the development of modern tennis in the late nineteenth century, competitors, when and where necessary, received contributions towards the costs they incurred in travelling to tournaments. In addition, in some instances winners and runners-up might receive prize money (Walker 1989). The growth of public interest in tennis and the entry of paying spectators at events contributed further to the game's transformation. At the first Wimbledon tournament spectators paid an entry fee of sixpence and a further sixpence for a programme that indicated the victor would receive 'a gold prize worth twelve guineas and a silver cup, presented by *The Field*, worth twenty-five guineas' (Gillmeister 1998: 194). In so far as 'amateur' at this stage signified social status as a gentleman, the acquisition of prizes did not, in and of itself, signify professionalism. Professional in respect of lawn tennis at this point in time tended to mean someone who was paid by a club for coaching (Gillmeister 1998: 355 n. 132). As in the case of other sports the term signified a lower social standing. While there was a degree of social stigma associated with professionalism, until the 1920s a number of tournaments sought to encourage the best amateurs and professionals to compete openly against one another.

Towards the close of the nineteenth century tennis tournaments were becoming more international with Englishmen competing in the Newport, Rhode Island tournament and Americans participating at Wimbledon. International tennis became firmly established with the inauguration of the Davis Cup in 1900. This tournament, initially between teams from America and England, institutionalised the payment of travel costs and other expenses. Increasing international exchanges led in 1913 to the formation of the International Lawn Tennis Federation (ILTF). In 1923 America was finally persuaded to join the ILTF and the championships of four member states, England, France, Australia and America were designated as the official championships, later to become known colloquially as 'Grand Slam' tournaments. From the 1920s 'the demands of the game, travel costs and opportunities for profit led inexorably towards the professionalisation of the sport' (1989: 168).

Participation in prestigious international tennis events required players possessing independent means, the support of patrons, or assistance with the considerable costs involved. While paying lip service to the amateur ethos tennis governing bodies tended to permit, if not encourage, '"shamateurism", usually paying amateurs liberal "expense" allowances for appearing in tournaments' (Rader 1983b: 318). The ambiguous nature of tennis's amateur status ultimately proved costly. The inability of the ILTF and the International Olympic Committee to establish an agreed rigorous operational definition of amateurism led to tennis being excluded from the Olympic Games from 1924 (Walker 1989).

Tennis really took off as a spectator sport after the First World War. In 1885 around 3,500 spectators watched the 'challenge round' at Wimbledon, yet by 1919, 8,000 spectators gathered to see Suzanne Lenglen, the French Champion, make her debut. In America the growth in spectator interest was no less spectacular. The rising popularity of tennis in the 1920s has been attributed in part to the emergence of two outstanding players, Suzanne Lenglen and Big Bill Tilden (Rader 1983b). From 1919 to 1926 Suzanne Lenglen won six ladies singles titles at Wimbledon and in the same period Tilden achieved comparable success in the United States men's championship. Their emergence and subsequent domination of women's and men's tennis has been described as marking 'the end of the conservative, casual and social age of tennis and the beginning of an age in which tennis players became public celebrities' (Rader 1983b: 220). Both players were controversial figures who drew spectators to events and attracted front and back page press interest. As well as being a strong player Suzanne Lenglen achieved notoriety for a liberated style of dress and her tendency to argue with officials. In 1926 she became a professional player, for a sum reputed to be $100,000, participating with other leading players in a tour of the United States organised by the sports promoter Charles C. Pyle, the man who had encouraged the footballer Red Grange to turn professional (Walker 1989).

Tilden was an outstanding player, an amateur for whom tennis was a full-time activity. As well as seven US national singles championships and five US doubles titles he won three Wimbledon singles championships. In addition to tennis Tilden had ambitions as an actor and took the lead in several shows. Like Lenglen he could be difficult with match officials and he had a reputation for being arrogant. But the biggest problem Tilden encountered within tennis was complying with the rule that prevented players from profiting directly from tennis by endorsing equipment, teaching or writing about the sport (Rader 1983b). Tilden accepted considerable sums of money for writing books, giving exclusive interviews and from time to time writing newspaper pieces and feature articles for magazines (Walker 1989). Writing for remuneration was a contravention of the amateur code and in 1924 the USLTA informed him that unless he ceased he would be suspended from tournaments. Furthermore, Tilden's homosexuality did not help his relationship with the USLTA which was working to eradicate the game's 'effete image' (Walker 1989).

In any event Tilden chose to ignore the demand to cease writing. Because he was such an important member of the American Davis Cup team and a player who drew significant numbers of people to events the suspension was not applied. Instead the USLTA compromised and advised that 'players could write about tennis as long as they did not "cover" the tournaments in which they were currently playing' (Rader 1983b: 222–223). True to form Tilden continued as before and in 1928 he was duly suspended. However, the reaction from the Fédération Française de Tennis, fearful that Tilden's absence from an imminent Davis Cup challenge round would reduce spectator interest, led to tennis officials in France turning to their government which sought help from the American administration. The diplomatic pressure exerted on the USLTA led to Tilden being allowed to play in the Davis Cup round in Paris but the suspension applied when he returned home. Reinstated the following year Tilden regained the US singles championship and also won the singles championships of Switzerland and the Netherlands. After failing to persuade the ILTF to allow an Open tournament in Philadelphia in 1930 Tilden turned professional and embarked upon a series of relatively obscure exhibition and international tours. A pattern was established that would see other successful amateur players joining professional tours.

In tennis the 'amateur' game remained the main attraction, the source of spectator interest, and 'shamateurism' constituted a necessary corollary, until the advent of Open tournaments in 1968. Why was this? Modern tennis started as a socially exclusive game and has largely remained so in England and America. Playing tennis in the late nineteenth century was the preserve of the wealthy, those who could afford their own courts or membership of an exclusive club. Those who participated in tournaments generally came from the wealthier sections of the community, as did those watching. From the beginning of the twentieth century, and especially after the First World War, tennis, like golf, attracted members of the growing industrial capitalist class, the upwardly mobile families of new money that sought to acquire social and cultural capital by gaining entry to exclusive clubs. These individuals had a vested interest in maintaining the social exclusivity of amateur tennis.

However, there was a significant and growing tension within tennis between the amateur ethos, which those in positions of responsibility within governing bodies, associations and clubs seeking to preserve the social exclusivity of the game worked to uphold, and the impulsion, if not imperative, common to competitive sport as a whole, to raise standards and improve performance. The latter required a serious commitment to the game that effectively began to transform it into a full-time activity, into something resembling a profession. The demands on participants in high profile competitive 'amateur' tennis tournaments were becoming considerable in terms of time, money and commitment. Major tennis tournaments were becoming increasingly international in character with competitors being drawn from around the world. While remaining amateur in status competitors effectively had to commit themselves full time to their sport and become increasingly professional in their attitude towards the game. The increasing potential for top players to earn a living, if indirectly, from the sport through expenses and other activities related to tennis aggravated the contradictions between the amateur ethos and the growing reality of 'shamateurism' or incipient professionalism.

Consider as an example the last Englishman to win the Wimbledon Singles title, Fred Perry (1909–95), who was champion in 1934, 1935 and 1936. Perry, the first player to win all four Grand Slam titles, described his attitude towards the game as at odds with the 'amateur outlook' of the time. As the son of a Lancashire cotton spinner who later became a Labour Member of Parliament, Perry, by virtue of his class background, was an outsider to the tennis establishment and regarded as, at best, uncouth. Reflecting on his difficulties with the LTA and committee members of the All England Club Perry remarked that he always had the feeling that he was 'tolerated but not really wanted' (quoted in Whannel 2002: 88). Perry's view of the LTA and the All England Club was undoubtedly influenced by a conversation he overheard when he won his first Wimbledon in 1934. A committee member of the All England Club apparently apologised to J. H. Crawford, Perry's Australian opponent, who had just lost in the final in three sets (6–3, 6–0, 7–5) in a mere 72 minutes, that 'This was one day when the best man didn't win' (quoted in Phillips 2002).

As a player Perry was argued to have a ruthless streak – 'I was always a believer in stamping on my opponent if I got him down ... I never wanted to give him the chance to get up' (http://www.wimbledon.org/features/fredperry. stm). He was considered supremely fit, a condition that was attributed to his training alongside members of the Arsenal Football Club. In addition to his Wimbledon titles, between 1933 and 1936 Perry won three US Championships and French and Australian titles. In attitude and commitment Perry was very much the professional and he campaigned, albeit unsuccessfully, to persuade the governing bodies of the game to accept professional tennis and move to open tournaments (Whannel 2001). After a victory over Australia in the Davis Cup in July 1936 Perry decided to turn professional, commenting that 'nothing had been done to encourage me to stay in the amateur game'. Perry's name had become synonymous with the finest tennis in the world and taking advantage of his additional reputation as the best dressed player of his day he proceeded to follow the example set by another player, Frenchman René Lacoste, who had formed a company to produce tennis shirts, and established a business of his own making *Fred Perry* sports shirts (http://www. wimbledon.org/features/fredperry.stm).

Perry was a very strong character, an individual who had the determination to 'push back the conventional limits of the sporting hero' (Inglis 1977: 120). Like outstanding individuals in other sporting fields, for example 'Babe' Ruth, Red Grange and Walter Hagen, Fred Perry sought to capitalise on his talent, reputation and image as a sportsman. After his playing career was over Perry was successful as a broadcaster and worked for 40 years for the BBC covering Wimbledon fortnight and the *Fred Perry* brand he established became very popular around the world, the wreath logo used on the merchandise becoming one of the most enduring in international sport.[2]

From the 1920s tennis grew in popularity and gradually became a significant spectator sport (Rader 1983b). To be successful in attracting spectators, standards of play had to be high and to that end players needed resources to cover equipment, travel, and tournament costs. Given that cash prizes and open tournaments continued to be prohibited, this meant that on a practical day-to-day basis regulations had to be gently bent as local clubs and third parties sought to sponsor individuals and cover their training needs and tournament expenses. Such covert arrangements continued until 1958 when modifications to regulations sanctioned a specific number of days per year – '240 ... of which not more than 150 could be spent abroad' – for which expenses could be granted (Walker 1989: 269). Finally in December 1967 the LTA announced that distinctions between amateur and professional were to be withdrawn and that in future all participants would be designated simply as 'players'. This initiative prepared the way for open tennis tournaments to begin the following year (Walker 1989).

The development of professional sport has been a long process, one marked by growing popular cultural appeal and increasing commercial significance. Professional sport is now very much a business, a commodity with considerable economic value, as well as an institutional form with enormous cultural significance. Located at the heart of popular culture in most countries around the world the appeal of professional sport is virtually unparalleled. Sport has the capacity to transcend cultural differences and bring people together in a way that few other activities can. Around the globe professional sport draws an impressive number of paying spectators on a regular basis to live matches, tournaments and competitions. Through the medium of television transmission sport attracts additional large global audiences. The rights to transmit sport events are now of considerable value to both sporting organisations and television corporations. But television transmission of sport events is also of value to an important third constituency, the growing number of sponsors, who have become increasingly significant players in the business of sport. It is in this commercial, media-rich environment that the sport star has not only grown in economic and cultural prominence but has been transformed into a celebrity figure whose significance in a number of instances has become global in magnitude.

Notes

1 In 1933 the 'hashmarks' were moved ten yards inside the sidelines and also in that year forward passes were permitted from any point behind the line of scrimmage. Coupled with the introduction in 1943 of free substitutions pro football began to look a more attractive proposition for spectators than the amateur college game (Rader 1983b: 253)

2 Several decades before Nike made its mark in the sport apparel business and succeeded in achieving street credibility as fashion wear the *Fred Perry* brand crossed over from sports clothing to become part of the 1960s 'mod' youth culture in England. Subsequently the *Fred Perry* casual shirt has become an essential fashion accessory for various youth sub-culture tribes, including skinheads, suede heads, ska and Northern soul boys.

As I have indicated *Fred Perry* was not alone in developing sport and recreational clothing after concluding a successful tennis career. René Lacoste (1904–96) won two Wimbledon titles, three French Opens and two US Opens in the course of his tennis career. In 1933 he set up a company, *Lacoste*, with Andre Gillier, owner of France's largest knitwear firm at the time, to produce a tennis shirt that he had designed with an embroidered alligator logo (www.lacoste.com).

4

Media, Sponsorship and Sport Stardom

The media and the making of modern sport

Sport, the media and sponsorship are closely articulated aspects of modern life without which contemporary forms of sport stardom and sporting celebrity would not exist. Modern professional sport is itself unimaginable without the media. Sport is now closely articulated with press, radio and television coverage of events, the results of matches, the performances of players, as well as the on- and off-field actions of sport personalities.

It was in the nineteenth century that newspapers and magazines first began to cover modern sport events on a significant scale, raising the status and profile of both the sports covered and the individual sporting figures singled out for special mention in reports. Indeed, in both Britain and the US modern sport and the modern press developed together (Mason 1993; Oriard 1993). The press had a significant early role in the promotion of modern sport in Britain and the USA. Not only did they provide free advance publicity of events and matches, as well as reports of games, including results, but they also 'helped to form sporting sub-cultures' (Mason 1993: 3). Press interest and press reporting contributed to the emergence of the specific forms of cultural life that came to be associated with each particular sport. In the nineteenth and early twentieth centuries in both Britain and the US it was principally through the newspaper that sports were discovered, that understanding developed and a familiarity with prominent, if not heroic figures was established.

In this chapter attention will be directed primarily to inter-relationships between the media and sport, but consideration will also be given to the associated impact commercial, endorsement and sponsorship activity has had on the world of sport. Drawing on examples from both Britain and the USA the focus will fall primarily on football. The game of football means different things in the British and American cultural contexts. The sport of association football ('soccer' in America) originated in England and is now played in most countries around the world. It can justifiably claim to be *the* global game. In contrast the cultural significance and popular appeal of 'grid-iron' or American football, played in North America, is largely confined to the US and Canada (Real 1989). But both football codes have a very high national profile. Association football, or soccer, is the national game in England as well as in a significant number of other countries and in America 'when the Super Bowl comes on television … highways empty of traffic and the shopping malls become barren of customers' (Wenner 1989: 157). Whether football can legitimately lay claim to be the national game in America is debatable, especially given the longstanding claim of baseball to that status and the more recent rise of basketball in national popularity. However, NFL football is acknowledged to be 'the most widely covered and lucrative of the major sports' (Bellamy 1989: 126) in the USA and the most popular sport on American television.

The present cultural status and meaning of any particular sport is a complex product of the various contributions of those directly and indirectly involved at all levels – clubs, players, associated organisations, governing bodies, commercial corporations, sponsors, advertisers, sportswriters, broadcasters, spectators, readers and viewers. The institution of modern sport has been shaped from the nineteenth century by the growing economic impact of the mass media and by the ways in which the media have reported matches, tournaments and events, highlighted specific features of play and drawn attention to particular players. In addition, following the growth in media interest in general and television coverage in particular modern sport has been transformed by the cultural and economic consequences of sponsorship.

Modern sport and the British press

Although there had been a sport magazine industry in England from around the end of the eighteenth century it was in the mid-nineteenth century that specialist sport publications began to emerge in significant numbers. In this period publications like *Sporting Life* (1859) the *Sportsman* (1865), the *Sporting Chronicle* (1871) and *Athletic News* (1875) emerged (Mason 1989: 1993; Whannel 2002). With the development of industrial capitalism and the growth of urban populations possessing rising levels of literacy towards the close of the century a potential mass market for a popular press began to exist (Mason 1993).

In 1896 the 'modern era of mass circulation popular [daily] newspapers began ... with the launch of the *Daily Mail*' and any paper aiming for a popular readership could not afford to neglect sport (Horne et al. 1999: 162). From the outset the *Daily Mail* had a page on sport and by 1900 was selling a million copies a day. From 1895 another popular mass circulation Sunday newspaper the *News of the World* had been devoting '14 per cent of its space to sport, especially racing and cricket, football and athletics in their seasons' (Mason 1993: 7). By 1905 it was devoting 15.75 per cent of its content to sport and in the same year another paper the *Umpire* gave 18.75 per cent of its content over to sport.

As the twentieth century developed the popularity of professional sport in Britain increased and this was reflected in press coverage. The growing popularity of sport and particular sporting figures was undoubtedly in part a corollary of sport's prominence within the popular press. In turn, for the press coverage of sport constituted a key element in the pursuit of increased circulation in an increasingly competitive marketplace. For example, in the mid-1920s the *People*, competing for readers with the *News of the World*, provided four pages of sport, more than a third of which were devoted entirely to association football. In the course of the 1930s around 10 per cent of the *People* was devoted to football and coverage of the national game in the paper had doubled by 1950 (Mason 1993).

By 1937 the average allocation of space to sport in daily and Sunday newspapers was averaging 11.4 and 17.7 per cent respectively. In 1955 it was estimated that sport related coverage accounted for 46 per cent of the *Daily Mirror* and 35 per cent of the *Daily Mail*, and increasingly a disproportionate share of that coverage was devoted to the national game of football (Mason 1989). As Arthur Hopcraft later remarked in a series of reflections on the relationship between the press and the national game,

> Readers' interest in football is insatiable, and it has been found to be intense at the level of chitchat. Newspaper circulations at their biggest are sustained by the unbroken flow of trivial detail as well as by occasional sensation ... No newspaper can afford not to write about football. (1971: 178–179)

The balance of press reporting of sport reflects the nation's popular cultural priorities and football continues to feature prominently in newspaper sport pages throughout most of the year. Even in the brief summer break, formerly known as 'the cricket season', itself interrupted by the annual ritual of Wimbledon tennis fortnight, football remains prominent on the sport news agenda. During the summer there are international matches and alternating tournaments (FIFA Confederations Cup, European Championships, World Cup), pre-season club tournaments and friendly matches to report on, not to mention the never-ending 'chitchat' about the transfer of players, the unfounded rumours, the inevitable denials and the generally less enthralling realities. The series of events associated with David Beckham's transfer from Manchester United to Real Madrid in July 2003 provides an appropriate example of the range of 'news' stories the subject of football can now generate. But football has not always exerted such an influence over popular culture, or occupied such a prominent place on the media agenda and its status as the national game has not gone unchallenged.

National games and national heroes: football v cricket

Football's claim to be the English national game is now beyond dispute. But towards the close of the nineteenth century it was in fact cricket rather than football that had a stronger claim to be regarded as the national sport in England (Holt 1996). Football in this period was a specifically winter sport, one that had been divided into 'association' and 'rugby' codes, the latter itself being 'further split both socially and regionally in the 1890s into northern working-class and southern middle-class formations' (Holt 1996: 48). Whereas cricket was the universal English summer sport and constituted the uncontested focus of the sporting public's interest, the winter sport of football was fragmented into different codes. Even the most prominent of the football codes, the association game, was not particularly popular beyond its core working-class support until the second half of the twentieth century when it began to increase its appeal among the professional and middle classes (Holt 1996). The contention is that up until then cricket had tended to be the primary source of truly national sporting figures. It was W. G. Grace and then 'gentlemen-amateurs' like C. B. Fry, A. C. MacLaren, Prince Ranjitsinhji, or 'Ranji' as he was generally known, and later professional players like Hobbs, Woolley, Sutcliffe, Hammond, Hutton and Compton who were feted in newspapers and magazines and came to be regarded by the public as heroic individuals (Holt 1996).

Newspaper and magazine reports cherished the public drama of cricket as the sport that most richly reflected the imagery of English countryside and history (Inglis 1977). It was through cricket journalism that the social mythology of the sporting hero was created. Cricket journalists like Neville Cardus, E. W. Swanton and John Arlott contributed significantly to the idea of the sporting hero (Inglis 1977). It was through the narratives of such writers that 'great performances [were transformed] into heroic myths' (Holt 1996: 52).

In contrast to their cricketing equivalents football players, until the inter-war period, were largely local heroes. Footballers, as one observer recalls,

> were part of the urban social fabric, unlike county cricketers who appealed to wider identities both regional, due to the county championship, and national, as a result of the already well-developed system of test matches between England and Australia or South Africa. (Mason 1996: 72)

There were international football matches between the four home nations, but these paled into insignificance compared to club football which 'fed parochial and civic pride and provided towns and players with hard-won celebrity' (Mason 1996: 72). In this period footballers generally came from the local town or community for whose team they played. The players in the team would be well known to supporters, their activities and their form being the subject of numerous tales (Hopcraft 1971).

As one observer has noted, 'this element of personality, hero-worship or star magnetism [has been] ... a longstanding attraction of the professional game' (Mason 1996: 71). The status of local hero or star was to a consider-able extent a reflection of outstanding performances, but the 'aura' of a star player was also to a significant degree attributable to local press reporting. Pre-match reporting alerted readers as to what to expect from a game and whom they should watch. Match reports served to identify and commem-orate particular features or attributes of individual players and specific moments of skill. Press 'judgement of who had played well and who badly influenced the public perception of "heroes" and "villains"' (Mason 1996: 76). Footballers remained local heroes and the game primarily a working-class cultural form until the 1960s when a series of factors began to have an impact. The ending of the maximum wage, abolition of 'the retention and transfer system', an increase in international football and the advent of the television age began to radically transform the game and players' prospects (Mason 1996: 84).

However, if from the late nineteenth century through to the 1960s cricket provided sporting figures of national standing and contributed significantly to the richness of English cultural imagery, association football throughout the period in question had a far greater mass spectator appeal. From the beginning of the twentieth century football matches regularly attracted large crowds and as the popularity of the game increased so did attendance at matches. Mason (1989) reports that 6 million people watched First Division matches in the 1908–9 season and that by the 1937–8 season attendance had risen to 14 million. In the FA Cup overall attendance from the first round to the final rose from 1.2 million in 1905–6 to over 2 million in 1935–6. Furthermore in the period between the two world wars 36 clubs registered record match attendance figures. And in the immediate post-Second World War period overall spectator numbers at professional football matches increased yet again to 36 million in the 1946–7 season, rising to a record total of 41.2 million in the 1948–9 season (Szymanski and Kuypers 2000). In the immediate aftermath of the war inexpensive forms of mass entertainment prospered and there was a substantial increase in attendance at a number of popular sport events. Dog racing and speedway events drew large crowds and in 'the summer of 1947 3 million spectators went to cricket' (Szymanski and Kuypers 2000: 44). While football might not have provided many truly national sporting figures up to this point, in terms of mass spectator appeal, exemplified by attendance at matches, its claim to be the most significant and popular national sport was becoming virtually incontestable. Indeed it might be argued that it had all along been the only serious contender for the status of 'the people's game' (Walvin 1994).

The 1950s represented the beginning of a period of growing consumer expenditure as the wealth of the population began to increase following the relative austerity of the post-war era. From 1953 there was a steady decline in attendance at football matches. Recreational and leisure pursuits that had been popular in the pre-war and immediate post-war periods began to lose some of their appeal as other attractions began to compete for consumer expenditure. The consumer goods industry increasingly attracted consumer expenditure with ownership of television sets alone increasing from 344,000 to 10.5 million in the ten-year period from 1950, reaching 15 million by 1968 (Szymanski and Kuypers 2000). As private forms of consumption grew in attractiveness and increased in scale there was a continuing displacement of 'old communal public forms of leisure' (Horne et al. 1999: 265). The prospect of an afternoon spent on the football terraces on a cold wet winter Saturday continued to hold its appeal for the die hard fan. But for a substantial number of former spectators there existed an increasing range of other more seductive consumer options, including the new form of entertainment provided by television.

Structural changes in the traditional pattern of the working week also affected attendance at football matches. In many parts of the country the spectators attending football matches on a Saturday afternoon typically would have finished work at midday in an inner-city area. After obtaining an appropriate beverage and sustenance – a pint and a pie – they would have proceeded to the football ground frequently located in the vicinity of their place of work. The winter Saturday afternoon ritual is effectively represented by the painter L. S. Lowry in *Going to the Match* which depicts an industrial landscape of smoke-shrouded factories, terraced houses, and workers making their way to a football stadium (http://www.millenniumart. co.uk/artwork/GoingToTheMatch.jpg). The end of Saturday morning factory work and the reduction of the working week to five days created the 'weekend' and with it new non-work responsibilities and leisure options emerged that began to compete with football's traditional attractions.

Increasing affluence, a growing emphasis on private consumption, the experience of home comforts and associated rising consumer expectations, coupled with the reduction of the working week and the consequences that followed for the pattern of non-work and leisure activity had significant consequences for football and for sport in general. As the traditional relationship between supporters and football clubs was exposed to new forms of social, cultural and economic life so attendance at matches declined. But football fared better than many other popular pre-war leisure activities, for while between the late 1940s and the late 1980s the game lost more than half its spectators, cricket lost three-quarters of its support. But by the mid-1990s both games had begun to attract an increasing number of spectators:

	Football	Cricket
1947–8	40,259,000	3,000,000
1971–2	28,704,000	984,000
1981–2	20,006,000	994,000
1988–9	18,464,000	751,000
1995–6	21,844,000	958,000

Source: Syzmnski and Kuypers 2000: 46

Football's rise to prominence as the national game and cricket's relative decline, and along with it the diminishing claims of individual cricket figures to national heroic status from the late 1950s onwards, is a reflection of wider social, cultural and economic transformations.

From the late 1950s the influence of American popular culture on British social life began to increase, this was particularly evident in the development of popular music, fashion styles and the growth of a consumer culture. There was also a not unrelated increase in the tempo of everyday life. With growing wealth, with affluence, there was an acceleration in the speed at which life was lived – work, communications, information transmission, transport, leisure, indeed everyday life as a whole became faster. The relaxed pace of traditional three day county and five day Test match cricket began to appear increasingly out of kilter with the tempo of everyday life in a developing modern society. Just as baseball echoing 'an older America, a leisurely paced past of farms and small towns' lost ground to 'grid-iron' football whose 'corporatism, rationalization and time-consciousness reflected modern America' (Rader 1983: 284), so in England cricket lost ground to football.

The very qualities that contributed to cricket's national stature and significance in the first half of the century, the evocative 'images of a vanishing pastoral England' it conjured up and the expressive 'moral vocabulary' (Holt 1996: 48) it provided, subsequently presented it with a problem. In an increasingly modern, consumer, fashion conscious era, one that witnessed the early manifestations of youth sub-cultural forms, cricket was increasingly regarded as lacking in street credibility, as having little, if any, popular cultural appeal. Furthermore, a game closely associated with the idea of an 'ordered and changeless social world' (Inglis 1977: 78) found itself increasingly at odds with and left behind by the reality of a fast-paced social world whose institutional features were subject to unrelenting processes of transformation. The 1960s ushered in a series of processes of transformation that would have enormous economic and cultural significance for sport. Increasing commercialisation, the prospect of and increasing need for sponsorship revenue, growing television coverage and significant developments in respect of the status and contractual conditions of professional sporting figures each had an impact on sport in general and the national game of football in particular.

Football from the 1960s: the English game in transition

In the specific case of football, abolition of the maximum wage, following a successful strike ballot of its membership by the Professional Footballers Association in the 1960–1 season, represented a very significant development. As did a judgment in the High Court in 1963 in favour of the plaintiff, George Eastham, that the retention and transfer system, to which players were subject at the time, constituted an 'unreasonable restraint of trade' (Nicholson 1992: 118). Both events significantly transformed the market situation of professional footballers allowing them to negotiate contracts with their clubs that better reflected their economic value and were more in line with the market value of their sport.[1]

In 1964 the British Broadcasting Corporation (BBC) started transmitting a weekly football highlights television programme, *Match of the Day*. Although attendance at matches was continuing to decline television coverage ensured football retained a popular appeal. In some respects TV coverage added to the game's attraction, especially for sponsors. Live television coverage of the World Cup Final between England and West Germany on 30 July 1966 was watched by a reported 400 million people around the world, the largest ever TV audience at the time. In England around 30 million people were estimated to be viewing the event. The game has been described as 'the greatest ... in the history of English football' (McIlvanney 1992: 152). It certainly represents one of the finer moments in English sport, if not the finest, and may well represent a defining cultural moment, serving as confirmation of football's indisputable status as the national game.

By the 1960s football had already provided a number of national sporting heroes, individuals like Stanley Matthews, Tom Finney and Billy Wright. The victory at Wembley in the 1966 World Cup Final elevated a number of other English footballers to the status of national sporting heroes. In particular Bobby Moore, Geoff Hurst, Bobby Charlton and his brother Jack Charlton became nationally known figures beyond the sport in which they had made their names. Bobby Charlton was already a heroic figure after surviving the tragedy of the Munich air crash in 1958 in which eight of his Manchester United team-mates had died (McKinstry 2002). What being part of England's finest sporting achievement did was to promote both the individuals involved in the team's success and the football industry as a whole. It also constituted one of those rare moments when people are brought together through the realisation of a common aspiration – 'a whole people knew by the victory of its football team that its sense of itself was confirmed in the outside world' (Inglis 1977: 34).

In the late 1960s the long-running decline in football attendance was arrested, albeit temporarily. In the 1965–6 season, immediately before the World Cup finals in England, attendance was 27.2 million and in 'the year of the World Cup they rose to 28.9 million and peaked at 30.1 million the season after England's injury time win over West Germany' (Szymanski and Kuypers 2000: 49). In addition to the national team's success English club football celebrated Manchester United's victory in the European Cup in 1968. By this time the signs that economic and cultural forces were beginning to transform the face of sport and the national game in particular were becoming more and more apparent. In the following year Rupert Murdoch purchased the *Sun* and transformed it into a tabloid newspaper to compete with the *Daily Mirror* (Whannel 2001). The increased competition for readers raised the profile of sport and football especially. Murdoch's defeat of the print unions and computerisation of the industry in 1986 further transformed the newspaper industry and created the conditions in which reporting styles and approaches were destined to change. As Gary Whannel notes,

> Full computerisation and colour printing accelerated the drift away from traditional page layout and towards a collage style in which headlines and photo displays came to dominate. This, in turn, heightened the force and impact of stories about easily recognised star figures. (2001: 35)

George Best: English football's first celebrity figure

Even before the 'tabloid revolution' the football star was beginning to be accorded a higher profile and being likened to prominent figures from the world of popular entertainment. Nowhere was this more in evidence than in the case of the Irish footballer, George Best, who became English football's first internationally recognised celebrity figure. After a memorable 5–1 victory against Benefica in the European Cup in the 1965–6 season the long-haired popstar-like Best was christened 'El Beatle' by the Portuguese newspaper *Bola*. In Best's words,

> Following that, everything went nuts. I even got my own column in the *Daily Express* and people wanted to know everything about me. Not just my football views but what clothes and music I liked and what clubs I went to. Suddenly everything I did was hip or cool. Everything was going mad off the pitch. Beatlemania was at its height ... and once the British press amended my nickname to the fifth Beatle, I became an instant target for them. I became an icon, I suppose. (2001: 100)

George Best not only exemplified the transformed status of the game, in turn he contributed to the game's transformation by demonstrating that footballers could provide regular front page as well as back page copy. Living the celebrity life of a superstar Best's news value was always good even if his conduct often was not beneficial for his football or for that matter the reputation of the game as a whole. The news value of popular cultural icons like Best increased as the tabloids fought to increase their circulation.

Continually questioning the authority of match officials, disputes with managers, frequenting nightclubs, heavy drinking and sexual promiscuity disrupted Best's playing career and ultimately brought it to a premature end. Best's career began with Manchester United, for whom he played for nearly 11 years, thereafter his career was in decline as he turned out for a series of lower league clubs, including Stockport County, Fulham and Hibernian, and played in the North American Soccer League for three teams (Best 2001). By virtue of his on- and off-field activities and the media attention they attracted Best firmly established the footballer as a popular cultural icon, a celebrity figure, a subject for talk-show interviews and documentary analysis. Best's popularity and newsworthiness also made him attractive to sponsors and companies seeking to promote sales of their products. Soon after acquiring the sobriquet of the 'fifth Beatle' Best was contracted to make a TV advert for an Irish sausage manufacturer, Cookstown, in which he delivered the predictable line 'Cookstown are the Best family sausages' (Best 2002: 103). Best featured in other advertisements for Spanish oranges, the Egg Marketing Board and, reflecting his image as football's leading Lothario, *Playtex* bras. Best also had various modelling contracts and was invited to make a record. If football had not quite yet become the new rock-and-roll the signs were beginning to emerge that it had the potential to make its leading figures as well known as their equivalents in the wider world of entertainment (Rojek 2001).

The media interest Best aroused both signified and contributed to the popular cultural appeal of high profile sporting figures and in the British setting footballers in particular. Others would follow Best and, attracting comparable levels of media interest, would become celebrity figures in their own right and begin to take advantage of the commercial opportunities a celebrity profile represented. The media spotlight Best had to endure increased both in scale and intensity as commercial competition between the tabloids grew. As competition increased the formerly relatively clear distinction between a public domain, regarded as fair game for reporting, and a private sphere, recognised as off-limits to reporters, began to be steadily undermined and eroded. In consequence,

> areas of life once resolutely private are now in the public domain ... scandal and gossip that has become a staple of tabloid content has featured sport stars, and has contributed ... to a public fascination with the personality and private life of sporting celebrities. (Whannel 2002: 35–36)

Henceforth high profile sport stars, and in Britain footballers in particular, have been both beneficiaries and victims of media spotlight exposure. Predictably the consequences for individuals have varied considerably as the experiences of three England international footballers whose careers have reflected changes affecting the game since the 1970s, effectively reveal.

Keegan, Gascoigne and Beckham

The rise to prominence of Kevin Keegan (1970s/1980s) has been described as signalling 'the arrival of the modern footballer-businessman' (Mason 1989: 163). Where Keegan exemplified the sober, professional, footballer-businessman, whose private life remained largely private and of relatively little interest to the press, Paul Gascoigne (late 1980s/1990s) represented an unpredictable and controversial multi-faceted figure – part genius, tragic-hero, fool and reprobate. Both have subsequently been overshadowed by the hyper-celebrity figure of David Beckham (late 1990s/2000s) whose media profile as a footballer and as a public figure is unparalleled in British sporting life as a whole and within the game of football in particular. From 1997 Beckham's relationship with, and subsequent marriage to, Victoria Adams (Posh Spice), a singer in a girl group, the Spice Girls, dramatically amplified media interest in him. The fusion of the worlds of football and popular music exemplified by the media frenzy over 'Posh and Becks' has ensured that David Beckham the footballer is virtually continuously in the news, although frequently not for his prowess on the field alone.[2]

While Beckham was not the first England international footballer to marry a prominent figure from the world of popular entertainment the economic standing and cultural profile of both the game and popular music were radically different from what they had been in the 1950s when Billy Wright (1924–94) married Joy Beverley who was the youngest of the 'Beverley Sisters', a popular singing trio. Wright of Wolverhampton Wanderers and England, for whom he played 105 times, 90 as captain, has been described as 'the idol of British football in the 1950s' (Huntington-Whiteley 1999: 235). While Wright was well known and had show business connections he never became a prominent celebrity figure. The cultural economy of sport, including football, in the 1950s was quite different, although there were emerging signs of change, in particular of sport stars beginning to be more widely recognised for the commercial value of their image. This was evident in the increased use that was beginning to be made of sport stars, including Wright, in product advertising.

Kevin Keegan was a successful club and England international footballer, he also captained his country. But by the late 1970s football had become a different game, it was on a different commercial footing, and the opportunities open to a high profile, media savvy, personable, hard working and uncontroversial figure like Keegan were considerable. In the late 1960s the rules of the Football Association and the Football League had prohibited players from employing agents but a decade later 'no top player was without a financial entourage of agent, accountant and bank manager' (Mason 1989: 162). The commercial opportunities awaiting the marketable player were beginning to make an agent a virtual necessity for the modern high profile star player.

Before the Second World War a few high profile footballers had derived income from lending their name to ghosted newspaper articles and some had earned additional money from advertising and endorsing products, including cigarettes and men's cosmetics. The first explicit sign of sponsorship in sport in Britain is argued to have occurred in 1898 when the league champions of the football league, Nottingham Forest, endorsed a beverage company, *Bovril* (Marshall and Cook 1992). George Camsell who provided an endorsement of 'Phosferine as the greatest of all tonics' in the late 1920s (Mason 1989: 163) offers another football related example. In the aftermath of the Second World War Dennis Compton, who played football for Arsenal and cricket for Middlesex and England, promoted the hair product, *Brylcreem*. Tom Finney who played football for Preston North End and England advertised the breakfast cereal *Shredded Wheat*, while Billy Wright endorsed *Quaker Oats* (Szymanski and Kuypers 2000: 67) and in 1951 Stanley Matthews was receiving £20 per week for endorsing a *Cooperative Society* make of football boot (Mason 1989). Earnings from commercial work outside of sport, in this instance football, then as now, compared very favourably with income derived directly from playing the game.

Players' salaries have increased dramatically in the intervening period, but so has the differential between income derived from playing sport and income from other commercial ventures such as advertising and sponsorship. In the 1970s and 1980s Kevin Keegan had contracts to promote an extensive range of products that included toiletries (*Brut*), sports goods and fashionable clothing, a breakfast cereal and canned food. He established a number of companies in his name and was also awarded a lucrative contract with BBC television (Mason 1989: 163).

Where Kevin Keegan cut an uncontroversial figure and was a safe bet for companies seeking endorsement of their products Paul Gascoigne, or 'Gazza' as he became known, seemed to continually court controversy. After the 1990 World Cup semi-final defeat by Germany, a match frequently recalled because of Gascoigne's 'tears in Turin' after receiving a second yellow card that would have prevented him from playing in the Final, 'Gazza' became a nationally known celebrity figure and his endorsement value soared (Hamilton 1993). Following the events in Turin Gascoigne became the focus of a process of commodification described as 'awesome in its intensity and scope' (Giddens 1990b). Commercial companies sought to associate themselves and their products with Gascoigne's rapid rise to celebrity status. For three months after the team returned from the tournament Gascoigne was rarely off the front pages of the tabloid press. In addition to a contract with the *Sun* newspaper, worth a reported £120,000, Gascoigne had endorsement contracts for various products including football boots, sportswear and *Brut* aftershave, about which, true to his unpredictable and commercially risky character, he commented 'It's for pooftahs isn't it?' (Hamilton 1993: 38). The 'tears in Turin' episode licensed the manufacture of Gazza 'real-tears crying dolls' and much later, as Gascoigne's career was drawing to a close, the tears re-appeared in an advertisement with Gary Lineker for *Walker's Crisps*. In the aftermath of that night in 1990 in Turin Gascoigne was able, for a time at least, to command substantial fees for opening fast-food outlets and supermarkets, appearing in advertisements and giving interviews.

The life and times of Paul Gascoigne as narrated in the press and displayed on TV has assumed the 'character of a long-running soap opera' (Whannel 2002: 145). From a high point in 1990 Gascoigne's career has taken a turbulent path. Gascoigne played football for his local team Newcastle United and then Tottenham Hotspur and was, for too brief a time, a key member of the England national team. At the peak of his career he moved to Italy to play for Lazio but after failing to settle moved to Scotland to play for Glasgow Rangers and then to Middlesbrough, Everton, Burnley and later a Chinese B league club side, the Gansu Sky Horses. Possessing a remarkable talent for the game Gascoigne would never quite realise his full potential. His playing career was diverted from its optimal course by a chaotic personal life, a poor choice of 'friends' and the detrimental effects of alcohol. But the constant presence of a media circus and the intrusiveness of the tabloid press in particular also played a pivotal role in shaping his career trajectory. As Whannel demonstrates in his analysis of the various media orchestrated constructions and subsequent dissections of Gascoigne's enigmatic celebrity,

> stars of all types play a very important part in the world of the tabloid press, and in the initial phase of fame they are typically celebrated for their ability, or achievements, or genuine charisma, or the spectacle of their appearance. Once they are established, however, further celebration becomes of low news value, whereas any whiff of sensation or scandal has a greatly enhanced news value. (2002: 148)

Initially Gazza, the unpredictable 'genius-clown' celebrity, represented an attractive if risky prospect for companies seeking a high profile sport star to endorse their products. However, the increasing frequency of reports of binge eating and excess drinking, followed by press stories of wife-beating, ultimately made Gascoigne virtually unmarketable. In turn, such behaviour and the public attention it received through media reporting served to undermine Gascoigne's reputation as a player by revealing him to be a figure at odds with the new more disciplined fitness regime that had gathered momentum within the game. The new regime has promoted an ethos of bodily maintenance and care that necessitates attention being given to diet, the practice of moderation in respect of alcohol and the adoption of a life-style conducive to optimising athletic performance. In many respects Paul Gascoigne appears as a figure out of his time, a figure whose fondness for an undisciplined life-style is reminiscent of players of an earlier era, when even stars were not subject to such intense media exposure and their indiscretions largely remained private affairs.

The heightened intensity of media interest in football and in football celebrity figures is itself a corollary of the new political economy of football and its growing cultural significance. If there have been costs in terms of a loss of a degree of privacy there have also been significant commercial benefits. Consider as an example the transformed endorsement value of the humble football boot. Increased participation in grass-roots football in the 1980s boosted the value of the football boot business and opened up lucrative endorsement prospects for a number of high profile players. Where in the 1950s Stanley Matthews had received £20 a week for wearing football boots from the *Cooperative Society*, by the 1980s Bryan Robson of Manchester United and England was receiving £25,000 a year for wearing *Balance Boots* (Mason 1989). Two decades later another United and England player, David Beckham, was receiving £3 million a year to be seen wearing *adidas* football boots.

In 2003 shortly before his transfer from Manchester United to Real Madrid David Beckham was reported to be earning in excess of £4.5 million per year from his club, around £1 million of which was reported to be for the use of his image (O'Connor 2003). Reported total annual income from endorsements was in excess of £11.5 million and was made up of the following:

adidas	£3 million per annum
Marks & Spencer	£3 million per annum
Pepsi	£2 million per annum
Vodafone	£1 million per annum
Brylcreem	£1 million per annum
Police sunglasses	£1 million per annum
Castrol	£0.5 million per annum

Source: O'Connor 2003: 5

This list is far from comprehensive and understates Beckham's actual income from sources outside football. For example it excludes a contract originally worth £1.5 million per annum with *Rage Software*, now a bankrupt company. There are also several contracts with other companies. In June 2003 Beckham's Asian tour with his wife Victoria took the couple to Japan, Malaysia, Vietnam and Thailand where they were involved in making advertisements and public appearances to promote a range of products. In Japan the Beckhams were reported to be the country's 'highest-paid foreign advertising icons, earning at least £10 million' through endorsement of a range of products that includes 'everything from beauty clinics to chocolates' (Parry and Lewis 2003).

Football now has a global appeal and a leading player such as Beckham has acquired a commensurate celebrity status. As the game's popularity around the world has grown the potential income available to leading players from non-sport activities such as advertising and product endorsement has increased considerably. In the late 1950s Johnny Haynes of Fulham and England was receiving 'an annual salary of only £1,000 as a footballer' but he was able to earn '£1,500 for three days' photographic work' for an advertisement for *Brylcreem* (Syzmanski and Kuypers 2000: 68). In 2003 the *Tokyo Beauty Centre* shot a 30-second promotional film over a period of two days in Adlington Hall close to Manchester for which David and Victoria Beckham were reportedly paid £2.2 million. This represents merely one manifestation of the changing political economy of football stardom, but it is one, in turn, that needs to be put in perspective.

The level of remuneration for top level sporting figures and the differential between earnings from sport and those from outside the game are even greater in the American context. When *Nike* first signed American basketball rookie Michael Jordan to endorse its sports footwear in the mid-1980s it was for a five year contract reported to be worth $3 million. At the time it was described as 'the endorsement coup of the century for the Bull's rookie and an indication that the whole endorsement game was careening out of control' (Katz 1994: 220–1). In 1996 American golfer Tiger Woods signed a five year endorsement contract with *Nike* reported to be worth $40 million (Rosaforte 2001). By 2003 the endorsement game had moved dramatically onwards and upwards into the commercial stratosphere. In that year *Nike* were reported to have awarded an 18-year-old American basketball prodigy LeBron James, who had yet to play a single professional game, a $90 million sponsorship contract. Also in 2003 *Nike* awarded 'Freddy Adu the 13-year-old wunderkind of American soccer', a game that as a male sport has yet to attract a mass audience in the US, a $1 million contract (Hannigan 2003).[3] Offering further confirmation of the extent to which the endorsement game was indeed totally out of control, *Reebok* were reported to have signed Mark Walker, the three-year-old self-professed 'future of basketball', to a lucrative sportswear marketing contract for an undisclosed sum 'believed to be well into seven figures' (Ayres 2003).

In the nineteenth and early twentieth centuries it was the popular press that helped to establish modern sports and promote sporting figures, subsequently other media, radio and television in particular, have played an increasingly significant role in raising the profile of sport and cultivating a culture of sporting celebrity. Before turning to a consideration of the role broadcasting media such as radio and more importantly television have played in the promotion and popularising of sport, attention will be directed to the contribution of the American press to the development of sport in America and grid-iron football in particular.

American sporting press

In America magazines on sport began to appear from the 1820s focusing on the more socially acceptable activities such as horse racing and less on those pursuits favoured by the lower classes. The *Spirit of the Times* founded in New York in 1831 was a pioneering sport publication that became the premier sporting weekly until it was displaced by the *New York Clipper* established in 1851 (Rader 1983b; McChesney 1989). It was through initially cursory coverage in *Spirit of the Times* in the 1850s and then the *New York Clipper* that baseball began to acquire national prominence. In 1862 Henry Chadwick was appointed to the *New York Herald* to report on baseball. He was the first full-time sport reporter to be hired by a daily newspaper (Oriard 1993). With the development of a modern national newspaper industry whose income derived from sales of papers and advertising space the growing popularity of sport proved to be an invaluable asset for increasing circulation. Sport began to receive regular coverage in papers such as the *New York Herald, New York Tribune* and the *New York Times*.

Growing press interest in and reporting of increasingly organised and commercial sporting activities contributed significantly to the establishment of sport as a legitimate cultural institution. From the 1880s intercollegiate football games attracted increasing press interest. In 1895 the *New York Journal* 'introduced the first distinct sports section' (McChesney 1989: 53) and by the 1920s it was an established part of every major daily paper. As the nineteenth century drew to a close newspaper circulation was rising and sport journalism had become an increasingly important feature of papers such as the *New York Sun* and the *New York World*. A dramatic growth of football coverage was a distinctive feature of the late-nineteenth century American press, a feature that contributed significantly to the creation of a '"mass" audience for college football, spanning the full range of social and economic classes' (Oriard 1993: 61).

In the 1880s collegiate games attracted rarely more than a few hundred spectators. Football was played in elite American universities and the wider public was largely unaware of or indifferent to the game. Baseball and rowing had been the most popular sports on elite university campuses until football became established, but unlike the latter they did not command such intense press interest (Rader 1983b). Football could not have achieved its popularity, its special place in 'the hearts and minds of Americans … without the agency of the modern metropolitan newspapers and their huge circulations' (Oriard 1993: 61). Indeed it has been suggested that the impact of the press on college football in the closing decades of the nineteenth century was greater than that of television on the professional game in the 1950s and 1960s (Oriard 1993: 57).

Sport provided entertaining copy and fitted in well with the popular press policy of increased sensationalism and illustration and from the mid-1880s Intercollegiate Football became visually and textually prominent in the Sunday *World* and the *Evening World* (Oriard 1993). By the 1920s four or five pages of sport coverage had become a routine feature of the daily press and the space devoted to football games had increased significantly. Placing emphasis on spectacular and sensational aspects of football the popular press were able to appeal to a cross-section of the American public, to the graduates of elite universities as well as middle- and working-class readerships. The prominence of football reports and illustrations in the press promoted an understanding of the game and substantially increased its popularity, ultimately transforming it into a nationally popular spectator sport and the football player into a 'seasonal hero' (Oriard 1993: 75).

The key factor that led to college football being accorded such prominence in the press was the decision taken in 1880 to play the season ending 'Big Game' in New York on the national holiday of Thanksgiving Day. The games provided an indication of the popular appeal of the sport and the potential financial gains to be made. In turn, extravagant reports in the press of the game and associated post-game celebrations created a popular audience for football and elevated it into a social event. As the *New York Herald* report of the events of Thanksgiving Day in 1893 serves to indicate, football was rapidly becoming a national sport:

> In these times Thanksgiving Day is no longer a solemn festival to God for mercies given. It is a holiday granted by the state and the nation to see a game of football. (cited in Oriard 1993: 95)

Few people were able to attend the games as spectators so it was through reports in the press that knowledge of football spread and its popularity increased. Towards the close of the nineteenth century football began to acquire a place in an emerging celebrity culture, big football games began to be places to be seen at, football was becoming fashionable. The game quickly spread across the country. Provincial newspapers began to report on the big games played between eastern universities and graduates took the game to towns and cities around America, organising local teams, playing and coaching. By the turn of the century football and football reporting was an established part of American national sporting culture. By 1905, 432 American cities had football teams and over the course of the first half of the twentieth century 'intercollegiate football became a truly national sport' (Oriard 1993: 132).

The narratives on football in the popular press offered a variety of views on the game, ranging from football as science to football as a gentlemanly pursuit. While it was the major college contests that attracted most attention matches involving professional teams also received press coverage. The press was not concerned about the erosion of amateur purity and professionalism was not regarded as a contentious issue. Professional players were represented 'not as mercenaries but as collections of all-stars, of football "giants" or "heroes"' (Oriard 1993: 177). Indeed press reports celebrated the professional game as offering the opportunity of witnessing football play of the highest quality.

The assumptions and values of scientific football were fully endorsed in press reporting of games. However, while endorsing the primacy of teamwork press reports demonstrated ways in which individual prowess could be recognised, how personal achievement and heroism still had a place in a 'new age of corporate industrialism' (Oriard 1993: 178; Rader 1983b). In the press football was represented less as a social, moral or economic matter and more as a spectacle, frequently containing gladiatorial narratives through which individual players were portrayed as larger-than-life heroes. Such narratives drew attention to football as a masculine sport, a sport in which aggression and violence contributed to the drama. In the early twentieth century wide-ranging processes of social and economic transformation associated with industrialisation, urbanisation and the closing of the frontier had given rise to anxieties about masculinity. The settings in which a vigorous and physical 'manliness' had formerly been routinely demonstrated were being rapidly transformed and it was in this context that sport and football in particular increasingly constituted a 'compensating validation of ... manhood' (Oriard 1993: 191).

Press narratives emphasised the game's manliness, physicality and roughness, the brawls involved and the necessity for 'heroic masculine force' to be employed. Football was represented as a rite of passage through which American boys would attain manhood. Accounts of football drew attention to the arduous character of the training, the intense demands associated with practice, as well as the rituals and the male bonding that were prominent features of the game. In a context where the world of work was being transformed and becoming less physical, football acquired increasing cultural significance, representing a 'union of the physical and mental that was difficult for men to find in modern America' (Oriard 1993: 201). Rationales for football frequently emphasised the ways in which moral benefits might flow from the physical demands placed upon players. But as the twentieth century developed a discourse of muscular Christianity, emphasising the moral and 'manly' character benefits of sport and football in particular was displaced by a growing 'culture of celebrity' that placed increasing emphasis on the individual player as a personality and a star.

In both Britain and America it was the popular press that created our modern sense of sport. Football, baseball, boxing, horse racing and other related activities achieved their generic identity as sports through the introduction and cultural mediation of specialist sports pages and sections in the press. From the 1890s in America press coverage of football, baseball, tennis and other sports was collected together in special sections and by the 1920s 'sports sections, simply designated "Sports", became conventional' (Oriard 1993: 275). Both football as an American spectacle and sport as an unrivalled American institution were in substantial part the product of the way the press promoted and reported on them.

It was through the coverage of intercollegiate games in the press that football acquired a prominent place for itself alongside baseball in American culture. However it took a while, until the 1920s, for football to achieve a comparable level of national popularity to that enjoyed by baseball. By that time colleges across the length and breadth of the country were able to fill 'enormous stadiums every Saturday, as the star players became media celebrities of unprecedented stature' (Oriard 1993: 277). Notwithstanding the formation in 1920 of a professional league the professional game continued to lag behind college football in terms of popularity until the 1960s when television began to have a significant impact on the preferences of fans. Football proved to be an ideal sport for television broadcasting. Whereas an effective appreciation of a baseball game required awareness of the playing area as a whole, with football 'much of the action of the game could be distilled to a small part of the field' (Rader 1983b: 245).

The 'Golden Age' of sports writing

The 1920s have often been described as the 'Golden Age' of American sport. However, in recognition of the contribution of sport journalism and sports writing to the rising popularity of sport in the opening decades of the twentieth century Robert Lipsyte has referred to the period as the 'Golden Age of Sportswriting' (1975: 170). The pre-television world of sport was one in which heroes predominated, it was a world in which writers and columnists made players into mythic heroes and through the quality of their writing became stars and celebrities themselves (Rader 1984). The press not only reported on sport they also promoted it, offering cups and medals for intercollegiate competitions and assistance in the organisation of tournaments. For example the Golden Gloves boxing tournament emerged in the mid-1920s with the help of the co-publisher of the Chicago *Tribune* and by 1928 it had become a national event (Rader 1984).

Sportswriters in the 1920s were literary craftsmen who sought to enhance the drama of sport events and colourfully embellish incidents involving prominent sporting figures. They contrived nicknames for high profile players that added to their cultural appeal and popularity. In the field of football Red Grange became the 'Galloping Ghost' and in baseball Babe Ruth was described as the 'Sultan of Swat' (Rader 1984: 21–20). In contrast with contemporary sports writing practice sportswriters sought to mask the frailties of performers. Rader suggests that 'sportswriters felt obligated to protect the private lives of the athletes' (1984: 22). However, with the advent of television coverage of sport events, press coverage of sport began to change considerably. Increasingly, and especially in the

British context with the growing competition in the late 1960s between the tabloid press, journalists turned to events and actions taking place behind the scenes, those events to which TV cameras could not gain access. And rather than masking the frailties of players and protecting their private lives from scrutiny the press began to capitalise on any signs of frailty and to treat the private lives of prominent sporting figures as eminently newsworthy (Whannel 2002).

Sport broadcasting

In the 1920s the advent of cinema newsreel and radio reporting added considerably to the coverage of sport. Cinema newsreel offered spectacular moving images of sport events and sporting figures. But radio offered immediacy in sport reporting inaccessible to the newspaper journalist or the retrospective view provided a week later in cinema newsreel coverage. Radio allowed people to follow the drama of sporting contests as they evolved, to experience, through the voice of a cultural intermediary, the commentator, what it was like to be there at the event.

If broadcasting of sporting events helped to popularise radio, the new medium in its turn contributed even more to sport's growing popularity. Through the national broadcasting of 'local' games the process that had been started through press reporting gathered momentum. Sport events, teams and individual players became known nationally and as sport reached the level of national popularity it acquired the status of a 'fundamental social institution' (McChesney 1989: 59). Sport is now a social institution of unequalled popularity. Shared knowledge and understanding, as well as commitment to sport have contributed to the development of national culture and national identity, to a sense of the nation as a community drawn together through sport.

With the growth in popularity of sport and the radio broadcasting of sport events in the 1930s advertisers began to recognise the marketing potential sport represented and started buying rights to broadcast major sports matches and tournaments. A broadcast of the 1921 heavyweight boxing championship between Georges Carpentier and Jack Dempsey demonstrated radio's potential. In 1923 two million radio listeners tuned in to hear a commentary on a heavyweight fight and in 1927 it is estimated that 50 million American fight fans heard a broadcast of the Jack Dempsey-Gene Tunney re-match (Rader 1984). The marketing potential of radio broadcasting of major sport events duly led corporations into broadcasting sport sponsorship:

> The Ford Motor Company paid $100,000 for the privilege of sponsoring the 1934 [baseball World] Series on all three major networks of the day: NBC, CBS, and the Mutual Broadcasting Company. In 1939 the Gillette Safety Razor Company began its thirty-two year stint as the regular sponsor of the Series. (Rader 1984: 25)

Initial worries that a broadcast of a game would reduce attendance meant that regular big league baseball games were not generally on the radio and in 1934 a number of New York City teams – the Yankees, Giants and Dodgers – prohibited radio commentary of their games for a period of five years. However, by the end of the Second World War all big league baseball teams were selling the rights for regular season coverage of matches to radio stations.

Two developments in the 1950s represented the turning point for radio sport broadcasting. First in 1955 a legal ruling required radio stations to pay a rights fee to sport franchises. The second development, the growth of television ownership and TV broadcasting, was of far greater significance for radio and for sport as a whole. Television coverage has transformed the culture of sport, how players, coaches, owners and fans conduct themselves, the financial infrastructure of sport, as well as the ways in which and the times at which games are played.

In Britain the first regular radio broadcasts had begun in 1922 when the British Broadcasting Corporation was established and granted a licence. Initially, as was the case in America, there was a degree of anxiety within sport about the impact BBC broadcasting of sport might have on attendance at events and in consequence sport broadcasts were limited. However, with the establishment of the BBC as a public corporation, following the Crawford Report of 1925, broadcasting of a range of prestigious sport events began to occur on a regular basis (Whannel 1992). From the mid-1920s the BBC began to bring radio coverage of sport to people in their own homes – by 1938 71 per cent of all households owned a radio – and contrary to the initial fears of sports organisations increasing coverage of sport did not lead to a drop in attendance. Indeed the period between the two World Wars was marked by a steady increase in spectators at sport events and by growing commercialisation in sport to which rising media coverage through cinema newsreel and radio broadcasts contributed significantly (Horne et al. 1999).

The BBC held a monopoly in broadcasting in Britain until 1955 when a commercial company Independent Television (ITV) was established. The BBC's monopoly over broadcasting began in 1922 and its regular coverage of major sporting matches and tournaments effectively made them part of national culture. By 1930 annual events such as 'the Boat Race, Test matches, Wimbledon, the Cup Final, the Grand National and the Derby … were being covered every year on the radio' and had become national occasions (Whannel 1992: 16). When BBC television coverage began many of the same events found their way onto the annual calendar of televised sports. With the emergence of satellite and digital television a comparable list of sport events deemed to be of national interest were 'reserved' for terrestrial television broadcast.

Initially in America it was sports such as boxing and wrestling that found favour with television, in good part because the limitations of the technology made it more difficult to adequately cover team sports. The use of only a few cameras with a single lens made coverage of fast, action-packed team sports like football played in a large stadium more difficult to cover than a boxing match involving two individuals in a relatively small ring. Notwithstanding such limitations companies were quick to recognise the potential of the medium and the popularity of boxing in particular led to commercial sponsorship of televised fights. Breweries, tobacco companies and *Gillette* the razor blade makers sought to promote their products through involvement with televised coverage of boxing.

As with other sports that would find their way onto the screen, the television promotion of boxing had significant consequences for the sport. The classic art of boxing began to be displaced by a more aggressive, brutal and spectacular style. The 'slugger' came to represent 'good TV style' and was the type of boxer producers and sponsors wanted on their programmes (Rader 1984). In addition, sponsors seeking to derive an appropriately positive association between their products and the boxing events with which their companies were associated wanted winners not losers in televised bouts. This represented a major problem, one that led to young and unknown fighters being required to fight opponents, 'winners', with far greater experience. The consequences for boxing and boxers were considerable; a poor performance and a defeat in a TV fight could effectively end a fighter's career and in 1956 an editorial in *Ring* magazine argued that television's insatiable appetite for boxing had 'depleted the ranks of professional fighters by … 50 per cent' (cited in Rader 1984: 44). Other sports such as wrestling and Roller Derby also accommodated television's requirement for spectacle and excitement by introducing fake and heavily stylised forms of physical violence. Such examples of the impact of television on sport led one analyst to conclude that 'whatever authenticity these "sports" had once enjoyed' had been reduced (Rader 1984: 46).

Television technology has developed rapidly since the 1950s. Video recording and editing, communication satellites, action replay and slow motion, along with the introduction of colour and innovations in camera design have transformed the medium and its coverage of sport (Horne et al. 1999). Initiatives in television programming have provided viewers with a variety of different views of sport, ranging from outside broadcasts of events, to highlights and magazine-style programmes, to quiz shows and documentaries on prominent players. By the mid-1960s over 80 per cent of British households and over 90 per cent of American households had televisions and sport programming had become an important element in television scheduling (Whannel 2002).

In Britain programmes such as *Sportsview*, *Grandstand* and *Match of the Day* quickly became established regular features of BBC programming and on ITV *World of Sport* and programmes such as *The Big Match* acquired a near comparable significance (Whannel 1992). However, while the nineteenth-century transformation of folk games through processes of codification and formalisation was first evident in England, the initial home of modern sport, the key features of the mid-twentieth-century revolutionary impact of television on sport, and all the consequences that have followed from that, first became apparent in America.

Sport and television in America

One of the early problems facing television in America was what to broadcast or how to fill the available time. In the absence of any real capacity to make programmes it was to sport events that television networks turned. Reflecting on the present close relationship between sport and television one former NBC director remarked that while sports now 'need television to survive … it was just the opposite when it first started. What some people forget is that television got off the ground because of sports' (cited in Leifer 1995: 127). Sport continues to be of great importance to the media as a whole, with sport broadcasting accounting for 25 per cent of network television revenues and sport news representing up to 33 per cent of the space in daily newspapers (Rader 1984; Leifer 1995).

While in the immediate post-Second World War period television networks regularly carried sport broadcasts none of them regarded such programming as 'critical to their success' and this was reflected in the lack of any specialist sport programming departments within the networks in this period (Rader 1984: 101). More often than not it was commercial companies or advertising agencies that acquired the right to broadcast a sport event and then a network partner would be sought for transmission. This relationship began to change in the 1960s when ABC backed its hunch that an increase in sport programming would raise its profile and go some way towards closing the ratings and advertising gap between itself and the bigger networks, CBS and NBC (Rader 1984).

In the 1950s NBC was the leading network as far as sport coverage was concerned with broadcasts of boxing and college football, including big intersectional college games like the Rose Bowl and the Orange Bowl. CBS was a close second covering the Kentucky Derby as well as professional football and baseball's 'Game of the Week' (Rader 1984). The turning point for the ABC network came in 1959 when the *Gillette* Safety Razor Company agreed to direct an advertising budget in the region of $8.5 million to the network in exchange for broadcast of its weekly boxing bouts. With such a secure additional revenue stream ABC was able to bid for rights to a range of sport events that had formerly been beyond its means. The first success was securing the National College Athletic Association (NCAA) football contract for 1960–1 a deal that led to the appointment of Roone Arledge who was soon to prove to be a pivotal figure in the world of TV sport in general and football in particular (Rader 1984).

Television and the popularity of the National Football League (NFL)

Baseball's traditional claim to special status, namely that it best exemplifies 'American character' (Levine 1985), was challenged by the rapid growth in the popularity of football. Baseball is a leisurely paced game, one that is not subject to the clock. It is in tune with an older, more traditional America. While in the immediate post-Second World War period new attendance records were set in both major and minor baseball leagues, by the mid-1950s attendance levels were falling dramatically as the impact of 'increasing privatization of leisure and the growth of television' began to have an impact (Rader 1984: 52).

With the growth of American consumer society new leisure patterns and life-styles developed. In particular the growth of television as the principal form of home entertainment on which big league baseball games were shown had a significant impact on attendance at games at all levels. While the development of new leisure interests and life-styles associated with the growth of consumption had a comparable effect on attendance at college football games in the course of the 1950s, both intercollegiate and professional football were to prove to be better equipped to accommodate television than baseball.

Before the advent of TV coverage, professional football lagged behind the college game in both popularity and financial status. Professional football was the sport of blue-collar workers, players' salaries were low and teams relied on the support of corporate sponsors for survival. For example, a meat packing company was the sponsor for the Green Bay Packers, while the Decatur Staleys relied upon the generosity of a starch manufacturer (Leifer 1995). Given their relatively parlous financial state club owners were ready to accept funds from television networks in exchange for the rights to broadcast games. In 1947 the owner of the Chicago Bears received $5,400 for television rights to six games and for the final game in 1948 against their local rivals the broadcast rights were sold for $5,000.

Football was well suited to television as breaks in play allowed for network advertising commercials and the spatial characteristics of the game and the field of play fitted in well with the features of the medium. A particular set of factors coincided to transform professional football, turning it into a nationally popular sport. Although in 1956 football teams were still closely associated with particular cities the CBS network experimented with nationwide transmission of selected NFL regular season games, an innovation that began the process of building a national audience for the sport. Football's national potential was confirmed in 1958 when CBS covered a crucial championship game that drew 30 million viewers. By 1960 it was evident that growing 'interdependencies between football and television were ... becoming irreversible' (Leifer 1995: 130). Instant replays and slow motion technology gave TV viewers a perspective on the game not available to fans in the stadiums. Colour television and artificial playing surfaces later added to the spectacular character of TV coverage. The prospect of television coverage also led to the formation of a new league, the American Football League (AFL) which quickly secured a contract with ABC for $8.5 million (Rader 1984; Leifer 1995).

The appointment of Pete Rozelle as NFL commissioner in 1959 was crucially important as he sought to persuade football franchise holders that they should negotiate TV rights through a single contract with revenues acquired being shared equally between clubs. The extension in 1961 of baseball's exemption from anti-trust legislation opened the way for football, and basketball and ice hockey, to pool 'individual franchise broadcasting rights' (Leifer 1995: 130). Early in 1962 Rozelle negotiated a contract with CBS for the 1962–3 season in which the broadcasting rights to all regular season NFL games were purchased for a total of '$4,650,000 or $350,000 per team' (Leifer 1995: 131). In 1959 at the top end of the market the New York Giants had earned $200,000 from TV rights, while at the other end the Green Bay Packers had made only $30,000. But after the Sports Broadcasting Act of 1961 and Rozelle's deployment of astute contract negotiating skills 'pro football opened the door to skyrocketing television contracts' (Rader 1984: 91). With TV audience viewing figures rising by 50 per cent between 1961 and 1963 Rozelle was able in 1964 to raise the price CBS paid for NFL annual broadcasting rights to $14 million. In the wake of the NFL-CBS deal the NBC network outbid ABC and agreed a contract with the AFL for broadcasting rights worth $42 million over five years. Such broadcasting contracts created the financial conditions for intense competition between the NFL and the AFL for the signing of college football stars in what became known as the 'Battle of the Paychecks' (Rader 1984: 92).

The cool medium of TV has made professional football into a hot sport and a major national cultural spectacle in both Britain and America. Football's ascent to national popularity in America has been explained in the following terms:

> Pro football … reflected its fans' work experiences. Most Americans now worked in large corporations, bureaucracies, universities, or institutes, and football was very much a corporate or bureaucratic sport … Like modern work, football embodied rationality, specialization, and coordination; the game required careful planning and preparation. (Rader 1984: 94)

A substantial part of the game's appeal is that it compensates for the sense of powerlessness individuals increasingly feel about their lives in a 'rationalized and systematized' world. The game's attraction is powerfully demonstrated by the response to TV coverage of the annual Super Bowl game that followed the merger between the NFL and AFL. The TV audience for the game quickly overtook other long established national sporting fixtures like the Kentucky Derby and baseball's World Series. By the 1980s over half the population of America was watching the game on TV, an audience size no other sport could approach, and ' "Super Bowl Sunday" became a national holiday' (Rader 1984: 97).

Football is undoubtedly the most popular sport on television around the world. In America and Canada North-American style professional football or 'grid-iron' attracts large TV audiences and advertising revenues. As the championship decider in American professional football the Super Bowl has consistently drawn the largest audiences to American TV with estimates ranging from 120 to 140 million viewers (Rader 1984; Real 1989; Wenner 1998). Unsurprisingly advertising costs during the game are regularly the highest of the year and were estimated to be in excess of '$500,000 per 30-second spot' in the late 1980s (Real 1989: 180). A decade later 'sponsors [were] paying up to $2.4 million per minute' (Wenner 1998: 4). For Super Bowl XXXVII (2003) between the Oakland Raiders and the Tampa Bay Buccaneers it was reported that there would be 61 commercial breaks and that the going rate for advertisers would be $4.2 million a minute. The US television audience was expected to be in the region of 130 million and the overseas audience about 650 million. The commercial attraction of such a large television audience led Anheuser-Busch the brewer of *Budweiser* beer to pay in the region of $15 million for eleven 30 second advertising slots (Anonymous 2003a).

Association football

Beyond North America it is the association code of football first formalised in England that can legitimately claim to be the undisputed global game, the game of the majority of people around the world. Affirmation of the association game's indisputable status can be gleaned from the survey FIFA conducted of participation in football around the world. The 'Big Count' survey returns submitted by the 204 national member organisations affiliated to FIFA revealed that 242,378,000 people are actively involved in playing the game. That represents roughly 1 out of every 25 of the world's population (FIFA-Survey: Big Count, at FIFA.com). Further confirmation that the association code is truly the world's game is provided by the rapidly growing popularity of the FIFA World Cup finals.

The game's global international tournament, held every four years, is appropriately named the 'World Cup' for it draws a significant number of supporters from around the world to matches and attracts the largest audience for any event shown on TV. The 1994 tournament was held in the USA in an attempt to increase the game's popularity on the North American continent. More than 3.5 million fans attended the matches. Over 30 billion people were estimated to have watched the games on TV and, drawn by the marketing potential, '40 multinational corporations paid US$400 million ... to gain "official product" status and guaranteed global advertising' (Manzenreiter and Horne 2002: 3). In 1998 the finals were held in France and FIFA estimated that 33.4 billion people watched the games on TV with 1.7 billion alone watching the final match between France and Brazil. Television coverage of the 2002 World Cup in Korea/Japan reached 213 countries and there were over 41,100 hours of dedicated programming. FIFA estimated that, notwithstanding the problem of difficult time zones for viewers in Europe and Central and South America, the cumulative audience over the 25 match days was 28.8 billion (FIFA World Cup and Television, FIFA.com).

The size of the potential TV audience for the World Cup finals has made the purchase of TV rights a big business issue and there has been a remarkable increase in the price paid for broadcasting rights since the 1980s. The TV broadcasting rights for the 1990, 1994 and 1998 World Cup tournaments held in Italy, the USA and France respectively were sold to an international consortium of public service broadcasters in Europe for US$310 million. The world TV rights (except for the USA) for the 2002 World Cup and the 2006 tournament in Germany were sold for US$1.97 billion (Horne and Manzenreiter 2002: 197).

As the twentieth century drew to a close the world's most popular sport and television, the world's most popular medium of mass communication and entertainment, were becoming increasingly closely connected. The television industry had come to appreciate 'the almost limitless potential of football's cross-cultural appeal' (Sugden and Tomlinson 1998: 82). As a result, money from the sale of TV rights and associated forms of income from marketing and sponsorship were quickly becoming a fundamental part of the new cultural economy of football and more broadly of sport as a whole.

Television and the new cultural economy of sport

Television coverage is now an essential part of modern sport as is sponsorship and rights marketing. Increasingly a vital objective for any major sport event is to sell exclusive marketing rights to a limited number of large corporations interested in promoting their products and services to a global television audience. In the period 1993–2003 the global sponsorship market grew from $10 million to $27 billion and at least two-thirds of that market, over $18 billion in 2003, is attributable to sport (Ruschetti et al. 2003). The 1978 World Cup in Argentina had six major sponsors, including *Coca-Cola*, *Gillette* and *Seiko*. At the World Cup in Mexico in 1986 there were twelve general sponsors including *Canon, Coca-Cola, Fuji, Gillette, JVC* and *Philips*. For the summer Olympics in Seoul in 1988 the IOC 'sold exclusive marketing rights to … Coca-Cola, VISA, 3M, Brother, Philips, Federal Express, Kodak, Time Inc., and Panasonic, for … more than $100 million' (Sugden and Tomlinson 1998: 86). At the World Cup in Italy in 1990 there were nine general sponsors with privileged access to stadium advertising, including many of the companies that had acquired exclusive rights for the Mexico tournament. For the USA tournament in 1994 there were eleven general sponsors including *Canon, Coca-Cola, Fuji, General Motors, Gillette, JVC, Mastercard, McDonald's,* and *Philips*. In France 1998 the twelve general sponsors included the nine identified above plus *adidas, Budweiser* and *Mars* (Sugden and Tomlinson 1998: 92–93).

The sale of television and marketing rights are now central to the political economy of sport. In the 1990s the Union of European Football Associations (UEFA) restructured 'the world's most important football competition' (Sugden and Tomlinson 1998: 74) involving leading clubs selected from its member organisations. Europe's annual club tournament, the UEFA

Champions League, is in terms of quality of football and calibre of players involved an event that can legitimately claim to be the world's premiere football tournament. Driven by a 'relentless commercial logic' UEFA have followed the exclusive sponsorship model (Sugden and Tomlinson 1998: 94–5). In the 1995–6 competition eight companies were able to avail themselves of the 'prestigious platform delivering volume audiences in prime-time programming' (Sugden and Tomlinson 1998: 95). The companies involved are household names and include *Amstel, Canon, Continental, Eurocard/ Mastercard, Ford, McDonald's, Philips* and *Reebok*. Through their association with the UEFA Champions League tournament these companies were able to reach a cumulative television audience of 3.5 billion people in Europe alone in the course of the 1995–6 season. The world-wide coverage the tournament attracted enabled sponsoring companies to reach additional audiences in Asia, Oceania, Africa, the Middle East and the Americas (Sugden and Tomlinson 1998).

Sport offers commercial companies the prospect of world-wide television exposure for their products and services. The money from the sale of television and marketing rights in turn has transformed sport. Football in particular has an unrivalled world-wide appeal and in consequence it is unequalled in global marketing potential. However the restructuring of the game made possible by the growth of marketing and sponsorship has raised concerns about the respects in which football culture is being 'shaped by an inexorable commercial logic' (Sugden and Tomlinson 1998: 97). Worries have also been expressed about the impact technological developments within television are likely to have on football in particular and sport in general.

The development of satellite and digital television has led to matches from the English *Premiership*, the Italian *Serie A* and the Spanish *La Liga* being transmitted around the world. The Premier League is the most popular national football league and is broadcast to 152 countries on a regular basis. Italy's *Serie A* is broadcast in 143 countries and Spain's *La Liga* is shown in 136 countries. Great games involving great players from the three best football leagues in the world represent a serious threat to lesser national leagues and their television broadcasting prospects. In the 2001–2 season a *Premiership* match between Manchester United and Liverpool drew an estimated global audience of half a billion people, or approximately one in twelve of the world's population (Campbell 2002). While *Serie A* and *La Liga* are popular in South America, southern Europe and south-east Asia, the attraction of the *Premiership* is strongest in Australasia, Africa and south-east Asia, with interest in countries such as Malaysia, Indonesia and Japan, not to mention China, growing at an especially rapid rate. Since 1992 and the formation of the Premier League the number of countries televising English football has quadrupled and the *Premiership* has become 'the biggest football brand in the world' (Campbell 2002: 46).

With the advent of satellite and subsequently digital television technologies there has been an increasing '"delocalization" of sporting tastes and loyalties' (Whitson 1998: 65). Just as national television coverage created the conditions in which sport fans could develop an affinity with and support for teams from beyond their local area, city or region, so global satellite television coverage of sport events has led to the development of international fan bases. As geography or place as the basis of identification with team has been eroded, so a variety of non-local sporting loyalties, expressed through the wearing of replica shirts, caps and other merchandise bearing club colours and logos, can be found along any street not just in America or Britain, but virtually anywhere in the world. Fans of any team can now be found anywhere and 'they contribute to the support of "their" teams not just by purchasing team paraphernalia but by uniting in front of the television' (Leifer 1995: 134).

With the process of 'delocalization' associated with first national and then global television coverage of sport events, visible symbolic signs of identification with a team have become increasingly important. As place or residence in a mobile, media-shaped late modern society provides less of a basis for sporting affiliation, it is to the purchase and display of team or club merchandise that those who want to publicly affirm their support increasingly turn. In the 1980s the sale of merchandise for nationally followed teams in the NFL and NBA created significant new revenue streams and in turn reinforced 'the place of sports logos and colours in the symbolic language and landscape of North American youth culture' (Whitson 1998: 66). As national markets have reached maturity leagues and clubs have sought to cultivate international publics and international markets for their merchandise.

The consequences of 'delocalization' for local or regional teams, those that have not been able to begin to generate an international following, have been considerable. Whatever the sport, undistinguished teams lacking any high profile players now struggle to attract media attention. As a FIFA report acknowledges in respect of football,

> while TV rights change hands for ever more colossal sums at the top of the football pyramid in Europe, the smaller countries, far from being able to capitalise on the knock-on effects of the sport's TV popularity, are *often obliged to pay their national networks to cover the local action* to a neo-discerning public. (cited in Sugden and Tomlinson 1998: 82–3 emphasis added)

The money from television and sponsorship coming into football at the top of the game in Europe has licensed a rapid rise in salaries and has led to the emergence of globally mobile superstar players. At the higher levels of the game 'football represents more and more graphically the triumph of the universal market ... it is an increasingly commodified product' (Sugden and Tomlinson 1998: 98). The prominence of sponsorship in all its manifestations (shirt, match, tournament and television coverage) clearly exemplifies the highly commodified status of the game, as does the transformed profile of leading players who have acquired the status of celebrities.

Football celebrity is a complex product of ability and performance on the field of play, cultural popularity, commercial value and crucially television exposure, without which the game would not have achieved its unrivalled level of global popularity. Prominent footballers have become cultural icons and much sought after endorsers of commercial products and services. But if television coverage is now vital for professional sport the increasing proliferation of television channels has simultaneously enhanced the value of sport to television. It is the wide-ranging cultural appeal of sport programming that accounts for its ability to 'break through the clutter of channels and advertising and consistently produce a desirable audience for sale to advertisers' (Bellamy 1998: 73). Major sports are increasingly highly valued by television because compared to other potential programming options they possess a valuable quality of authenticity, they are in relatively limited supply and consistently offer the prospect of drawing predictable and demographically desirable audiences. Major sports present television with an increasingly scarce opportunity to broadcast genuine, competitive events whose dramatic development and outcome cannot be pre-determined.

Sport retains a substantial degree of authenticity. It has been described as 'the last frontier of reality on television' (Bellamy 1998: 73). No matter how hard commentators, analysts and sponsors work, and the very codes and conventions of television coverage itself operate, if unwittingly, to subordinate the ethos of sport to the values of entertainment and commerce, sport retains a significant measure of authenticity. While the experience of sporting events may have been transformed by the cultural prominence accorded to spectacle, entertainment and commerce following the increasingly close articulation of sport, television and sponsorship, sport nevertheless retains its distinctive quality and unique appeal.

Sport television: from terrestrial to satellite

Live sport coverage was identified as crucial to the growth of non-terrestrial television by Rupert Murdoch who described it as the '"battering ram" for the expansion of his global television network' (Szymanski and Kuypers 2000: 62). In Murdoch's view sport represents the most powerful and attractive of all entertainment genres and among the various sports football ranks number one (Syzmanski and Kuypers 2000). The success of Rupert Murdoch's BSkyB network in winning an auction for the rights to televise live English Premiership football matches from the 1992/3 season radically transformed football finances as well as the traditional fixture schedule. The new contract involved a partnership between BSkyB and the BBC. At £304 million over five years the contract cost 'six times more than the previous arrangement with terrestrial TV' (Williams 1994: 384). BSkyB paid £191.5 million for the right to show 60 live matches each season and the BBC paid £22.5 million for a regular highlights package to be shown in its Saturday evening flagship *Match of the Day* programme. Sponsorship and the sale of overseas rights made up the remaining £90 million (Giulianotti 1999). On renewal of the contract in 1996 Sky paid the Premier League £670 million to show live matches and the BBC paid £73 million for its package (Sugden and Tomlinson 1998).

The entry of BSkyB into the market for TV rights for live coverage of Premier league football has transformed the political economy of the game. In 1978 the BBC paid the Football League in England £9.8 million for a four-year football highlights deal. In 1983 the first live football television contract was for five matches a year for two years and cost £2.6 million. From 1992 television rights revenue has constituted a significant new source of income, especially at the higher levels of the game. This has contributed to the emergence of a small upper echelon of wealthy clubs which now possess the capacity to pay high transfer fees and to offer lucrative contracts to players, a factor which post-Bosman has led to an influx of overseas players into the Premier League.

As well as playing a significant part in transforming the economic infra-structure of professional football in England, Sky TV has had a significant impact on the culture of the game. The new TV contract was for transmission of 60 live games and in consequence the fixture schedule had to be revised. Saturday afternoon would never again carry quite the same cultural significance as matches to be televised live might be scheduled for Saturday lunchtime, Sunday afternoons and/or a prime-time slot from 7pm-10pm on Monday evenings. The idea of regularly covering football live in prime-time television was not novel. At the time it was being introduced into Britain in the 1990s it was already a well established feature of television coverage of the National Football League in America.

In America in the 1960s and 1970s Roone Arledge was employed by ABC to direct and produce NFL television coverage. Arledge set out to transform the television viewer's experience of football. He used 'cranes ... and heli-copters' to get better views of the stadium and its location, 'hand-held cameras for close-up shots ... of nervous coaches', as well as 'rifle-type micro-phones to pickup the roar of the crowd ... or the crunch of a hard tackle' (Rader 1984: 247). Subsequently BSkyB have employed comparable innova-tions and embraced associated entertainment production values in their coverage of Premier League football in England and subsequently UEFA Champions League. BSkyB use airships to provide an aerial view of the sta-dium and its neighbourhood, hand-held cameras for close-up shots of fans, a multiplicity of remote pitch-side cameras to better follow the action, as well as a battery of microphones to bring the sounds to the sights the cameras provide.

Roone Arledge introduced another radical innovation into television sports coverage in 1970. An ambitious new national television program-ming format was devised for NFL:

> 'Monday Night Football' outstripped all other regular sportcasts in popularity ... this prime-time sports show altered the Monday-night habits of a large portion of the American people. (Rader 1984: 248)

Precisely what impact Sky's equivalent programme to ABC's Monday Night Football has had on the habits of English viewers is open to debate. Certainly pubs have recognised the potential benefits associated with advertising their satellite television provision and the possibility that 'Monday Night Football' might increase bar sales on an otherwise conventionally quiet night. Extension of licensing hours along with Sky TV's coverage of Premier League football has contributed to the 'rapid growth of a cultural form – collective viewing of sport – not previously a major feature of English social life' (Horne et al. 1999: 165). Undoubtedly increased live coverage of games, profiles provided of players, pre- and post-match interviews, analysis and replay of key players' contributions and significant moments in the action, have changed not just television coverage of football but the game itself. Top clubs and leading players in particular have been beneficiaries of the new cultural economy of football. Players' salaries have increased significantly and so have their profiles both within and beyond the game. In turn, BSkyB's association with Premier League football has provided the broadcaster with an economic and cultural platform from which to build a profile as the leading sport network in Britain and thereby carve out a distinctive identity for itself.

The potential for sport broadcasting to offer networks a way of differentiating themselves from their rivals was first recognised in America, ABC's NFL Monday Night Football and the 'NBA on NBC' representing two prominent examples of such 'brand identification' (Bellamy 1998). In America the major television networks, ABC, CBS, NBC and Fox continue to dominate coverage of major professional baseball, football, basketball and hockey leagues, although ESPN, an ABC subsidiary has a significant global sport broadcasting presence.[4] As an American terrestrial television network ABC has had access to a far greater potential national audience than a satellite television network like BSkyB has had in England to date – in 2003 an estimated 12 million households, a minority, and 40,000 pubs were BSkyB subscribers. However, the television industry is changing as it becomes multi-channel and increasingly international and in America the market share of the major networks is declining as new channels come on line and this has led the networks to 'pursue an aggressive strategy of acquisition of overseas broadcasting companies' (Leifer 1995: 303).

In a comparable manner there is an increasing recognition in professional sport that as home markets appear to be approaching maturity or saturation point, further growth has to be sought in overseas markets, effectively through the cultivation of new fans, audiences and consumers via global television coverage and merchandising. In this context how well games travel, how attractive games are beyond the cultural context in which they developed their initial appeal becomes a critically important issue. For example, the association code of football has proven to be far more popular around the world than 'grid-iron' football. To date, attempts to promote North American sports – the World League of American Football and NFL and NHL exhibition games – around the world have had only very modest levels of success (Whitson 1998).

Major team sports in America have been transformed through processes of modernisation, reluctantly in the case of baseball, eagerly in respect of football and belatedly, yet positively, as far as basketball is concerned. One of the difficulties major leagues have encountered is working out whether it is possible to cater simultaneously to local, national and potential international publics. Traditionally major league baseball has been based on teams attached to local cities and with the introduction of a 162 game season from 1961 it has found itself disadvantaged in an era of televised sport. Commercial logic and advertising revenue led American television networks to place emphasis on national publics for sport programmes and this meant that 'broadcasts had to be limited so that baseball fans *everywhere* would feel compelled to watch *any* baseball broadcast' (Leifer 1995: 161). In the absence of any organisational control over broadcasting the big problem for baseball has been how to limit television coverage. Baseball team owners have continued to try to build a loyal local following and to this end have sold rights to broadcast their games to cable and local television. At the end of the 1980s only 75 baseball games, including play-offs and World Series games, were being broadcast nationally but '1,700 of the 2,200 played each season were being shown on a regional or pay-per-view basis' (Leifer 1995: 165).

A comparison with the NFL, 'the modern prototype' (Leifer 1995), is very revealing. Football teams do not have city attachments in the way that baseball teams do and there are no local television contracts. From the 1950s the NFL had been quick to embrace television and through nationwide broadcasts became a truly national sport. In consequence teams were able to build national publics and in due course 'the "Super Bowl" was initiated and became the first sports championship event staged primarily for television' (Leifer 1995: 132). The later introduction of ABC's Monday Night Football served to confirm football as the national sport in late modern America. The NFL policy has been for a limited number of televised games that would be viewed by fans from all locales and it is a policy that has been financially lucrative for the sport, so much so that in the late 1980s 'the NFL received more for its 57 broadcasts than baseball did for its 1,800' (Leifer 1995: 165).

However, the very success of professional football's adaptation to American national network television may constitute a problem as the networks themselves face competition from new television technologies (cable, satellite, pay-per-view) and the necessity of creating an international public becomes an increasing commercial imperative. Professional football's relative cultural marginality meant that it was better placed to take advantage of the potential represented by the new medium of television and in so doing it displaced baseball in popularity. Network television provided the platform on which professional football was able to secure and mobilise a national public. NFL teams might have city associations by virtue of their names but each aspired 'to be watched by the nation' (Leifer 1995: 149) and the medium of television made it possible for fans to be drawn from across the nation. How well placed the NFL is to make the adaptations and accommodations that might be necessary to secure an international public is another matter.

The global sport marketplace

The creation of committed global audiences for sport represents a special challenge. Analysis of the prospects for the major leagues in American baseball, football, hockey and basketball, suggests that the latter may be best placed to penetrate international markets precisely because it 'failed to emulate either early Major League Baseball or the modern NFL' (Leifer 1995: 188). The NBA was relatively slow to respond to the opportunities represented by network television and when it did so in 1965 ratings were relatively low, reaching only 6 per cent of the viewing audience. In the late 1970s revenue from television contracts with CBS increased, rising from $840,900 per team per year in 1978 to $1.2 million per team per year in 1982. Comparable figures for the NFL were $5.5 million and $14.5 million respectively, the differences reflecting the gap in cultural status and appeal of the two sports in the period in question (Rader 1984).

The appointment of David Stern as commissioner of the NBA in 1984 coincided with two other events that were to have a substantial effect on basketball's future. One was the purchase by ABC of the Entertainment Sports Programming Network (ESPN), a relatively new cable broadcaster that had already established itself as 'part of the fabric of life for the nation's sports fans' (Halberstam 2001: 129). The second was that Michael Jordan left university and signed for the Chicago Bulls. ESPN had been broadcasting college basketball from 1979 and those college players like Jordan who went on to play in the NBA were already well-known figures, stars in the making. On becoming NBA commissioner Stern, following the example of the NFL, moved quickly to limit the number of NBA games shown on television (down from 100 to 50) and as basketball's popularity in America grew the NBA began to explore international markets. Basketball had reached a low point in the 1960s, when NBC abandoned a television contract because of lack of viewer interest. The game suffered further ignominy in the late 1970s when the NBA world championship was not shown live. From the mid-1980s however, basketball began to achieve a 'status in American popular culture that now rivals that of the NFL' (Whitson 1998: 65).

In the 1980s the NBA sought 'to associate the game with the skills and personalities of a series of stars: Magic Johnson and Larry Bird, Michael Jordan and Charles Barkley, Shaquille O'Neal and Grant Hill' (Whitson 1995: 66). Television coverage not only highlighted the exceptional ability of such players but contributed to them becoming stars and personalities. Whitson notes that the NBA and companies like *Nike* and *Reebok* were quick to take advantage of the raised cultural profile individual players acquired through television coverage. One important consequence of which has been the creation of 'an unprecedented series of black American celebrities, whose celebrity has in turn augmented the visibility of the league and the game in American (and now global) popular culture' (Whitson 1995: 66–67).

Basketball, more than any other American sport, has been considered to have the potential to extend its popularity beyond America (Halberstam 2001). Because the rules of the game are relatively straightforward, far more so than either baseball or American football, the game has travelled more easily across national and cultural boundaries. Global diffusion of the game has been further assisted by a combination of the powerful market penetrating capacity of American broadcasting media, language accessibility, and the prior diffusion around the world of many other American cultural forms such as popular music, film, fashion, fast-food and television programmes. NBA games are now on television in over 70 countries and star players have acquired international popularity and celebrity status (Leifer 1995; Bellamy 1998). The NBA brand is now marketed internationally through caps, t-shirts and basketballs and over the period 1981–91 the sale of videos alone grew in value from $40 million to $1 billion (Leifer 1995). In many respects the NBA is now the late modern prototype and is regarded as the 'most television and marketing-savvy of all the major sports leagues' (Bellamy 1998: 82).

However, while there has been an expansion of the league to Canada and attempts have been made to establish a viable global competition (e.g. *McDonald's* Open tournament), to date the NBA's global profile remains largely a marketing phenomenon. And the claim that basketball rather than soccer is the 'ascending new sport in the world ... winning ever greater popularity with the young' is difficult to sustain (Halberstam 2001: 130). Even within America the continuing grass-roots growth in the popularity of soccer among women and girls and the interest aroused by Freddy Adu, described by some as the future of American soccer or the 'soccer saviour', render the claim, at best, premature (Chadband 2004; Hannigan 2004).[5]

While the claim made about the rising global popularity of basketball is controversial, the observation that 'it was inevitable that sooner or later some American athlete would become a signature commercial figure' (Halberstam 2001: 130), is not. The first commercial representative of the 'new athletic-cultural-commercial empire' was Michael Jordan, an American and a basketball player (Halberstam 2001: 131). To understand why an American basketball player was the first to achieve this status it is necessary to consider a number of factors. These include the greater cultural and commercial significance of sneakers or trainers in contrast to football and baseball footwear in 1980s' America and the associated commercial rivalry that existed between *Nike, adidas* and *Converse* as they sought to increase their share of the sneaker market. Advances in television production and reception technologies led to bigger and better pictures and a greater 'sense of physical and emotional intimacy' with sporting figures (Halberstam 2001: 131) and this proved to be especially significant in a game like basketball where play is fast and physically intense and where, because there are only five members on a team as compared to baseball's nine and football's eleven, each individual player features far more prominently in the action. The combination of improved television coverage and associated forms of commercial exposure through advertising campaigns, plus the fact that the NBA and its players had acquired a unique level of popularity and street-credibility with young American males in particular, served to raise the status and profile of individual players. NBA players became highly marketable commodities and the combination of their on-court prowess and on-screen performance in games and advertising campaigns duly elevated them to the status of stars and in the case of Michael Jordan to super-stardom.

There are currently three outstanding globally significant signature commercial sporting figures. Two are American, former basketball star Michael Jordan and golfer Tiger Woods. The third is an Englishman and a footballer, David Beckham, an individual who is as celebrated a figure as Jordan and Woods everywhere around the world with the exception of America. The global promotion of such high profile star figures in television coverage of games and through commercial campaigns in which they feature produces benefits for all parties involved. Sport stars and their images, their clubs and the leagues they play in, the television coverage they receive and the commercial endorsement and advertising campaigns in which they are involved, constitute 'circuits of promotion' (Whitson 1998). The network that connects the figure of Michael Jordan, the NBA and *Nike* effectively illustrates the mutually reinforcing promotional processes that have become a feature of the contemporary world of sport:

> Nike ... attached its corporate persona to images of Michael Jordan ... [and] when Jordan appeared in Nike advertisements in the early 1990s he was adding to the global visibility of the Chicago Bulls, the NBA, and the game of basketball, as well as promoting Nike shoes. He was also, not incidentally, promoting himself and adding to his value as a promotional icon. (Whitson 1998: 67)

Jordan's high visibility has been beneficial for his team, the NBA, *Nike* and not least of all for the man himself as 'Jordan' the brand has emerged through the promotional process.

With the 'delocalisation' of sporting loyalties associated with national television and subsequently global television coverage, the sport star has become an increasingly important figure around and in respect of whom identification and loyalty can be constituted and expressed. The growing commodification of sport is exemplified by and associated with the search for new global audiences, markets and competitions for television coverage and merchandise sales. And it is in this context that the figure of the sport star has come to assume such trans-cultural significance and to exemplify potential global economic value.

American major league sports have made significant efforts to expand internationally and as well as the licensing of products, each of the leagues sells television broadcasts of games around the world. In England *the* major league sport by a considerable distance is football and its most prestigious product is the *Premiership* which has been very successful in finding international markets for merchandise and the sale of rights to live television broadcasts. *Premiership* clubs benefit from the fact that their game is the world's game. They are able to participate in effective and well-established international competitions such as the UEFA Champions League and the UEFA Cup. Teams derive significant revenue, substantial in some cases, from participation in such international competitions. Revenue comes directly from spectator attendance at games and in addition from a share of the sale of television rights around the world. Indirect revenue streams may arise from the sale of merchandise associated with international promotion of a club and its players through global television coverage. In the case of the American major leagues there is a significant difference in so far as most of the revenue derived from international activity comes from the sale of merchandise carrying league and team logos rather than from international competition. In acknowledgement of this the NBA increased the number of its staff engaged in international marketing from 25 in 1983 to 300 in 1991 and it currently maintains offices in Switzerland, Australia, China and Spain. In a comparable manner the NFL since 1988 has been devoting considerable attention to international marketing and currently licenses in the region of '350 manufacturers ... to produce over 2,500 items that bring in over $2.3 billion in worldwide retail sales' (Leifer 1995: 287).

Attempts to build an international following for American sports, through the staging of regular season games overseas or the promotion of international competitions, or global leagues, have proven far from successful in attracting either viable television ratings or an acceptable level of match attendance. Baseball and American football do not have solid international bases on which they can cultivate an international public in the way that association football (soccer) has been able to do. As Olympic sports the prospects for basketball and hockey may look better, but to date the 'marketing genius' of the NBA and the NHL has not led to an international public regularly following competitions (Leifer 1995).

In both America and England major professional sports and television corporations now work to extend their global reach in order to enhance their value to sponsors and advertisers. Taking stock of this situation Whitson argues that 'the stakes are almost unlimited, in terms of merchandising and television revenues and ... allied promotional revenues' (1998: 69). Unlike its other cultural products, for example *Coca-Cola* and *Pepsi*, *Levi* jeans, popular musical forms, film genres and television programmes, American sports and teams appear to be rather more limited in significance and appeal and confined largely to audiences within the USA cultural heartland.[6]

Does sport constitute a cultural form that signifies the limit of American cultural imperialism? The answer seems to be a qualified 'yes' in so far as attempts to attract live global audiences for specifically American sports have generally not been very successful. In consequence it has been argued that the 'outcome of globalization is less likely to be the hegemony of American sports' (Whitson 1998: 70). However, processes of extensive commodification that first became apparent in American sport following the growth of television coverage and sponsorship are destined to continue to be a powerful influence on any sport that seeks to maintain its 'place in a mediated global culture' (Whitson 1998: 70–71). Marketing, merchandising, a culture of celebrity, the values of entertainment and accommodation to the demands of television are now part and parcel of major sport events around the world, part of the new cultural economy of sport.

The consequences of the new cultural economy of sport

The sport industry in both Britain and America is now to a substantial degree a 'media-made phenomenon' in so far as television's capacity to 'manufacture "stars", sell products, alter lifestyles, and ... commodify audiences [has] made spectator sports an element of mainstream culture' (Bellamy 1998: 74). Television has undoubtedly transformed sport, but it has been argued that the prominence of show business and entertainment values intrinsic to a medium operating in a commercial marketplace, where audience ratings are crucial, has led to 'a trivialization of the traditional sports experience' (Rader 1984: 101; see also Lasch 1991).

The tendency to build up an event in order to generate a TV audience that extends beyond the particular game's fan base may lead to trailers that exaggerate the significance of an event and pre-match comments that risk raising expectations to a level that may prove unrealisable. The codes and conventions intrinsic to a medium that operates primarily in terms of entertainment values have led to sport television coverage being criticised for its degeneration into 'spectacle'. Indeed, television's dramatisation of sport has been argued to threaten the very quality that may distinguish sport from so many other aspects of contemporary social life, namely its authenticity (Rader 1984).

As the scale of potential television and sponsorship revenue has grown, sports have sought to introduce a number of changes deliberately designed to broaden their popular appeal and to promote their attractiveness to the medium. Sports have carefully repackaged themselves for television by modifying rules to increase fan and viewer interest (association football's penalty shoot-outs), adopting new playing schedules (Monday Night Football) and introducing new formats to increase end of season excitement (play-off systems). Television coverage brings exciting images of professional sport directly into people's homes and into the bars and cafes where, with the advent of satellite television, communal viewing has become increasingly popular. In so far as the medium has a tendency to single out and focus on individuals, even in team sports, one important consequence is that the profiles of all players featured in televised sports are likely to be raised. In short, with television coverage the chance of an individual player becoming more widely known is likely to increase significantly. In the case of outstanding or star players the frequent use of pre-match analysis of previous performances, close-up shots and pre- and post-match interview material, contributes significantly to their transformation into very well-known figures, both on and off the field of play, in short into celebrities.

As the cultural economy of sporting celebrity has developed the status of leading sportsmen and sportswomen has increased and their cultural profile has risen significantly. In the cultural-commercial force field formed by the close articulation of sport, television and sponsorship the character of the sporting hero has been displaced by the celebrity figure of the sport star.

Notes

1 In 1995 Jean-Marc Bosman's successful legal action through the European Court of Justice led to footballers being accorded the same freedom of movement as other European workers (Giulianotti 1999).

2 Beckham's off-field activities began to attract significant media attention when he dated Victoria Adams, one of The Spice Girls. Press coverage of their subsequent engagement, wedding, and family life elevated 'Posh and Becks' to celebrity status as Britain's most popular couple (Whannel 2002). But in the spring of 2004 the tabloid press in Britain ran a series of stories about Beckham's private life in Madrid. Details of alleged mobile phone text-messages to a former female personal assistant and reports of alleged relationships with other young women placed Beckham on the front pages of the tabloids and on radio and television news agendas for several days running and threatened to transform his carefully cultivated image and damage the Beckham brand.

3 By the time he was 14 Adu, who was selected by DC United in the 2004 Major League Soccer SuperDraft, was reputed to be the best paid soccer player in the USA, earning $500,000 a year. Press speculation about Adu's potential to become 'bigger than Pele' gained momentum when he was selected by *Pepsi* to appear in a commercial alongside the former Brazilian international footballer (Hannigan 2004).

4 The elevation of Fox to major network status alongside CBS, NBC and ABC confirmed the importance of sports rights for television companies. It was when it became the 'Home of the NFL' in 1994 that Fox signalled to the financial and advertising communities that it was growing in power and ranked as a major television network (Bellamy 1998).

5 There was a women's professional soccer league in America and following the success of the USA team in the 1999 Women's World Cup its leading players became stars. For example, in 2000 Mia Hamm was reported to be earning over $1 million from endorsement contracts with a range of companies including *Gatorade, Pepsi, Quaker Oats, Nike* and *Nabisco* (St. John 2001: 18). However in 2003 the professional game in America began to suffer from falling attendances and declining television ratings and sponsorship interest which led to investors withdrawing their support. As a result the Women's United Soccer Association (WUSA) League was disbanded and the players' contracts were cancelled just before the start of the 2003 Women's World Cup (Leighton 2003). Nevertheless soccer in the USA is considered to be 'getting bigger and bigger particularly at the grassroots level ... The number of youth that are playing ... has quadrupled in the last 10 years and ... for women it is absolutely the fastest growing sport' (http://www.footballculture.net/teams/feat-bethany.html).

6 Baseball is played in Puerto Rico, the Dominican Republic, Cuba and Japan and attempts were made in 1969, 1974 and 1989 to create a viable yet modest international league, but to no avail. American football is played in Canada and on Japanese University campuses and since 1991 there has been an NFL European League of six teams based in Germany (4), the Netherlands (1) and Scotland (1) (see nfluk.com and http://wwwwbs.cs.tu-berlin.de/user/tiny/history.html). As with baseball attempts to form a commercially viable international league attracting an international public have proven largely unsuccessful. If there are small pockets of enthusiasm for American sports around the world they have not to date extended to regular season MLB, NFL and NBA games (Leifer 1995).

5

Corporate Culture and the Branding of the Sport Star: *Nike*, Michael Jordan and Tiger Woods

Sport, culture and economy

In the closing decades of the twentieth century the popular appeal and cultural and economic significance of sport grew to unprecedented levels. During the 1980s sport became more and more highly commercialised and mass media dependent and since then it has occupied an increasingly prominent economic and cultural position (Wenner 1989). Assessing the rise of sport during the 1980s one analyst remarked that 'the economic foundation for the modern sport-media boom will remain intact until advertisers find some source of programming radically superior to sport' (McChesney 1989: 67). Subsequently the popularity of sport has continued to grow and sport events, programmes, products and personalities have become an established part of both the commercial and the cultural landscape.

Professional sport constitutes a form of work, a business or industry, one that is simultaneously of enormous economic and cultural significance. With their organisational forms, division of labour, professionalism and competitiveness modern sports replicate 'the structure of the workplace' (Kellner 1996: 459). As a form of service work sport constitutes an 'assemblage of practices built up from parts that are economic and non-economic (but always already cultural)' (du Gay and Pryke 2002: 4). Sport is at the very heart of the articulation of culture and economy and plays an increasingly prominent part in the provision of services and the promotion and marketing of commodities in the new 'cultural economy'. As sport has come to 'define the culture of the world' it has also become of increasing economic significance (Katz 1994; Kuper 2003). Indeed, sport serves as an institutional exemplification of the way in which there has been a 'fusing, blurring and interaction of practices' that conventionally have been designated as either economic or cultural in substance (Negus 2002: 116).

Symbols, signs and meanings occupy an increasingly prominent place in contemporary economic life (Baudrillard 1981). Economic transformations have led to 'economies of signs and space', to the 'recasting of meaning in work and in leisure' and the growing importance of cultural intermediaries operating in advertising, styling, branding and marketing (Lash and Urry 1994: 3). Sport has come to occupy an important place in the production and consumption of a proliferating range of commodities and services as well as in respect of the generation of popular meanings and values with which commodities are imbued (Negus 2002). In particular sporting associations and sporting figures have been identified by advertising agencies and management consultants as offering highly effective means for establishing a distinctive 'set of emotional meanings and values around products' that will contribute to the process of 'brand building', if not enhancement of 'brand value' (Nixon 2003: 40).

Sport has not featured significantly in social scientific analyses of the transformation of contemporary economic life. Analysts have discussed advertising culture, the emergence of a cultural economy and the increasingly significant role of cultural intermediaries, but the institutional domain of sport offering corporations high visibility, an unrivalled aura of authenticity, and an unequalled capacity to 'burnish corporate images and sell brands' has been marginalised, if not neglected altogether (Miciak and Shanklin 1994). A notable exception is Naomi Klein's analysis of the ways in which multinational corporations have extended their global influence by redirecting their energies and resources away from the production of goods and towards the cultivation and promotion of '*images* of their brands' (2001: 4, emphasis in original).

In tracing the process through which corporations moved from making things to cultivating their brands Klein makes a distinction between advertising and branding. Whereas the brand is described as 'the core meaning of the modern corporation', advertising constitutes merely the means for delivery, effectively the conductor through which brand meaning is conveyed to consumers (Klein 2001: 5). The early roots of competitive branding, the association of proper names with generic goods and the introduction and deployment of corporate logos can be traced back to the late nineteenth century. In outlining the processes through which a 'new branded world' has developed Klein draws attention to a four-fold increase in advertising expenditure in the USA between 1979 and 1998, rising from $50 billion to around $200 billion. In the case of one particularly prominent sport goods company, the 'attitude brand' *Nike*, advertising expenditure increased twenty-fold, from around $25 million in 1987 to around $500 million in 1997 (Klein 2001: 16–19). Reflecting on this period Klein remarks that companies such as *Nike* and *Reebok* and their competitors in the sneaker business were 'signing star athletes to colossal sponsorship deals' (2001: 16) to promote their brands.

Corporations have attempted to associate their brands with events and figures that evoke a 'feeling of authenticity' (Klein 2001: 36) and the cultural form that has been identified as most readily exemplifying authenticity has been sport. The association between branding and sport has been pivotal in the development of *Nike* the sport goods corporation and, in turn, the elevation of basketball player Michael Jordan to a level of economic and cultural significance that extends far beyond his particular sporting field, if not the world of sport as a whole. However, before discussing *Nike*'s economic and cultural impact on the world of sport and the circumstances in which Jordan emerged and subsequently acquired iconic status, consideration needs to be given to the history of basketball before Michael Jordan became a major player within the game. The cultural and economic significance of basketball before Jordan was rather different to what the game became after Jordan, after the emergence of the cultural phenomenon to which *Nike's* compellingly powerful imagery made such a formative contribution.

The origin of basketball

Basketball as a formally organised modern sport originated in America in the late nineteenth century. The first officially recognised game is reported to have taken place in 1891 between two nine-man teams. One team was captained by a physical education instructor James Naismith, who is credited with developing the new game as an indoor winter sport that would help both to entertain and to build the fitness of students, the captain of the other team was a faculty colleague. Naismith worked at the International Training School in Springfield Massachusetts to which prospective leaders of local Young Men's Christian Associations (YMCA) came to study (Baerwald 1995). The early national development of the game took place through a process of diffusion around the network of YMCAs and it began to be an international sport after it was introduced overseas by members of the American military. The game was introduced in France (Paris) in 1893, England (London) 1894 and Brazil 1896, it was being played in China by 1898, and had been 'demonstrated in Japan, Iran, and India by 1901' (Baerwald 1995: 174).

The rules of basketball were gradually formalised. Naismith had produced 13 rules in 1891 and initially movement with the ball was prohibited. In 1893 some movement was permitted providing one foot remained pinned to the spot. By 1895 teams tended to limit the number of active players to five on each side and by this stage a rectangular backboard to which the hoop and basket were attached had become a standard feature of the game. A year later greater movement was allowed as players were permitted to dribble with the ball. In 1915 the three principal organisations that had played an early role in trying to develop a formal system of rules – the YMCA, the Amateur Athletic Union (AAU) and the National Collegiate Athletic Association (NCAA) – formed a committee to establish consistent national codes and standards. And in 1932 an international governing body – the Federation Internationale de Basketball Amateur (FIBA) – was formed (Baerwald 1995; Leifer 1995).

While initially basketball games were played in gymnasiums the monopolisation of a scarce resource by a sport involving as few as ten players led to conflicts with the greater number of other potential users and ultimately to a number of YMCAs refusing to allow the sport to be played on their premises. In consequence as the game developed a variety of other venues had to be used. Lofts above stables, an opera house, abandoned churches, a lumberyard driveway, a roller-skating rink, dance halls and concrete floor armouries provided early settings for games (Baerwald 1995). In the course of the 1920s college basketball benefited from the multi-purpose gymnasiums which had begun to be constructed in many high schools and universities.

While the college game grew in popularity in the 1920s and 1930s there were only a few professional basketball teams. A number of attempts were made to establish professional leagues, the first being the American Basketball League (1926–31). Subsequently the National Basketball League (NBL: 1937–49) and the Basketball Association of America (BAA: 1946–9) were established and with their merger in 1949 the National Basketball Association (NBA) was formed. Initially major league basketball, the professional game, was a relatively marginal sport, one that frequently served 'as a way to better utilize hockey arenas in large cities' (Leifer 1995: 171–172). The sport allowed ice hockey arena owners and owners of other multi-purpose facilities in big cities to fill winter schedule vacancies and generate extra revenue (Rader 1983b; Baerwald 1995). Being dependent on multi-purpose arenas meant that basketball teams often found themselves displaced by other more popular and lucrative events, so much so that from 1946 to 1951 the New York Knickerbockers played less than 50 per cent of their home games at their Madison Square Garden venue. And in the 1952 NBA seven-game playoff series four different arenas had to be used because the teams involved found that other events had priority. In the case of the New York Knickerbockers for two of the games it was a circus that had first call on the facilities (Rader 1983b; Baerwald 1995).

The prospects for the professional game improved in the early 1950s as gambling violations and recruitment scandals were exposed in college basketball allowing the relatively newly established NBA to turn the tables on the amateur game and promote itself as the '"clean" alternative' (Leifer 1995: 172). But while professional basketball started to acquire a higher profile it continued to be beset by a number of problems. Throughout the 1950s the number of franchises that had made up the league declined from seventeen to eight and by 1960 only teams from major sporting cities in the East remained. By the 1966–7 season the league was merely ten strong with only two teams based in the west of the country (Leifer 1995). Moreover, while there had been television contracts in the early 1950s they were insubstantial, reflecting the relatively poor audience drawing power of the game. Indeed in 1962 NBC decided to abandon broadcast of regular season games on the grounds that they were boring the audience, so much so that ratings were deemed to be too low to report (Rader 1983b).

It was not until the late 1960s that the NBA began to make headway by securing improved television contracts. As the game's national profile and prosperity grew so in 1967 a rival professional organisation, the American Basketball Association (ABA), was formed. Competition between the two leagues forced up salaries as the leagues sought to outbid one another for the signatures of leading players. While the rival league lasted for nine years the losses it sustained eventually led in 1976 to its dissolution. Following closure of the league four ABA teams applied for and gained entry into the NBA (Rader 1983b; Leifer 1995). By 1980, largely in order to deter other potentially interested parties from establishing rival leagues, the NBA had increased the size of its league to twenty-three and had extended its coverage nationwide. Revenue from television contracts had by this time increased, reflecting a rise in audience viewing figures, but the sums involved remained relatively modest when compared to the revenue the NFL received from television.

In the mid-1960s the NBA contract with ABC for Sunday afternoon television transmission of regular season games was reputed to be worth $600,000 per year for the entire league, rising by $100,000 every year for the duration of the five year contract (Leifer 1995). By 1972 each franchise was receiving around $325,000 from the ABC contract but from 1974 with the signing of a new contract with CBS this rose to $535,000 per year (Rader 1983b). Over this period the percentage of the television audience viewing basketball matches rose from 6 per cent in 1965 to 8.9 per cent in 1969 and then moved above 10 per cent in 1973, only to fall back again in 1974 to 8.1 per cent (Leifer 1995). Between 1978 and 1982 the television contract with CBS grew in value by approximately 42 per cent (from $840,900 to $1.2 million per team per year). In comparison television rights revenue received by each NFL franchise between 1964 and 1978 increased over five-fold (from $1 million to $5.5 million per team per year) and between 1978 and 1982 increased again by a factor of just under three (from $5.5 million to $14.5 million per team per year).

The increase in the number of basketball teams and the geographical expansion of the NBA league led to an 82-game season, increased travel and, in turn, to players appearing fatigued, lethargic and indifferent in regular-season games – qualities that a predominantly white television audience tended to attribute to the racial origin of some of the players. Black players were accused of not trying hard enough and 'the inability of whites to iden- tify with black players threatened to reduce fan support for the sport' (Rader 1983b: 299). Lack of viewer interest in regular games led to television cov- erage being directed to play-off games involving the strongest big-city teams and as the 1980s began the future of basketball appeared uncertain.

Until 1950 there had been no African-Americans playing professional basketball in the BAA, a fact that has been attributed partly to racial prej- udice and partly to the league's franchise holders not wishing to disturb their 'profitable relationship' with the owner of the Harlem Globetrotters who virtually monopolised 'top black talent' (Rader 1983b: 295). In con- trast to other sports like baseball and football, basketball's equipment and spatial requirements are very modest and its history shows that it has been 'the sport played most seriously by residents of poorer neighbourhoods in large American cities' (Baerwald 1995: 206). A ball, a hoop and a little space is all that is needed and such minimal requirements have made basket- ball the definitive inner-city or 'ghetto' sport. Reflecting on the particular significance of basketball for black communities in the late 1960s one observer remarked that the game seemed almost 'more religious rite than sport' and that kids playing for hours on end during the course of a summer would 'wear out four or five pairs of sneakers' (Tarshis 1972: 14, cited in Baerwald 1995: 205). The latent commercial potential of the sport would in due course be recognised by both television networks and commercial corporations.

Nike and the world of sport

The *Nike* brand emerged in 1972 at the Olympic trials in Eugene, USA. At the time *adidas*, a German company, monopolised the sport footwear industry, their dominance being illustrated by the fact that 80 per cent of medal winners at the summer Olympic Games held in Montreal were wearing their products. Although at the time athletics remained an amateur sport it was widely believed that under-the-table payments were being made to persuade competitors to wear running shoes made by the German company. Such payments provided amateur athletes with some contribution towards training costs but they were never officially acknowledged. Early in the 1970s Steve Prefontaine, an American distance runner, was using *adidas* running shoes when Phil Knight *Nike*'s CEO offered him 'five thousand dollars, above board, in exchange for wearing Nike shoes and a competition shirt that said Nike' (Katz 1994: 63). The American Athletics Union (AAU) did not take kindly to the exposure of the hidden payments system and warned Prefontaine as to his future conduct. When asked what he intended to do about the warning Prefontaine is reputed to have said 'Screw 'em', exemplifying an attitude that would become synonymous with *Nike* endorsers. Tragically in 1975 Prefontaine died at the age of 24 in a car crash. At the time he held seven American records (Katz 1994: 64).

In its early days *Nike*, which was closely associated with long-distance running, sought to present itself as anti-establishment, unlike *adidas* which was regarded as closely associated with the governing bodies of international sport. *Nike* set out to market itself as the champion of the athlete, as standing for something different to the aristocratic elites and bureaucratic constituencies that dominated the world of sport. Within the company there was,

> an internal obsession with 'authenticity'. The company would be dedicated to the proposition that authentic athletic desires would help to create authentic products for authentic athletes. The cause of the individual athlete would become the company's cause. (Katz 1994: 25)

By 1990 *Nike* had seven times more sporting figures contracted to it than any other company in its field. It had overtaken *adidas* in the worldwide sale of sport footwear and controlled 33 per cent of the American market compared to *adidas*'s 3 per cent. In the course of the 1990s *Nike*'s presence in a variety of sports grew significantly. In this period over 50 per cent of teams playing NCAA basketball wore *Nike* shoes, in the NBA 25 per cent of players were contracted to *Nike* and over 60 per cent of the players wore *Nike* shoes. In addition 275 NFL players and 290 major league baseball players wore *Nike* (Katz 1994). The *Nike* view was that sport had become a more significant popular cultural force than music and 'had so completely permeated the logic of the market place in consumer goods that by 1992 the psychological content of selling was often more sports-oriented than it was sexual' (Katz 1994: 26).

The attitude brand

In 1992, celebrating the company's twentieth anniversary, Knight acknowledged Steve Prefontaine's significance and the special qualities he possessed:

> Pre was a rebel from a working-class background, a guy full of cockiness and pride and guts. Pre's spirit ... is the cornerstone of this company's soul. (Katz 1994: 64)

'Attitude' has been synonymous with *Nike* from the very beginning. 'Just do it' – rebellion, irreverence, cynicism and an ironic self-referential quality are all part of the *Nike* (anti-)corporate style. *Nike* sought to sign sporting figures who were more than winners, more than just players. They had to possess something more, signify something more, and that something more was a 'special attitude'.

In 1977 Phil Knight sitting at Wimbledon watching a men's singles tennis match found that 'something more' that would in due course lead to an 'anti-country-club, "rock-and-roll" tennis surge' (Katz 1994: 220). It assumed the form of a fiery 18-year-old American raised in New York. John McEnroe raged on court, sometimes smashed his racquet on the ground, and 'let off plenty of steam at visually challenged linesmen' (McEnroe 2002: 105). McEnroe – 'Super Brat', 'McBrat' or 'McNasty' as he later became known to the British tabloid press – represented a very different kind of tennis player (McEnroe 2002). His tennis was played with attitude and Knight immediately identified McEnroe as a 'Nike guy', as someone who would break the mould of tennis, who would transform the game's image. McEnroe duly received an endorsement 'windfall package' of $100,000, a figure that at the time was considered to be 'scandalously large' (Katz 1994).

In the early 1980s professional tennis became a more youthful game, a sport in which the 'great rivalries were between players who *looked* like kids' (Katz 1994: 224). By the mid-1980s tennis codes and conventions were increasingly being challenged, for example, in the 1985 Master's tournament McEnroe appeared on court wearing black shorts and a navy blue shirt rather than the conventional whites, and the game was becoming more popular, moving beyond the elite circles of exclusive clubs and attracting a wider public. As its popularity grew so did the sales figures for tennis goods.

Nike's signature sporting figures, the likes of Ilie Nastase, John McEnroe and Andre Agassi in tennis, Eric Cantona and Ian Wright in soccer, the NFL player Lester Hayes who 'reached inside opponent's helmets and slapped them in the face', and NBA star Charles Barkley who also conformed to the 'bad-boy-with-attitude Nike tradition' were 'combustible players' and *Nike*'s executives loved them (Katz 1994: 37). The key qualities *Nike* executives looked for were attitude and a fiercely competitive drive to win and McEnroe was a perfect early embodiment of such qualities. His volatile reputation and use of expletives allowed the company to develop a series of compelling advertisements that played on the public's knowledge of the extent to which his greatness as a tennis player was coupled with an anti-establishment and rebellious streak. In 1981 tennis shoes were being marketed through advertising campaigns that informed the prospective customer that 'McEnroe Swears by Them' and in another version 'Nike' was represented as 'McEnroe's Favorite Four-Letter Word' (Strasser and Becklund 1993: 353).

Although *Nike* is known as a sport goods company the manufacturing of its products is located off-shore in low-overhead/low-wage, under-regulated, export processing zones (EPZs) in countries such as Indonesia, the Philippines and China (Klein 2001). The company has been described as a 'model of the global, postindustrial enterprise' and, following the abandonment of the manufacturing sector, as exemplifying the hollowing out of American industry (Katz 1994: ix, 10). The goods bearing the *Nike* logo are made by overseas contractors. It is a complex of meanings and associations, the implication of a certain way of being, an attitude or image, perhaps the insinuation of a particular style of life, that *Nike* has invested its resources into creating.

Nike and many other well-known companies 'no longer produce products and advertise them, but rather buy products and "brand" them, [and] these companies are forever on the prowl for creative new ways to build and strengthen their brand images' (Klein 2001: 5). To that end the company has employed a carefully selected number of sporting figures to promote its brand and through a combination of sporting prowess, media exposure and high visibility marketing campaigns the individuals involved have been elevated to a status that is on a par with show business celebrities, Hollywood film legends and rock-and-roll superstars.

Jordan, team Nike *and the battle of the brands*

There can be few people around the world who would not now readily recognise the 'swoosh' logo employed by *Nike* or who would not have heard of and be able to recognise Michael Jordan the basketball phenomenon. The global prominence of the *Nike* brand and the cultural iconic status accorded to Jordan are closely connected. If global branded celebrity status is personified by Michael Jordan it has not been achieved through extraordinary basketball ability and determination alone, but in substantial part is a result of the way in which television and sponsorship have transformed professional sport. Jordan's status and meaning derived not simply from his on-court performances for the Chicago Bulls, from his game plays and their television screening (slow-motion replay, repetition and freeze-framing), but also from the off-court commercial endorsement and advertising roles he played for *Nike* on television. There was a synergy between the ability, skill, bravery and competitive drive and will to win displayed on the basketball court by Jordan and the myth-making television advertising campaigns created by *Nike*. In short, Jordan not only played for the Chicago Bulls but also, and in an important sense simultaneously, for team *Nike* and both organisations were beneficiaries of the circuits of cross-promotion that were created (Klein 2001).

The significance of being a member of team *Nike* is perhaps most vividly illustrated by events that took place during the 1992 summer Olympic Games held in Barcelona. The Federation Internationale de Basketball Amateur (FIBA), the sport's world governing body, had made it possible for professional players to participate in the Barcelona games and believed that the presence of the American superstars would help further the international diffusion of the game. The USA basketball team that entered the games was known as the 'Dream Team', it was a team composed of the best players in the world. Half of the players in the team were contracted to *Nike* for endorsement purposes. Along with Jordan there was Charles Barkley, David Robinson, John Stockton, Scottie Pippin and Chris Mullin.

The United States Olympic Committee (USOC) had received sponsorship funding of $4 million from *Reebok*, a close competitor of *Nike* in the sport footwear and clothing business. The deal was that American medal-winning competitors would wear jackets bearing the *Reebok* emblem when participating in award ceremonies, such high profile events would provide the company with valuable and prestigious global television exposure. *Nike* and *Reebok* had been in intense competition for over a decade, they were arch rivals in the 'sneaker wars', and the brand loyalty of the *Nike* endorsing players in the team was exemplified by Jordan who is reputed to have stated bluntly that 'We won't wear Reebok' (Katz 1994: 16) and 'I don't believe in endorsing my competition' (LaFeber 2002: 100). Another player, Charles Barkley, argued that he had 'two million reasons not to wear Reebok' (Halberstam 2001: 298).

The president of the USA Basketball organisation who had drafted players for the team was left in no doubt about Jordan's feelings on the matter – 'All of us in this team are hired guns, so let's not pretend we're anything else. All of us have endorsement deals with different companies ... I'm not stepping up on any platform in Reebok' (Katz 1994: 20). For Jordan the matter was one of 'ethics and pride' and given what has been described as his 'atavistic incapacity to back away from anything that looked remotely like a competitive challenge' (Katz 1994: 21) the prospect of a resolution to the stand-off appeared to be, at best, slim. If the *Nike* 'Dream Team' members refused to wear the *Reebok* jackets on the presentation rostrum they were advised that they would not be allowed to formally receive their medals.

A few days before the basketball finals, which it was anticipated would be watched by 600 million television viewers across 193 countries, the

American team members were informed through a joint press release from the IOC and USA Basketball that all members of the US team must wear the *Reebok*-made track suits but 'some players may choose to wear the awards suit in a manner that does not reveal any commercial identification' (Katz 1994: 30). Taking advantage of this get-out clause the *Nike* contracted players decided to roll the collars of their jackets back so that the *Reebok* emblem could not be seen. Jordan and Barkley went further and draped themselves in the American flag, a gesture which served to obscure even a small *Reebok* emblem on their track pants (LaFeber 2002). A patriotic symbol was employed to affirm corporate loyalty and the publicity the stand-off received reduced an Olympic event to a contest between two sneaker companies, *Nike* v *Reebok* (LaFeber 2002).

In the aftermath of the 1992 Olympics Charles Barkley confirmed that commercial loyalty occupied a prominent place in the contemporary athlete's list of priorities – 'you play a sport very well and that takes you to a certain level by itself. But Nike can take you way beyond that. Nike has helped me make a whole lot of money, and I'm not about to forget it' (Katz 1994: 17). Just in case anyone failed to get the point Michael Jordan emphasised how strongly he felt about 'loyalty to my own company' and explained that he was simply standing up for what he believed in (LaFeber 2002: 100–101).

Swoosh – high visibility exemplified

Nike is representative of a new stage of capitalism. With the development of a global cultural economy, economic growth is bound up with the generation of sign value, with enhancement of the symbolic capital value of commodities through advertising, and in the case of *Nike*, sport marketing and branding in particular (Goldman and Papson 1998). *Nike* has acquired the status of a 'superbrand' and has been so successful in closely associating itself with the world of sport, presenting itself as virtually synonymous with sport culture, that the distinction between sponsor and sponsored appears at times to have dissolved completely (Goldman and Papson 1998; Klein 2001).

The aim of *Nike*'s commercial campaigns has been to weave the 'swoosh' logo and an associated constellation of meanings into 'the cultural fabric of sports' (Goldman and Papson 1998: 169) and in so far as this has been achieved the *Nike* brand has been a beneficiary of sport's authenticity and unique cultural significance. The diverse games and events that are part of the institution of modern sport cut across social divisions and cultural differences and have a significant influence on the lives of the majority of people around the world. The institution of modern sport is global in scale and scope and it represents a powerful and persuasive medium through which to promote and market images and cultivate a 'global desire for things' (Katz 1994: 199). In turn, the way in which *Nike* has created a series of mythic narratives featuring prominent sporting figures in television advertising campaigns to enhance its brand sign value has elevated those individuals who have featured and the sports they represent on to another plane.

Airing Jordan

Leading sports figures already have a high degree of visibility by virtue of their sporting prowess and the media coverage sport attracts. What promotional narratives like those introduced by *Nike* have managed to achieve is to elevate particular individuals to a celebrity status that is not directly associated either 'with their teams or even, at times, with their sport' (Klein 2001: 51). The early *Nike* commercials featuring Jordan were relatively conventional, concentrating on his athletic ability and basketball playing skills. It was the 'Jordan Flight' television commercial to promote the 'Air Jordan' line of shoes in which Jordan is shown leaping to the basket to the sound of roaring jet engines that constituted the beginning of his cultural ascent to iconic status. It was not necessary for the commercial to say anything about the shoes, the first in a long line that would become the all-time best selling sneakers, simply showing Jordan taking off was sufficient (LaFeber 2002).

Subsequent commercials sought to broaden Jordan's appeal by focusing on other qualities – his likeability, charm, coolness and elegance. In the commercials directed by and starring Spike Lee *Nike* sought to promote Jordan as more than an exceptional athlete by cultivating a storyline in which he was the central character. Spike Lee had already inadvertently prefigured the idea in his feature film *She's Gotta Have It* in which he played the character Mars Blackmon whose idolisation of Michael Jordan is represented by a Jordan poster on the wall of his apartment and by his unwillingness to be parted from his Air Jordan shoes, even when he is in bed with the seductive Nola Darling, whose favours he has been ardently pursuing in competition with two other young black men (Halberstam 2001).

Lee's Jordan commercials feature the character Mars Blackmon representing 'the Fan'. In one of the earlier commercials Mars is shown in the foreground with Michael Jordan standing in the background with his arm around Nola Darling the woman Mars desires. Mars facing the camera asks bemusedly what she sees in him and then poses a series of questions trying to find out whether it's the shoes, his height or his athletic prowess, to each question Nola replies 'No'. In the end Mars excitedly concludes that 'It's gotta be the shoes!' Such commercials served not only to promote the performance enhancing potential represented by *Nike* shoes but also portrayed the company as playfully aware of the tendentious character of the connections that are made in advertisements between commodities and people's identities. And in so far as this reflexive awareness was recognised and appreciated by viewers *Nike* came across as an unconventional corporation.

For a culturally influential and commercially significant target group – 'young, media literate consumers' – such commercials served to raise the company's 'authenticity quotient'. In a broadly comparable manner the later commercials that featured Jordan reflecting on his failure to hit winning shots, or that presented him ruminating on the motivational importance of criticism, served to balance his 'celebrity with humanity' and to signify a self-effacing and authentic personality (Goldman and Papson 1998: 48–49). Showing Jordan talking about missed shots, lost games, the criticisms he has faced and the doubts he has encountered signifies openness and honesty, the integrity of the man behind the celebrity, and simultaneously accords authenticity to Jordan and the economic and cultural forms of life with which his sign is closely articulated.

Jordan, basketball and the new cultural economy of sport

The big commercial sport goods endorsement contracts in the late 1970s and early 1980s had tended to favour tennis players, in particular prominent American players like Arthur Ashe, Jimmy Connors and John McEnroe. In the mid-1980s David Falk a junior partner at the Dell sports agency began to represent a basketball rookie from North Carolina who had been drafted by the Chicago Bulls, a long losing team, one that ranked behind their ice hockey (Chicago Black Hawks) and NFL (Chicago Bears) peers in popularity within their home city. Falk's aim was to secure for his client Michael Jordan a commercial status comparable to that of a tennis player (Strasser and Becklund 1993).

In the late 1970s and early 1980s basketball had a poor reputation with mainstream corporate America. The game's marketability was restricted by virtue of the fact that '[m]any white fans … found it difficult to identify with a sport in which the players were more than 75 per cent black', its players were thought to be overpaid and it was believed that many were taking drugs (Rader 1984: 148; LaFeber 2002). Prior to becoming commissioner David Stern worked hard to transform the image and viability of the game. Recognising the value to the NFL of close corporate connections Stern sought to reposition basketball and to acquire endorsements from major American corporations. To that end Stern secured the agreement of the Players Association to introduce team salary capping (set at 53 per cent of gross receipts) and a drug-testing regime, measures that signified basketball was serious about improving its reputation and changing its public image. Stern was duly appointed to the position of commissioner of the NBA in 1984, the same season Michael Jordan turned pro.

In 1984 when he was drafted to the Chicago Bulls Jordan was already something of a national figure and had been described as 'the finest all-around amateur player in the world' (LaFeber 2002: 32). The technological developments that had led to satellite television broadcasting of sport by ESPN from 1979 had by the mid-1980s raised the profile of sport in general and basketball in particular. In the year that Jordan left university to join the Chicago Bulls ESPN was already reaching 34 million households in America, providing sport fans with a regular diet of sport programmes

(Halberstam 2001). ESPN, purchased by the ABC network in 1984, had been covering college basketball since 1979 and in 1982 it secured a two year agreement to show NBA games. ESPN's satellite television network played a key role in raising the profile of basketball, especially through its coverage of the college game which served to introduce new basketball faces, including many like Jordan who would subsequently graduate to the NBA, to those fans watching at home.

In the mid-1980s *Converse* and *adidas* were the big sport footwear companies and by comparison *Nike* was a small company, a relatively minor player in the sport goods business (LaFeber 2002). Professional basketball players wore *Converse* shoes and unsurprisingly it was *Converse* sneakers that boys aspired to own, although the market for basketball shoes was relatively modest as baseball remained 'America's most deeply rooted sport and football [NFL] its most exciting one' (Halberstam 2001: 141). It was in this context that Falk sought to secure a contract for Jordan by adopting an aggressive 'convince us we should sign with you' approach. From their very first meeting Falk had felt that Jordan was special, that he might be able,

> to transcend the narrow boundaries of his sport, that he had a charismatic quality that ordinary people would understand and respond to, qualities that placed him in a special elite of athletes like Pele [soccer], Muhammed Ali [boxing], and Arthur Ashe [tennis], whose fame and celebrity were greater outside the United States than within it. (Halberstam 2001: 140)

However, *Converse* the market leaders, with such established professional basketball players as Magic Johnson, Larry Bird and Isiah Thomas already endorsing their products, were unmoved, indeed they found Falk's pitch for a contract for Jordan arrogant and audacious (Halberstam 2001). *Converse*'s best offer was that Jordan would become one more athlete in their stable and would be paid what others were receiving (Strasser and Becklund 1993).

Nike's basketball policy had been to offer small endorsement contracts in the region of $8,000 to a number of good players, but in the mid-1980s the policy was changed in order to try increase commercial benefits. It was decided to put all the resources into one player who would become 'Nike's signature athlete', but as all the great players were already under contract elsewhere it had to be a rookie. After some prevarication *Nike* chose Jordan who was guaranteed around $1 million a year for an initial period of five years. As his agent is reported to have commented 'the realm of commercial endorsements for basketball players [before Jordan] was like the world before Columbus, when many people still presumed the earth was flat' (Halberstam 2001: 141).

Without doubt Michael Jordan possessed exceptional talent as a basketball player but other factors were in play in his elevation to the status of global cultural icon. In addition to those identified above these included the relative simplicity of basketball and its potential accessibility to a global audience, the suitability of the game for promoting individual players as stars, the global broadcasting capacity of America, the impact technological developments in television coverage had on the sport, the communicational benefits of an internationally accepted language and the presence of a well-developed popular culture that had long proven attractive to the world's youth.

Jordan's performances during his first season led to him being compared to other longer-established star players like Julius Erving, Magic Johnson, and Larry Bird. With a more attractive image, a group of star players possessing on court prowess, personality and charisma and ESPN offering increased television exposure the NBA began to acquire the status of a 'hot sport', one whose rising popularity with the young was especially appealing to corporate America which identified basketball as providing greater potential access to the 'world youth market' than either baseball or NFL (Halberstam 2001).

With the entry of Jordan into the professional game and *Nike*'s very substantial investment in him as their signature commercial athlete the focus on individual star players increased significantly. But it was not only sport goods companies such as *Nike* that sought to protect their investment by raising the profile of their stars, the league itself actively sought to promote individual players and to encourage an emphasis on personalities to broaden the professional game's popular cultural appeal and increase its commercial value. And as its cultural and commercial appeal grew so the league extended its vision beyond the world of sport and began to compare itself with the wider entertainment industry.

A sense of the league's more ambitious view of its potential prospects is evident from the comparison drawn by Stern between the NBA and Disney:

> They have theme parks, and we have theme parks. Only we call them arenas. They have characters: Mickey and Goofy. Our characters are named Magic and Michael. Disney sells apparel: we sell apparel. They make home videos; we make home videos. (cited in LaFeber 2002: 64)

The potential synergy between the NBA and the world of popular entertainment was effectively demonstrated in the summer of 1995 when Michael Jordan co-starred with Bill Murray, Bugs Bunny and other cartoon characters in the commercially successful Warner Brothers film *Space Jam*, along with a number of other pro basketball players, including Larry Bird, Charles Barkley and Patrick Ewing. This event represented the culmination of a process of transformation that from the mid-1980s had turned basketball games into spectacles with 'laser shows, dramatic player introductions, energizing music, half-time contests and sideshows', transformations that signified an equation of Disney productions with 'wholesome entertainment' and demonstrated the extent to which the NBA had indeed become 'Disneyfied' (McDonald 1996: 349).

Jordan's image took on a life of its own as the combination of exceptional basketball ability, illuminated and elaborated by television coverage, with its array of camera angles, slow motion and replay facilities and associated forms of analysis, and commercials that emphasised his 'transcendent skill and iron determination' elevated him to a unique cultural position (Goldman and Papson 1998: 49). Numerous figures from the worlds of sport, film, television and popular music have been accorded celebrity status by virtue of qualities and performances attributed to them. However, in contrast to the frequently artificial or synthetic character of qualities and performances attributed to celebrities from the world of entertainment the actions and achievements of figures from the world of sport retain a significant measure of authenticity.

The athletic prowess of leading sporting figures like Jordan was demonstrated on court, on the field of play, again and again, in big games against gifted teams and players who tried their hardest to disrupt moves and prevent their opponents from succeeding. Television coverage of the exceptional quality of Jordan's performances in game after game, alongside the series of imaginative, popular and commercially successful advertisements in which he featured, had the effect of creating a cultural icon 'who had the power and force and charisma of a major movie star' (Halberstam 2001: 184). However, there is an important difference between sporting figures like Jordan and figures from the world of entertainment. Jordan's poorest moments on court, his errors and failures, or those of any other sporting figures for that matter, were there for all to see in the stadium or on television. In contrast the mistakes of figures from the world of entertainment – film, television and music – are generally concealed, consigned to the cutting room floor, left behind in rehearsals or in the editing booth, or digitally erased so that no trace of error remains. The contributions of sporting figures like Jordan – the accurate pass, effectively completed move, winning game and successful season – have an authenticity that makes them unique and sets them apart from the wider world of entertainment. But while such factors may begin to account for Jordan's high profile they do not exhaust the question of his cultural and economic significance.

Jordan: athlete and commodity sign

As a basketball player Jordan's achievements are remarkable. The season before he joined the Chicago Bulls they had lost twice as many games as they had won. In Jordan's first season he was rookie of the year and the Bulls won ten more games than in the previous year. In the following season, 1985–6, Jordan set a play-off record point score of 63 against Boston Celtics, the eventual NBA championship winners. The 1987–8 season saw further improvements as the Bulls won 50 of their 82 games and Jordan won both Most Valuable Player and Defensive Player of the Year, becoming the first NBA player to hold both awards simultaneously. Match attendances also grew as the team improved but there was relatively little progress on the play-off front until a new coach, Phil Jackson was appointed in 1989. In Jackson's second season as coach, 1990–1, the Bulls, with Jordan outstanding, reached the NBA Finals where they defeated the Los Angeles Lakers led by another superstar Earvin 'Magic' Johnson. With Jordan's growing dominance on court the Bulls achieved further NBA Championships in the following two seasons (1991–2 and 1992–3). Then a few months after his father's death in 1993 Jordan, 30 years of age, declaring that he had 'nothing more to prove in basketball', announced his retirement from the game (LaFeber 2002: 121).

Jordan had fulfilled the hopes of *Nike* CEO Phil Knight by capturing the imagination of the sporting public with his superior athletic ability and, by becoming so closely associated with the company and all it stood for, the cultural and commercial figure of Jordan came to signify that great athletic performances were articulated with great products. Jordan's fans became customers and *Nike*'s customers joined his legion of fans. When asked by the NBA commissioner for his initial thoughts on Jordan's retirement Knight replied that he was 'concerned about the impact on the company' (Katz 1994: 311). In due course however Jordan's retirement from basketball was transformed from a potential disaster to a commercial opportunity.

Nike has prided itself on its celebration of the potentiality present in sport for a 'pure form of sociality', that is, on the way in which sporting ability expressed in games may be able to transcend differences of 'class, race, gender and age' (Goldman and Papson 1998: 62). Notwithstanding the fact that it contributed powerfully to processes that were continuing to transform sport and sporting figures into media spectacles and commodities, *Nike* sought to promote the idea of sport as possessing sacred or spiritual qualities that simultaneously allowed individuals to express their 'true' selves and affirm membership of a community. The associated tensions are contained within the figure of the celebrity athlete who simultaneously exemplifies the transcendental spiritual qualities of sporting performance and the material values and interests of the world of commerce as they are conveyed in media representations configured by cultural intermediaries acting on behalf of multinational corporations. In so far as the economic rewards received by sportsmen and sportswomen from the games in which they are involved and the endorsement contracts they have secured have increased dramatically over the past ten years or so there has been growing concern that material interest rather than an inherent love of the game has become the 'prime motivation' (Goldman and Papson 1998: 63).

Wanting to gain as much value as it could from the Jordan 'brand' *Nike* proceeded to present Jordan's retirement as a purification rite, to portray the star as wanting to escape the media hype and commercial pressure of the professional game and recapture the essential essence of basketball by returning to playing. Campaigns sought to promote both Jordan and *Nike* as, in the final instance, motivated by an intrinsic love of the game, rather than commerce. The implication of *Nike*'s post-retirement ads was that Jordan simply wanted to play the game and that notwithstanding 'the commercialization and spectacularization of sport … Jordan and his fellow players remain[ed] pure at heart in their love of the game' (Goldman and Papson 1998: 64). Such campaigns conveyed the impression that the shared culture of the game remained unchanged, that the essential aspects of sport and the motivation of sporting figures remained uncontaminated by processes of commercialisation unleashed by corporations such as *Nike* and exemplified by the metamorphosis of Jordan into a brand.

The reality was very different as the various biographies and critical analyses of Jordan's high profile sport career revealed. Rather than a purification rite Jordan described his retirement from the game in 1993 as brought about not only by his feeling that in respect of basketball there was nothing left to prove, but also that media and commercial pressures had made it difficult for him to achieve even a small measure of privacy. Being constantly exposed to scrutiny on and off the court drove Jordan to 'near-despair' (Greene 1996). But being a competitive sportsman Jordan could not resist playing for long and within a few months of retiring he was playing minor league baseball for the Chicago White Sox. His unremarkable performances on the baseball diamond proved that he was indeed mortal and 17 months after leaving basketball Jordan announced that he was returning to the Bulls.

His first game back after retirement attracted the biggest television audience ever for a regular season NBA game and it quickly became apparent that notwithstanding the unsuccessful baseball episode Jordan remained a highly popular figure and

> an immensely profitable commodity in a society that, especially with the end of the Cold War, seemed to value profit, celebrity and marketability above all else. He and Nike thus became post-Cold War symbols – indeed phenomena – of American culture, American globalization, American marketing, American wealth, American headquartered media, [and] American based transnationals. (LaFeber 2002: 128)

However, by the mid-1990s Jordan was being subjected to increasing criticism as analysts began to express concern about the growing commodification and spectacularisation of sport and to reflect on his wider social and cultural significance. As the 'greatest endorser of the twentieth century' (LaFeber 2002) became a focus of critical inquiry, so too did *Nike* and the consequences of American economic and cultural imperialism to which the company contributed.

The Jordan phenomenon

The social and cultural phenomenon 'Michael Jordan' was the focus of considerable analytic attention in the course of the late 1990s. Analysts sought to reflect on Jordan's place within sport, to determine his local and global significance, to deconstruct associated media representations and reflect on his 'blackness' (Andrews 1996a, 1996b, 1998; Andrews et al. 1996; Armstrong 1996; Kellner 1996; McDonald 1996). Although he was elevated to the status of national icon for the way in which he came to be regarded as embodying American values and ideals, with the growth of satellite television and developments in information technology Jordan became a globally popular figure, the 'first great athlete of the wired world' (Halberstam 1991: 76).

Media descriptions of Jordan as 'bigger than basketball', as a 'pop icon', or as a 'hero of the wired world' (Andrews 1996b: 315; Halberstam 1991) serve to distract attention from the wider economic and cultural processes that contributed to the formation of the Jordan phenomenon. A number of analysts have noted that the Jordan phenomenon emerged in a particular historical conjuncture, one powerfully influenced by neo-liberal economic thought and the resurgence of conservative or 'New Right' forms of political philosophy and popular culture (Andrews 1998; LaFeber 2002). The neo-liberal agenda placed emphasis on individual achievement and promoted the personal qualities of the individual as the most important determinants of success. In effect Jordan's rise to sport stardom and wealth was represented as confirmation that American society remained open to talent whatever one's social origin, in short that 'the American dream was alive and dunking' (Andrews 1998: 201).

The profile of basketball, Jordan the player, his team and the league, each benefited from the economic and cultural phenomenon constituted by *Nike* and represented by the commodity-sign 'Jordan'. As well as *Nike* numerous other corporations which associated their commodities with the sign 'Jordan' derived significant interest from his cultural capital. *Nike*'s expensive advertising campaigns and those created by *McDonald's* and *Coca-Cola* quickly turned Jordan into a household name, into a familiar commodity-sign, from which other companies employing him could benefit through 'rub-off' or 'transference' of the positive associations already in play within the wider cultural economy (Patton 1986). And in so far as Jordan has tended to be associated with popular American products the 'All-American aura' that was attributed to him from his first days at the University of North Carolina has grown in intensity (Patton 1986: 52). Jordan has had links with a wide range of American commercial concerns as the following far from comprehensive list compiled in the early 1990s indicates:

> CBS-Fox video, Chevrolet, Coca-Cola [and subsequently Gatorade], Electronic Arts computer games ... Hanes underwear ... Wrigley ... Illinois State Lottery, McDonald's ... Wheaties, and Wilson Sporting Goods. (Andrews 1998: 203)

The advertising narratives constructed around the figure of Jordan exemplify two central aspects of American life, namely the virtues of competitive individualism and 'a devoted allegiance to the family as a metaphor alluding to the simulated harmony of American society as a whole' (Andrews 1998: 205). In other words Jordan not only endorsed a wide range of products and services, simultaneously he endorsed 'the American way' both within the USA and, with increasing satellite television transmission of NBA games and associated commercials, around the world.

Jordan's popularity seemed to know no bounds. In 1995 the *Chicago Tribune* described him as 'the most recognised American figure on the planet' (cited in Armstrong 1996: 326). Shortly before his return to basketball from his first retirement in 1995 a mass circulation paper in China, the *China Sports Daily*, described Jordan in a front page feature as 'still the most popular sports star on earth' (Armstrong 1996: 326). In the late 1990s a survey conducted in China had Jordan placed narrowly second to Thomas Edison in a list of the best-known Americans. In Germany, South Africa and Japan Jordan's iconic status raised interest in NBA basketball, helped to move significant quantities of merchandise and increased the number of people playing the game. Even in France where criticism of and resistance to forms of economic and cultural 'Americanisation' had been longstanding Jordan attracted public acclaim and enormous media interest. As one observer remarked on the conclusion of his team's trip to Paris,

> It was fitting that Jordan climaxed the visit by posing under the Eiffel Tower wearing Nikes and promoting McDonald's. Beneath an industrial wonder of the nineteenth century posed three wonders of the post-industrial era. (LaFeber 2002: 137–138)

The figure of Jordan clad in *Nike* apparel and promoting American products and values exemplifies the transformed global economic and cultural significance of sport following the emergence of satellite and cable television and the recognition of a potential global market for sport programming. The global popularity of sport delivers huge television audiences for advertisers and in turn helps promote the sale of both sport-related and other merchandise marketed through coverage of sport events and the endorsement appeal of high-profile sporting figures.

As Jordan's career progressed throughout the late 1980s and 1990s sport products and sporting figures assumed an increasing economic and cultural significance. As the 1990s were drawing to a close it was estimated that Jordan alone had had a $10 billion impact on the American economy. Jordan was not simply a basketball player, nor even just a basketball star he had become a commodity-sign, a brand, and a consumer-cultural icon.

23 and 45 (and 7): commodified signs of the times

Jordan began his career with the Chicago Bulls wearing uniform number '23' which as his reputation soared adorned numerous replica shirts sold to fans in America and around the world. One estimate is that Jordan was responsible for $3.1 billion of 'increased sales of NBA-licensed clothing (especially jerseys with No. 23 on them) (LaFeber 2002: 137). Jordan and his 'No. 23' has been the focus of a great deal of speculation, mythmaking and analysis. The Reverend Jesse Jackson, demonstrating the mystical and quasi-religious qualities that have been attributed to the player, is reported to have described Michael Jordan as taking 'light into dark places' and as having suggested that black and white children 'find in No. 23 success and achievement' (Armstrong 1996: 328). Numerous other quasi-religious metaphors have been employed to describe Jordan's performances and the reception he has received from his legion of fans. Larry Bird of the Boston

Celtics remarked after a play-off record score of 63 points at the end of the 1985–6 season that 'I think he's God disguised as Michael Jordan' (cited in LaFeber 2002: 51).

Regarded by some of his peers as 'Black Jesus', Jordan was reported in the *Chicago Tribune* in 1995 as having visited a fan confined to a wheelchair who then began to walk again. There are other stories of people kneeling and praying in front of a bronze statue of Jordan and of a fan getting on court before a game and kissing Jordan's feet (Armstrong 2001: 17). Somewhat predictably Jordan's return to basketball after retirement led reporters to write of 'the second coming'. Clearly caution needs to be exercised in interpreting such reports for it cannot be assumed that sport journalists or sport fans are lacking in irony or a sense of humour. What such reports signify is the respect in which journalists and fans were moved by Jordan's exceptional talents to attribute to him a supernatural aura and to accord him a mythic status.

On returning to the Chicago Bulls in 1995 Jordan chose another number, his trademark '23' having been 'retired' when he left. The switch to '45', the number he had worn in his brief baseball career, offered further commercial benefits as fans once again sought to 'be like Mike' by wearing jerseys bearing his new number. The choice of a new uniform number was described as 'the greatest marketing ploy in the history of sport' (quoted in Armstrong 1996: 341). Jordan's explanation for the switch from '23' was that it was 'the number my father last saw me in' before he was murdered (quoted in Armstrong 1996: 329). Whatever the reason for the switch, the number 45 jersey quickly became the fastest selling sport garment and demand was described as 'unbelievable' (Armstrong 1996: 339).

The unnecessary change of number attracted criticism and complaints, notably that 'the 45 seemed like a contrivance baldly intended to move a product in a way that 23 never had' (Greene 1996: 247). To make matters worse, and seemingly oblivious to the fans who had invested in 45, after a below par performance in the play-off series against the Orlando Magic which led to the Bulls losing game one, Jordan, who scored a mere 19 points, turned out in game two wearing his old number 23. One of his opponents remarked after game one that 'Number 45 doesn't explode like number 23 … he revs up but he doesn't really take off' (Greene 1996: 258), but in game two wearing 23 Jordan scored 38 points and the Bulls won. As one reporter wryly commented of the Jordan 'brand', 'just like the change in Coca-Cola, "New Mike" just didn't have quite the same flair as "Mike Classic"' (quoted in Armstrong 1996: 340). Any fears that the number change might present a public relations or marketing problem soon disappeared as sales of number 23 took off again (LaFeber 2002).

Less than a decade later there would be another comparable shirt number story involving an even more popular global sport and another sport star who had acquired the status of a global cultural icon. In 2003 David Beckham left Manchester United, for whom his number 7 shirt had been a very lucrative merchandising item with more than 1.7 million being sold each year, to join Real Madrid whose number 7 was worn by local hero and club captain Raul. On joining Real Madrid Beckham chose number 23 and was reported to be 'ecstatic to be able to choose his new shirt number because it is the same as that of his ultimate sporting hero, basketball legend Michael Jordan' (Bolton 2003). Subsequently Beckham's number 23 replica shirt has proven to be a lucrative merchandising item for his new club Real Madrid, for whom merchandising sales provide 40 per cent of their revenue, as well as for the manufacturer *adidas*, with whom Beckham has had a longstanding football boot endorsement contract (Carlin 2003).

In 2003 Beckham was described as 'the most famous athlete in the world', although in commercial terms he ranked behind the American 'sporting megastars' Michael Jordan and Tiger Woods (Syed 2003). Undoubtedly the way in which Beckham's career has developed does bear comparison with the sporting and commercial career trajectories of both Jordan and Woods, although there are also notable differences, not least of all the ways in which questions of race and ethnicity have surfaced in analytic reflections and media and advertising narratives on the American stars.

On the (in)significance of Jordan's 'blackness'

At times it has seemed as though Jordan has wished to avoid the issue of race, if not to erase it. For example he is quoted as having remarked that his aspiration was 'to be seen as "neither black nor white"' (Patton 1986: 52). Certainly in respect of his popularity and the success of his commercial endorsements it has been suggested that he may be regarded as a 'crossover hero' (Halberstam 1991), or as an athlete possessing attributes and qualities that allowed him to be perceived as 'beyond race' (Patton 1986). Without doubt his fame extends beyond the African-American community from which he emerged and he has received 'more commercial endorsement deals from the predominantly white, middle-class purveyors of public taste than ... white athletes' (Halberstam 1991: 76). To some extent observations such as these reflect a 'color-blind credo', exemplified by the owner of the Bulls, Jerry Reinsdorf, who is reputed to have remarked that 'Michael has no color', a view that appears to have been shared by Jordan's agent David Falk who commented of Jordan that 'he transcends race' (quoted in Andrews 1996: 125, 139).

Four distinct aspects or moments of Jordan's racial signification have been identified (Andrews 1996a). First, there is a notion of the 'natural athleticism' of Jordan the African-American athlete – muscular physique, strength, gracefulness and endurance – which in respect of basketball performance informs accounts of why 'white men can't jump' yet black men like Jordan can fly. Second, there is the carefully culturally constructed media representation of Jordan as an 'All-American', which in the context of late 1980s America led to Jordan being represented as a 'Reaganite racial replicant: a black version of a white cultural model who ... would ensure the submergence and subversion of racial Otherness' and thereby 'appeal to the racially sensitive sensibilities of the American mass market' (Andrews 1996a: 137). Portrayed as exemplifying the valued qualities of personal motivation and integrity, responsibility and sporting and commercial success, Jordan seemed to signify that black Americans could realise the dream, could cross the racial divide and achieve upward social and economic mobility. Accorded a status no black man had ever acquired before when he was recognised as 'America's favourite athlete' (Andrews 1996a: 139), Jordan's social elevation has cleared the way for others to acquire a comparable standing. Perhaps the clearest example is provided by Tiger Woods, whose popularity transcends the world of golf, and whose status is that of 'America's son', a perfect embodiment of America's multiculturalism (Cole and Andrews 2000).

However, the notion of racial transcendence with which the figure of Jordan has been associated has been described as a fatally flawed notion, a consequence of 'the reactionary, color-blind cultural politics that nurtured it' (Andrews 1996a: 140). In contrast to the ways in which most other black sporting figures have been portrayed, Jordan's blackness has been deliberately underplayed in promotions that have sought to emphasise his All-American virtues and his status as a role model. Generally Jordan has been represented as a 'paragon of American virtue' in contrast to other black sporting figures whose media and promotional caricatures have tended to reinforce 'stereotypically violent and threatening images of young black males' (Andrews 1996a: 141). For example, Charles Barkley of the Phoenix Suns and one of Jordan's colleagues on the 'Dream Team' was portrayed as 'not like Mike', not a paragon of American virtue, but as an irreverent figure, a 'bad-boy-with-attitude' (Katz 1994). In a provocative *Nike* advertisement Barkley declared,

> I am not a role model
> I am not paid to be a role model
> I am paid to wreak havoc on the basketball court
> Parents should be role models
> Just because I can dunk a basketball
> Doesn't mean I should raise your kids.
> (quoted in Goldman and Papson 1998: 84)

Barkley's image was one of unconstrained force and aggression promoted in various advertising campaigns in which journalists, referees and even Godzilla were his victims. Although such advertisements were amusing they implicitly drew upon and served to reinforce cultural stereotypes of African-American males as threatening.

A third form of racial signification to which the figure of Jordan became subject emerged with media identification of evidence of departures from the All-American 'racially neutered identity' which had been ascribed to him (Andrews 1996a: 142). In the 1991–2 season Jordan began to receive media criticism for appearing to fall short of the standards expected of a 'paragon of American virtue' (Andrews 1996a: 141). Jordan was portrayed as arrogant and selfish, as being obsessive about game statistics and as treating players on his team without the consideration and respect they deserved (Smith 1994). In failing to attend a reception for his team at the White House, appearing to have become excessively competitive in his sport and overly preoccupied with protecting commercial rights to his image, being less than enthusiastic about participating in the 1992 USA Olympic basketball team, and perhaps most significantly of all, being identified as a high-stakes gambler, Jordan's virtual whiter-than-white image became tarnished (Andrews 1996a: 143–4; LaFeber 2002: 96–99, 113–116).

Ultimately it was the identification of Jordan's problems with gambling that led to a media feeding frenzy with reporters drawing attention not only to the sums of money involved but also the lack of judgement he had displayed in his choice of friends (Halberstam 2001). However, the possibility that the censured figure of Jordan would be redrawn as vulnerable, weak and deficient, as after all conforming to the stereotype of the African-American male, receded as stories of Jordan's gambling problems were displaced by reports of the championship series between the Chicago Bulls and the Phoenix Suns which the Bulls won. In helping the Bulls to register their third consecutive championship and, in the course of the series of matches, achieve an average of 41 points per game, an NBA record, Jordan took the heat out of the gambling story (LaFeber 2002). The gambling story did however regain newsworthiness in the summer of 1993 following the murder of his father. Press reports implied that a motive for the murder might be retribution for Jordan's gambling debts. Once again it was being implied that Jordan, who had been trying to get people to view him 'more as a good person than a good Black man' (Denzin 1996: 321), had a darker side and there was a suggestion that his fame and/or gambling may have contributed to his father's murder. News media narratives at the time seemed, in Jordan's own words, to be bringing about his 'metamorphosis from "Michael Jordan the person to Michael Jordan the black guy"' (quoted in Andrews 1996a: 147).

With the arrest of suspects for the crime, one of whom was African-American, media speculation about deviant aspects of Jordan's lifestyle diminished and the wholesome All-American image began to be resurrected. Jordan's announcement of his retirement from basketball in the October of the year in which his father died confirmed his restoration as the national celebrity who exemplified the possibility of realising the American dream. Within a short period, some four months, Jordan announced that he was to try his hand at baseball the game that most white Americans were infatuated with and, notwithstanding the television generated popularity of NFL, would consider constitutes the national game (Rader 1984). In so far as for many (white) Americans baseball exemplified the distinctive qualities of American character – courage, combativeness, discipline, determination, energy, eagerness and enthusiasm – then Jordan's decision to sign for the Chicago White Sox served as confirmation, if any were needed, of his All-American credentials.

While Jordan struggled to get anywhere in the Birmingham Barons AA team (two levels below the major league game) to which he was sent by the White Sox to learn his trade, the very fact that he had chosen baseball drew much needed attention and publicity to the game and it also enhanced his reputation by demonstrating that he was prepared to put his athletic reputation on the line. The baseball 'sabbatical' lasted nearly two years and during that time full advantage was taken of the new commercial opportunities that presented themselves. Both *Nike* and *Gatorade* ran advertising campaigns that made a commercial virtue of Jordan's baseball fallibility. Furthermore, Jordan continued to hold lucrative endorsement contracts for *McDonald's*, *Wheaties*, *Chevrolet* and *Hanes*. The corporate world knew that 'even without basketball, Jordan stood alone as a salesman' and a year after retirement from basketball his place as the highest earning athlete was confirmed once more (LaFeber 2002: 123).

While Jordan was away from basketball its image had deteriorated. As a new populist Republicanism set the political agenda of the country, so 'a racist, reactionary traditionalism' led to a younger generation of basketball stars being subjected to criticism 'for being self-centred, spoilt, brash, arrogant, and irresponsible' (Andrews 1996a: 150). Reporters drew parallels between the unacceptable conduct of many young urban African-American males and the ill-disciplined, unruly and disrespectful behaviour of NBA players. Playing standards were considered to be on the slide and the very soul of the game was considered to be threatened by the behaviour of the younger players. It was in this troubled context that Jordan returned to the game and it is here that a further form of racial signification has been identified (Andrews 1996a).

Jordan's return to the game led to media narratives that once again promoted 'Jordanmania' and emphasised the extent to which his excellence derived from his All-American qualities, notably his competitive individualism, sense of responsibility, rigorous work ethic, loyalty and commitment to his team's cause. Jordan, or 'SuperMichael' as he was described on the cover of *Sports Illustrated* in March 1995, was positively contrasted in the media with 'the NBA's vilified "spoilsports and malcontents"' (Andrews 1996a: 152). After his comeback game against Orlando Jordan described in a press-conference some of the things he wanted to achieve:

> I really felt I wanted to instil some positive things back to the game. You know, there's a lot of negative things that have been happening to the game … the young guys are not taking care of their responsibilities in terms of maintaining that love for the game, you know, and not let it waste to where its so business-oriented that the integrity of the game's going to be at stake. (quoted in Andrews 1996a: 152)

Where an older generation of players, the likes of Jordan, Scottie Pippin, Dennis Rodman and even 'bad boy' Charles Barkley were revered for working at their game, even after obtaining lucrative playing contracts, the new younger generation of NBA stars were considered to be petulant, seemed to take things for granted and generally displayed a carelessness that troubled the league and represented a turn-off for the public. While Jordan, Magic Johnson and Larry Bird had acquired a status comparable to that enjoyed by high profile entertainers and rock stars they remained committed and hard working athletes. In contrast the emerging younger generation 'seemed not to understand the difference between being a rock star and a basketball player and believed they were both' (Halberstam 2001: 385).

It is somewhat ironic that someone who has been called the 'greatest endorser of the twentieth century' and who was described by another basketball legend Julius Erving as 'less a person than "something of a 24-hour commodity"' (LaFeber 2002: 130, 85) should have expressed so much concern about the impact of business on sport. It is indisputable that during his playing career Jordan continually demonstrated his commitment to the game. As a number of observers have reported, playing basketball was Jordan's main source of pleasure, indeed he was one of the very few professionals who insisted that 'a love-of-the-game clause' be included in his contract so that he could 'stop by any playground in America, put on a pair of sneakers, and play in a pickup game' (Halberstam 2001: 167). But notwithstanding his intrinsic commitment to, interest in, and passion for the game, exemplified by his fondness for pickup games, Jordan continually demonstrated a keen appreciation of both his and the game's commercial potential. For example, while cycling with friends in California after his first retirement from the NBA, Jordan came across a pickup game and following street protocol got the right ('getting next') to play the winner of the four-on-four game that was taking place. Word spread and very soon a large crowd, with estimates ranging from 500 to several thousands, was watching Jordan and friends taking on a group of local players (Katz 1994; Greene 1996). Recalling how good it felt Jordan, recognising the marketing potential of the event, told one of his biographers 'I think we're going to re-create it for a commercial' (Greene 1996: 3).

While the Jordan image has conformed in many respects to the tenets of athletic masculinity – strength and power, competitiveness, comradeship and bravery – his off-court image has encompassed other more family-friendly qualities that suggest 'a kinder, gentler masculinity' (McDonald and Andrews 2001: 28). Even where there has been a suggestion of the black body as erotic in advertisements featuring Jordan, as in one of the commercials for *Hanes* underwear – 'Just wait until we get our Hanes on you' – any allusion to sexual performance has been rendered 'safe' by the affirmative presence of family members, notably father James and wife Juanita, signifying stable family relationships and sexual responsibility (McDonald 1996).

The figure of Jordan simultaneously signifies sport as play and as work or business. Jordan is promoted as embodying the possibility of sport retaining its integrity, its play spirit, its meaning and authenticity, notwithstanding commercial pressures that have led to games and sporting figures becoming commodities. Despite all the hype, all the spectacle, Jordan the cultural icon signifies that at the very heart of sport there is something that remains uncontaminated by the intrusion of corporate sponsorship, marketing and a capitalist commercial logic and that is the enthusiasm and 'pure' love of the game displayed by players (Greene 1996; Goldman and Papson 1998). Within a 'dual America' transformed by neo-liberal economic policies, social reorganisation and wide-ranging reductions in welfare provision that have led to a rapid growth in inequality, new forms of poverty and social exclusion (Castells 1998), the Jordan family has come to signify that 'the American Dream is available to those people of color who are apparently committed enough to pull themselves up by their bootstraps' (McDonald 1996: 361). The exhortation to 'be like Mike' is not simply about purchasing the sneakers, the underwear, the drink or the burger, it suggests that there are opportunities to be realised, lifestyle choices to be made and that ultimately individuals are responsible for their own fate. As Andrews observed,

> The harsh realities and entrenched inequities of the American racial formation are conveniently obscured by the Jordan hypermythology, as white America congratulates itself for Jordan's very existence, and simultaneously demonizes the amassing victims of America's racial hegemony for not being like Mike. (1998: 214)

Sport and politics: Muhammad Ali an African-American hero

Some African-American athletes have used a public profile acquired through sport to engage in politics, but Jordan has carefully avoided political involvements. 1960's America provided a number of examples of political responses by high profile African-American sporting figures to the social issues of the time. The track and field competitors Tommie Smith and John Carlos gave black power salutes on the medal rostrum at the 1968 Olympic Games in Mexico City to draw attention to the plight of black Americans. Another, perhaps the most celebrated example of an African-American sporting figure using cultural prominence associated with sporting prowess to make a significant political impact, is provided by Muhammad Ali. Ali has been described as one of three American sporting figures, the other two being Michael Jordan and Tiger Woods, who in an era influenced by television have acquired a popular appeal that extends beyond their individual sporting fields (Rosaforte 2001: 286).

A few days after winning the heavyweight boxing championship in 1964 Cassius Clay joined the Nation of Islam and a week or so later changed his name to Muhammad Ali, declaring that Clay was his 'slave name'. Ali's conversion to Islam came amid rising social conflict in America and growing concern about an ongoing war in Vietnam. Called to an army induction centre in 1967 and facing the prospect of going to serve in the US armed forces in Vietnam, Ali completed a statement outlining his grounds for refusal – 'I refuse to be inducted into the armed forces of the United States … because I claim to be exempt as a minister of the religion of Islam' (Remnick 2000: 291). Ali's stand led to him being sentenced to prison, fined and stripped of his boxing title. He did not fight again for over three years.

While court appeals were being prepared on Ali's behalf he appeared frequently on ABC's *Wide World of Sport* and began to acquire something of the status of a national media celebrity (Rader 1984).

When Ali had taken his original army induction aptitude test in 1964 his score was very low and he was classified as '1-Y' and ineligible for service. On hearing in 1966 that, in the light of escalating requirements for troops in Vietnam, his score had been reclassified as '1-A', signifying eligibility for service, Ali remarked 'I ain't got no quarrel with them Vietcong' (Remnick 2000: 287). As Ali became increasingly politicised from this point on he emphasised his African roots, his blackness and in addition drew attention to the politics that lay beneath the surface of sport. In time the qualities Ali displayed, the combination of phenomenal boxing ability and unrivalled boxing success, a principled political standpoint and a charismatic personality, 'established him as the biggest boxing star ever and perhaps the biggest sport star ever' (Whannel 2002: 121). For the way he fought, both in the ring and beyond it, the designation 'sporting hero' seems entirely appropriate, far more so than for sporting figures for whom fears about commercial costs appear to take precedence over involvement in politics.

In 1990 when the arch-conservative Senator Jesse Helms was standing against a popular African-American, Harvey Gannt, in a race for the Senate in North Carolina, Jordan was asked by a number of influential African-Americans, including former Wimbledon and US Open tennis champion Arthur Ashe, to lend the campaign his support. But Jordan never responded. The explanation given by those close to him for his unwillingness to lend support was that it might alienate a significant number of consumers towards whom his commercial endorsements were directed. The comment attributed to Jordan was that 'Republicans buy sneakers too' (Crowley 1999: 5).

Jordan's unwillingness to get involved in anything that might prejudice his commercial endorsement activities was further confirmed when his company *Nike* came under criticism in 1997 from an international anti-*Nike* movement for its use of export processing zone sweatshops in south-east Asia. Jordan remained 'politically neutered' as Arthur Ashe remarked, declaring that 'his job was to shoot hoop, not play politics' (Klein 2001: 369). Later in the year Jordan appeared to recognise that there might be a case to answer. In an interview given to the *Sporting News* Jordan gave the impression that he might go to Asia to see for himself what conditions were like in the factories, but he never went (Crowley 1999). *Nike* had made Jordan wealthy, by 1998 his earnings from the company over his career were estimated to be around $130 million and, in turn, Jordan had helped to transform *Nike*'s cultural profile and commercial standing (Halberstam 2001). Reflecting on Jordan's apolitical stance one critic commented that,

> He has never used his platform to pursue social or political change; indeed, he's gone out of his way to play it safe. This is, of course, precisely how the corporations he endorses want it. Politics and marketing don't mix: a loose cannon like Muhammad Ali could forget about big endorsement contracts. (Crowley 1999: 5)

Jordan retired once more in January 1999 and received plaudits from the media for being not just 'the most popular athlete' in American sport history and around the world, but also for becoming a celebrity figure, a global cultural icon who had transcended the world of sport. But history was destined to repeat itself and in the shadow of the tragedy that befell New York on September 11 2001 Jordan returned, yet again, to the NBA to play for the Washington Wizards, one of the worst teams in the league.

On leaving the Chicago Bulls Jordan had bought a stake in a company that had a controlling interest in the Wizards franchise and became vice-president of their basketball operations, but the team's poor performances and the attractions of getting on court again led him to announce his return to playing. Jordan played for the Wizards for two seasons and they failed to make the play-offs each time (LaFeber 2002). However, commercially Jordan's return was a great success with sell-out crowds at home and on the road. Club merchandise sales also took off with replicas of the Washington Wizards number 23 becoming popular with basketball fans. And back in action on the television screen Jordan could offer a greater level of exposure for the products and companies he endorsed. Indeed, where in the late 1990s Jordan's impact on the economy had been estimated at $10 billion, by the end of his brief playing career with the Wizards it had been revised upwards to $13 billion (Engel 2003).

Other high profile sporting figures have been beneficiaries of Jordan's colossal impact on the world of sport and one American of colour in particular, Tiger Woods, has followed his example by combining an exceptional level of sporting success with a range of lucrative commercial endorsement contracts.

Tiger Woods

By the time Eldrick 'Tiger' Woods turned professional he was already a golfing phenomenon. At the age of 11 Woods entered 33 junior tournaments and won them all and in 1991 at the age of 15 he became the youngest winner of the US Junior Amateur Championships. Woods made more history by winning the tournament in the following two years and thereby became the first to have won the event three years in succession. Woods, two years younger than the great Bobby Jones had been when he first won the event, then proceeded to win the US Amateur Championship for an unprecedented three years in succession – 1994, 1995 and 1996. In the summer of 1996 Woods turned professional and in 1997 at the age of 21 he became the youngest player to win the Masters. Later in the same year and only 42 weeks after turning professional Woods was accorded number one position in the Official World Golf Ranking (Stodghill and Grover 1997; Owen 2001).

There are a number of respects in which the career profile of Woods resembles that of Jordan. Both quickly acquired a reputation for unrivalled athletic ability in their respective sporting fields and both have been credited with comparable qualities of character – competitive toughness, coolness under pressure, determination and a willingness to give time and energy to practice in order to perfect their playing techniques. Like Jordan's impact on basketball, the entry of Woods into the professional game of golf has been described as unique in its transformative effect (Stodghill and Grover 1997; Owen 2001; Rosaforte 2001). Ticket sales and attendances for golf tournaments rose as did audience ratings for television coverage of golf events, even for those tournaments in which Woods was not participating. As one observer reported, 'Woods took golf and put it on the front page of the *New York Times*' (Rosaforte 2001: 27). The rapid rise in his popularity led to Woods being invited on to television talk shows, offered appearances in television sitcoms, and accorded front cover and interviews in popular magazines. The comparisons with Jordan also extend to offers of endorsement contracts, the most significant initial agreement for Woods being with *Nike* who offered a five-year contract in 1996 reportedly worth $40 million (Enrico 1997; Rosaforte 2001). As Hughes Norton of International Management Group (IMG), who represented Woods, remarked '$40 million for five years ... is more than Nike pays any athlete in salary, even *Jordan*' (Smith 1996: 49, emphasis in original).

In 1996 it seemed that *Nike*'s signature athlete Michael Jordan's basketball career was coming to a close and that meant there was a commercial slot to be filled. In terms of his achievements, potential, appearance and ability to handle the media, not to mention his multi-ethnicity, Tiger Woods represented an ideal subject for endorsement and marketing activities. *Nike* CEO Phil Knight quickly recognised the potential, remarking that 'What Michael Jordan did for basketball, [Woods] absolutely can do for golf' (quoted in Rosaforte 2001: 62). Prior to signing Woods *Nike* had a very low golf profile and Knight, appreciating that endorsement of clothing, clubs and balls is commercially more significant in relation to golf than many other sports, sought to change that. A high proportion of those who attend golf tournaments or watch television coverage also play the game and in so far as marketing has a significant impact on their clothing and equipment purchases Knight believed that 'Woods would turn Nike instantly into a global force in golf' (Owen 2001: 96).

Phil Knight saw in Tiger Woods a unique character, someone destined for greatness, an athlete whose determination to win every time coupled with a capacity to get the crowd to identify with him signified that he was a 'Nike guy' (Stodghill and Grover 1997). At the point that Woods signed with *Nike* golf-related sales represented merely 1 per cent of the company's overall turnover. In 1996 it was reported that Woods had helped to double the sales of *Nike* golf shoes and the expectation was that in terms of commercial impact Woods would be to the 1990s what Jordan had been to the 1980s (Enrico 1997).

Early in his professional career Woods identified Jordan as his role model, commenting 'How could you not at least set your sights on being like him?' (Rosaforte 2001: 26). However, an important difference between the two was that Jordan was playing in a sport that was dominated by African-American players and in that respect basketball was the very antithesis of the world of golf in which Tiger Woods operated. Woods had to confront forms of prejudice and discrimination that led to golf being 'stereotyped as an uncool white-man's game' (Rosaforte 2001: 27). As Woods's career has progressed the comparisons with Jordan have multiplied. Like Jordan, Woods has been described as a phenomenon the likes of which we may never see again. In winning his second Masters tournament in 2001 Woods, having won the PGA Championship, the US Open Championship and the British Open Championship in 2000, became the first golfer in history to hold simultaneously all four major professional championships. The closest comparison that can be made with the 'Tiger Slam' is the sequence of victories in major tournaments achieved by the amateur golfer Bobby Jones in 1930. Jones practised law for six months of the year and was virtually a part-time golfer. However, that did not stop him from winning '13 of the 21 major championships that he entered' between 1923 and 1930 (Rubenstein 1997: 2). Then in 1930 Jones achieved what became known as the 'Grand Slam' by winning the US and British Opens and Amateur tournaments in the same year.

Racism in golf

When Bobby Jones was playing racism was prevalent in the world of golf and most of the tournaments and courses, including the Masters and the Augusta National Golf Club, both of which he had helped to establish, were off limits to African-Americans. Indeed the history of golf in America has been described as one of 'exclusion and racial intolerance' (Owen 2001: 177).

While there are no conclusive historical records it has been speculated that the birthplace of American golf was probably in South Carolina in the late eighteenth century and that African-American slaves were probably used 'as caddies by members of the South Carolina Golf Club' (Sinnette 1998: 4). Historical evidence confirms that African-Americans did participate in the game from the late nineteenth century. For example, George Grant patented a wooden peg golf tee in 1899, 25 years before a white golfer, William Lowell, obtained a patent for a golf tee that he exploited commercially. Lowell was regarded as the inventor of the golf tee until 1991 when the United States Golf Association (USGA) belatedly gave Grant the recognition he deserved (Sinnette 1998).

The experiences of a number of other late nineteenth, early twentieth century figures who acquired golfing skills through their roles as caddies highlight the difficulties African-Americans faced when trying to pursue a playing interest in the game. In 1896 John Matthew Shippen Jr. was encouraged to enter the second US Open Championship but the day before play was to start a number of professional players threatened the tournament director that they would withdraw if Shippen, an African-American, and Oscar Bunn, a close friend and full-bloodied Shinnecock Indian, were permitted to play (Stevens 2000). Theodore Havemeyer, the tournament director, stood firm, indicating that the event would proceed as scheduled, including Shippen and Bunn. Other accounts of the incident suggest that Havemeyer 'stated that Shippen was only "half black" implying that he would have prohibited [him] … from playing if he were a full-bloodied African-American' (Sinnette 1998: 18–19).

There are many other examples of discrimination against African-American golfers. Walter Speedy and three other black golfers were prevented from participating in a public links tournament in Chicago in 1910. And in 1921 Speedy and a group of black golfers found that their names had been erased from the register for a citywide tournament to be held in Chicago and replaced by white golfers (Sinnette 1998). Such experiences led in 1925 to Speedy helping to establish an organisation, the United States Colored Golf Association (USCGA), to promote the interests of black golfers. By 1928 the organisation had abbreviated its name to the United Golfers Association (UGA).

The treatment of Dewey Brown by the Professional Golfer's Association (PGA) provides a further example of the problems encountered by African-Americans. From the age of eight Brown worked as a caddie and assisted with cutting the fairways at Madison Golf Club. As well as acquiring golf playing skills and demonstrating an aptitude for giving lessons Brown became an accomplished golf club maker and repairer. Brown held positions at a number of golf clubs in Pennsylvania, New Jersey and New York and participated as a golf professional in a number of local tournaments. In 1928 he became a member of the PGA, the first African-American to do so. The question of his racial identity did not arise at the time, more than likely because he possessed 'very light skin'. However, in 1934 for no reason, 'without any explanation or forewarning', his eligibility for membership of the organisation was withdrawn (Sinnette 1998: 32). In the absence of any explanation at all from the PGA it has been suggested that the organisation was probably unaware of Brown's African ancestry at the time they awarded membership. After Brown's expulsion the PGA scrutinised applications more carefully to avoid further possible 'oversights' (Sinnette 1998).

A number of factors contributed to the growth in the number of African-Americans playing golf. Being a caddie was a significant early entry route into the world of golf for African-Americans, especially the professional game. Caddies acquired a fine knowledge of the rules, codes of conduct and etiquette, an understanding of the way weather conditions affected courses and the playing of the game, and by observing players close-up they gained knowledge of techniques and psychology. Furthermore, in their free time they could use golfing equipment to which they had access to develop their playing skills. Movement of black populations from remote regions of the South to the North in the period leading up to the First World War, the spread of municipal golf courses, plus the development of black golf clubs and tournaments had a significant impact on participation rates in amateur golf. In the course of the Second World War golf instruction became a part of military service recreational programmes. However, continuing racial segregation meant that there were relatively few opportunities for African-Americans to play until President Harry Truman issued Executive Orders which desegregated the armed forces and the civil service:

> Almost immediately Truman's executive orders changed the atmosphere for African-Americans on military golf courses ... African-Americans began to use military golf facilities in greater numbers and with greater frequency. Within a relatively short time, black golfers also became members of military golf teams and participated in military tournaments. (Sinnette 1998: 81)

For most of the first half of the twentieth century organised sport in America had an 'apartheid-like structure' and in respect of golf a series of 'parallel structures' – organisations (USCGA/UGA) and golf clubs – emerged to meet the needs of the growing number of black golfers (Sinnette 1998: 58–59).

In 1943 the Professional Golfer's Association introduced a clause, Section I of Article III, into its constitution which specifically limited membership of the organisation to 'Professional golfers of the Caucasian race' (Owen 2001: 179). By virtue of their exclusion from membership of the PGA African-American golfers were prevented from participating in lucrative PGA tour events. In 1948 two African-Americans, prevented from participating in a PGA tour event, for which they had qualified by finishing in the top 60 in the Los Angeles Open, one of only three predominantly white tournaments that accepted entries from black professionals, filed a lawsuit against the PGA. The suit was eventually dropped in response to the PGA appearing to agree not to discriminate against black golfers. However, the 'Caucasian clause' was not removed and the PGA adopted a new strategy of describing its co-sponsored golf events as 'Open Invitationals',

> the new name allowed a host club to refuse to 'invite' a black golfer to an event, whereupon the PGA could wring its hands and declare it had no control over a private club's policies. (Sinnette 1998: 127)

Unrestricted PGA membership would not become a reality until November 1961 when the 'Caucasian' clause was finally removed from the PGA constitution, but only after the intervention of the California Attorney General Stanley Mosk who indicated that the PGA would not be allowed to hold tournaments in the state if it continued to discriminate against African-Americans (Sinnette 1998: 131–132). Removal of the discriminatory clause allowed golf to become formally integrated, the last major American sport to do so. However, when Tiger Woods was born in 1975 the mind-set that had long fostered prejudice against non-white players remained 'very much a part of the culture of golf' (Owen 2001: 181).

Hello world: I am Tiger Woods

When Tiger Woods entered the world of professional golf in 1996 he was already a fairly well-known figure in the golfing community, having participated as an amateur in PGA Tour events and having attracted the attention of the press, television, and specialist golf publications such as *Golf World* that featured him on the cover of its 2 August edition as it speculated about the possibility that he might turn professional. Wearing cap and shirt bearing the 'swoosh' logo Woods announced his decision to become a professional on 20 August. At that time Jim Thorpe was the only African-American on the PGA Tour circuit. Simultaneously Woods indicated that he had signed up with the International Management Group (IMG), an organisation that had been closely monitoring his progress for several years through his father Earl Woods who had a position with IMG as '"talent scout" for the American Junior Golf Association' (Cole and Andrews 2000: 113). On turning professional Woods also signed a five-year endorsement deal worth $40 million that IMG had brokered with *Nike*. As one observer remarked, Woods 'was now a packaged product, a corporation and an icon' (Rosaforte 2001: 70–71).

Tiger Woods's opening words at the press conference at the Brown Deer Golf Club arranged to announce his decision to turn pro appeared innocuous enough – 'I guess, hello, world' (Rosaforte 2001: 70). However, the very next day *The Wall Street Journal* and television commercials on ESPN and CBS carried *Nike* commercials featuring Tiger Woods declaring 'Hello world'. Moreover, *Nike* had decided to make race and golf's reputation as a sport that had yet to become fully inclusive the focus of its opening promotion of the nation's leading black golfer. The television campaign showed images of Woods playing golf and over a musical score he described major events in his career to date, including successes like his three consecutive US Amateur titles. Then towards the conclusion of the advertisement Woods remarked:

> Hello world.
> There are still courses in the US I am not allowed to play because of the color of my skin.
> Hello world.
> I've heard I am not ready for you.
> Are you ready for me?
> (quoted in Cole and Andrews 2000: 114)

The advertisement was greeted with precisely the kind of response *Nike* would have anticipated and desired. The golfing establishment were on the defensive and demanded to know where Woods was unable to play. *Nike* were required to issue press statements explaining that a literal interpretation of the text would be misleading and that the passage in the advertisement represented '"a metaphor" with Woods representing other [less privileged] black golfers' who were still being denied the right to play on some courses (Goldman and Papson 1998: 113).

The press reported on and amplified reaction to the *Nike* advertising campaign as did television programmes that covered the 'Hello World' advertisement and the question of racism in golf, as well as the impact Woods had begun to have on the game. The publicity surrounding Woods's dramatic entry into the professional game served to further raise awareness of the *Nike* brand, but it also left the company exposed to the criticism that the advertising campaign had quite deliberately attempted to exploit golf's bad record on racial issues in order to promote the sale of golf products within the black community. *Nike* was accused of employing a crude 'race carding' strategy and Woods's marketability was argued to derive less from any exceptional playing ability he might possess and more from the fact that he was a black player (Cole and Andrews 2000). However, notwithstanding reservations about the company's motives in running the ad and the commercial benefits they might have derived from it, the narrative served to draw attention to the presence of racism in golf and by implication American society as a whole. The ad also represented Woods as incontrovertibly African-American.

When questioned on the subject of racism raised in the 'Hello world' advertisement Woods remarked that the message was long overdue and true (Smith 1996). Woods described how when younger he was 'always treated as an outsider' and denied things at school, socially and in golf because of the colour of his skin (Rosaforte 2001: 48). On the specific question of racism in golf Woods experienced problems from an early age, especially at the Navy Golf Course in Long Beach California where his father Earl, as a retired army lieutenant colonel and former Green Beret, had playing privileges. Earl Woods was subjected to racial abuse at the course by white golfers in the late 1980s and there were several attempts to ban his son from playing there (Smith 1996; Sinnette 1998). Interviewed in 1990 at the PGA Junior Championship, a 14-year-old Tiger Woods commented on the treatment he received at his home course, 'They try to shut me out. I think it's my skin color' (Rosaforte 2001: 48). In 1994, only two years before the 'Hello world' ad appeared and the same year in which Woods won the first of his US Amateur championships, he was still having problems at the Navy course (Rosaforte 2001).

Tiger Woods's racial identity has been a matter of considerable comment. Journalists responding critically to the 'Hello world' ad recalled how Woods had previously commented that the only time he thought about race was when the media asked him about it (Smith 1996). Moreover, as an amateur at the 1995 US Open Woods had issued a statement to reporters indicating that to call him 'black' or 'African-American' would not be entirely appropriate or accurate as his ethnic background was more complex, his father being African-American and his mother Thai. Pressed later on his racial identity Woods would describe himself as multi-ethnic, but that in itself does not represent a denial of his blackness. A clue to his views on the issue emerged from one of his responses to the controversy provoked by the 'Hello world' ad,

> What I realized is that even though I'm mathematically Asian – if anything – if you have one drop of black blood in the United States you're black. (Smith 1996: 50)

Without doubt the first *Nike* campaign had made a mark and not necessarily one that was entirely to the liking of Hughes Norton, Woods's IMG agent at the time, who would have noted that other companies, such as *McDonald's*, who were considering offering endorsement contracts might have been deterred by the effect *Nike's* 'edgy ads' had on his client's commercial image.

The first campaign simultaneously identified the problem of racism and presented Woods as a signifier of racial progress and national transformation comparable to other historic African-American sporting figures, such as Jackie Robinson who broke the 'colour ban' in major league baseball in 1947 and Arthur Ashe who from the late 1960s demonstrated that African-Americans could succeed in a sport that had been almost entirely 'white' by winning major tennis titles (Lipsyte and Levine 1995; http://www.geocities.com/dblimbrick/ashe.html). Woods confirmed his status as a signifier of racial progress when he won the Masters at Augusta National on 13 April 1997, becoming the first black man to win a major golf championship. There had been no black competitors in the Masters until 1975 when Lee Elder was permitted to play. Moreover there had been no black members at Augusta National until 1991 and there were only two in 1997. Lee Elder described Woods's victory as representing the emancipation of the sport:

> This is so significant sociologically. It's more significant to me, even, than Jackie Robinson breaking the [baseball] color line ... After today we will have a situation where no one will even turn their head to notice when a black person walks to the first tee. (quoted in Rosaforte 2001: 156)

The 'Hello world' campaign did not deter consumers, to the contrary, consumer interest in *Nike* products and in Woods was raised as consumers were invited to find in the company and in the figure of Woods an exemplification of 'the American way' and 'the American Dream' (Cole and Andrews 2000).

The second campaign – 'I am Tiger Woods' – represented Woods as 'the unequivocal embodiment of America's future multicultural citizenry' (Cole and Andrews 2000: 118). The advertisement featured a cohort of multi-racial children – the 'new' America – engaged in various golf scenes interspersed with shots of Woods with whom they were shown to identify through repetition of the words 'I am Tiger Woods'. The advertisement concluded with Woods, exemplifying America's new multi-ethnic face, playing a golf shot followed by the on-screen text, 'I am Tiger Woods' (Goldman and Papson 1998). The advertisement effectively anticipated the description of his multi-ethnicity that Woods proffered in an *Oprah Winfrey Show* interview in 1997 – 'I'm a Cablinasian: Ca, Caucasian; bl, black; in, Indian; Asian – Cablinasian' (quoted in Cole and Andrews 2000: 120). The way in which Tiger Woods has exemplified and embraced diversity has articulated perfectly with the global branding and marketing objectives of the new consumer capitalism.

America's son: 'an industry all by himself'

Nike's subsequent campaigns featuring Woods have moved away from issues of race and ethnicity and become less confrontational and more self-effacing.

The later advertisements for *Nike* and other companies have sought to employ ironic twists to humanise Woods while continuing to allude to and/or display his exceptional golfing skills. For example, in a 1999 advertisement *Nike* showed Woods keeping a golf ball in the air by tapping it off the face of his 60-degree sand wedge 49 times with the ball going between his legs, behind his back and even being stopped on the club before being hit with a baseball swing 120 yards down the driving range (Ratnesar 2000: 52). The advertisement received near universal acclaim for the exceptional skill Woods displayed as well as for the amusing and entertaining character it revealed. The ad has been credited with doing 'more for Tiger's mass appeal than all the words that had been written' and as having 'burned images of the *Nike* brand into the pop culture psyche' (Rosaforte 2001: 42). A subsequent series of *Nike* ads have featured Woods with a cartoon tiger puppet golf accessory called 'Frank' who comments critically on his golfing ability. Then in the aftermath of reports of Woods responding to a poor run of form by discarding his *Nike* driver and returning to his 975D *Titleist* club, with which he had so much success early in his professional career, *Nike* produced a series of ads featuring Woods in which a prominent theme was his freedom to play with whatever equipment he chooses, notwithstanding his contractual obligations (Chaudhary 2003; Davies 2003a).

Demonstrating that any publicity is good for brand awareness and confirming an ability to incorporate criticism and turn it to commercial advantage *Nike* produced a series of ads in which Woods was shown categorically stating:

'I am not a "Nike" athlete I am a "whoever makes the best equipment in the world" athlete'.

'You know what my Nike contract says? I don't have to play their equipment if I've found something better. How's that for pressure?

'Dear Nike, all I wanna do is win Majors. I'll do whatever it takes including switching equipment if necessary. These are my terms, they are non-negotiable'.

Predictably in each of the ads the swoosh logo was clearly visible on at least one item of Woods's clothing – cap, shirt and/or golfing glove – and to avoid any misunderstanding the *Nike Golf* logo appeared prominently in the final frame (http://www.nike.com/nikegolf/). The ultimate message that the ads conveyed is that free to switch to something better, the athlete who favours the best equipment in the world and whose terms are non-negotiable remains firmly wedded to *Nike*.

Undoubtedly Tiger Woods has already carved out a secure place for himself in the history of golf. He is a highly gifted player, an individual who has been described as having changed the face of golf, as having transcended all races, and as having become more than an athlete as he has crossed over 'into the realm of icon' (Rosaforte 2001: 9, 12–20, 44). In a manner that resembles Jordan, Woods has indeed become an industry. Woods has lucrative commercial contracts with a range of prominent corporations that have helped to make him the highest paid athlete in history. In 1999 reported earnings were in the region of $50 million and in 2000 $65 million. In 2002 Woods held endorsement contracts with *American Express, Asahi, Buick, Electronic Arts (EA), TAGHeuer, Wheaties, TLC Laser Eye Centers,* as well as more directly golf and/or sport related contracts with *Nike Golf, Golf Digest, Upper Deck,* and *Famous Photography Inc.* (http://www.tigerwoods.com).

As well as receiving sizeable appearance fees to participate in events – for example in 1999 $2 million to play in Dubai and $1 million to participate in the Deutsche Bank SAP Open and the Johnnie Walker Classic – Woods has been able to earn additional income from amateur golfers keen to be on the course with him. For example in 2000 one individual reportedly paid £1.1 million to play a round of golf with him. And in 2001 Woods flew to China where 72 amateur golfers from Hong Kong, Singapore, China and Taiwan paid up to $80,000 a hole to play golf with him at the Mission Hills club (Brown 2001). In addition golf tournament successes have provided Woods with an additional substantial source of income and in 2000 his PGA Tour earnings of $8,286,821 represented a single-season record (Owen 2001: 172).

Woods, like Jordan, constitutes no threat to the corporate world, any potential Woods might have had to become a 'progressive cultural figure has effectively been neutered by the forces of corporate capitalism' (Cole and Andrews 2001: 84). It has been estimated by *ESPN Magazine* that Woods will 'make $6 billion before he's through with 75 per cent of that coming through endorsement income' (Rosaforte 2001: 38). The various contracts Woods holds mean that there are corporate responsibilities that have to be met. There are golfing clinics and tournaments organised by his corporate sponsors at which attendance is required and other events held by corporations that are in competition with his sponsors which he will not attend. For example, the contractual commitment Woods has to *Amex* explains why the only week of the PGA Tour season that he regularly misses is the *MasterCard* Colonial (Rosaforte 2001). In a comparable manner the contract Woods signed with the Disney Corporation in 2001 has led to him playing a schedule that favours tournaments televised by ABC which is owned by Disney (Davies 2001).

The consequences of the very lucrative *Nike* Golf endorsement contract have become increasingly evident since Woods achieved the 'Tiger Slam'. When Woods first signed with *Nike* in 1996 they did not make clubs or balls, but there was an understanding that should they eventually do so, and providing they proved to be better than those made by other companies, he would use them (Davies 2003b). From a reputed $40 million contract in 1996 *Nike* raised their investment in Woods to a reported $80 to $100 million for a five-year contract in 2000. Also in 1996 Woods had signed a $20 million contract to play with *Titleist* equipment, including a *Titleist* golf ball, the Tour Professional 90, but the *Nike* advertisement that went out during the 1999 US Open showing Woods juggling a golf ball on his Nike club before hitting it with a baseball swing caused *Titleist* to begin legal action against *Nike* because the implication was that the ball used was not the one he was contracted to use. The controversy led to a renegotiation of Woods's contract with *Titleist*. He would continue using, for the time being at least, *Titleist* prototype blade irons but his bag would bear the *Buick* brand. It had also been agreed that Woods would be paid $50,000 for each tournament in which the *Titleist* Professional golf ball was used. However, in the *Nike Golf* Sales Meeting in 2000 Woods announced he would be switching to the *Nike* Tour Accuracy TW golf ball.

The golf ball market was worth $1 billion in 1999 and *Titleist* was the market leader with 45 per cent, followed by *Spalding* with 23 per cent and then *Maxfli*, *Wilson* and *Precept*, with *Nike* on 1 per cent (Harris 2000). In 2000 Woods won ten tournaments with the new *Nike* ball but after *Titleist* had introduced their revolutionary solid core ball, the Pro VI, Woods lost his aura of invincibility and the games of his rivals began to improve significantly. Then in 2002 Woods switched to *Nike* irons, but after winning the Masters and US Open that year his driving accuracy slipped and he did not win any of the next five Majors and controversially he returned to his old *Titleist* 975D driver in July of 2003, only to switch yet again a few months later to a new driver, the *Nike* Igniter prototype (Anonymous 2003b).

Golf is a sport in which technological innovations in the design of equipment has played a significant role throughout the game's history. Golf has tended to be a game for the privileged few, a game to which it is relatively difficult to gain access without sufficient resources and social capital. For disadvantaged young African-American males it was caddying that provided access and a gradual introduction to the game. The majority of the early African-American professional players acquired their golf knowledge and playing ability through their roles as caddies. However, shortly after the end of the Second World War caddies began to decline in number and by the mid-1970s there were very few African-Americans playing the game (Sinnette 1998; McDaniels 2000). Indeed no African-American had made an impression on the professional game for almost 20 years until Tiger Woods made his entry in 1996.

A number of factors have been identified as contributing to the steady decline in the number of caddies in general and African-American caddies in particular. These include the practice of professional golfers hiring their own personal caddie, sometimes a family member, who would accompany them to every event, a practice which reduced the potential income stream for club caddies; the poor image of the caddy among younger African-Americans; and finally the impact of the motorised golf buggy (Sinnette 1998). The motorised golf buggy was more economical and convenient for the golfer and offered golf clubs a new rental income stream while simultaneously removing the need for a large pool of caddies. The introduction of the motorised golf buggy reduced the requirement for caddies and thereby significantly reduced the golfing prospects of young African-Americans (McDaniels 2000).

There is an irresistible commercial imperative that leads corporations in a competitive capitalist marketplace, including those with a stake in the golf equipment and accessory market, to continually seek to innovate to gain an advantage over their competitors in the quality and performance of their products. The performances of high profile players, like Woods, may derive considerable benefit from technological advances achieved in club and ball design, but then again access to the potential benefits associated with new advances in club and ball design may be restricted by contractual responsibilities that confine players to a particular brand. Likewise, corporations that have introduced innovations in club and ball design may benefit from the successful playing record and performance of signature athletes using their products, but a lack of playing success may, in turn, reflect badly on endorsed product ranges. In the course of his professional career Tiger Woods has experienced both the benefits of advances in technology and design with *Nike* as well as the disadvantages associated with being contracted to a company that has been playing catch up with its competitors in the golf equipment field.

Concluding remarks: on the sport star as role model

Sport stars are frequently treated by the media as role models (Whannel 2002). Sporting ability and success is greeted with media acclaim and the individuals involved are then elevated to star status and represented as influential figures, as examples to others, especially the young. Once elevated to the status of role model the conduct of sport stars is closely monitored and subjected to what amounts to virtual surveillance by doorstepping journalists, with any indiscretions or departures from what is deemed to be appropriate behaviour being regarded as newsworthy and attracting media criticism. In the majority of cases sport stars are involuntarily accorded the status of role model. Such a status appears as an unavoidable consequence of a high profile acquired through sporting success. Few openly welcome being placed on a pedestal as a role model and, as the response of Charles Barkley described earlier confirms, some reject the very idea (Goldman and Papson 1998). However, Tiger Woods has embraced the idea, remarking that 'I've been very blessed to have the opportunity to become a role model. Not too many people in this world have that opportunity' (Rosaforte 2001: 72).

The idea of Tiger Woods as a role model was anticipated by his father Earl's references to his son as destined to become more influential than the prophet Muhammad and Mahatma Gandhi (Rosaforte 2001: 28). Woods learnt to play golf at his father's side and as he grew his father helped him to concentrate and to prepare for competition by deliberately attempting to distract him. Early in his career observers thought Woods might be overly dependent on his father and some critics have drawn parallels between Earl Woods and Stefano Capriati the 'overbearing father of Jennifer Capriati' (Rosaforte 2001: 85, 317). However, rather than taking advantage of his son or pushing him too far, Earl Woods has been described as all too frequently 'sacrificing his own well-being for what he clearly believes to be a higher cause' (Owen 2001: 79).

In 1996 Woods and his father began holding golfing clinics for inner-city children, a forerunner of the Tiger Woods Foundation that would be set up to introduce to the game young children who might otherwise never get the opportunity. By transforming the image of golf Woods has been credited with making it more likely that gifted young athletes might take up the game. The foundation Woods has helped to establish provides opportunities for those who are interested in golf to participate in one-on-one instruction sessions with him (Owen 2001). By 1999 Earl Woods was describing his son as a 'world figure ... a world celebrity', someone whose fame and influence extended far beyond the game he played, someone who he firmly believed was destined 'to make a difference in people's lives all over the world' (Owen 2001: 63).

While a number of observers have shared some of Earl Woods's views of his son's potential, describing him as the 'chosen one', as comparable to Jackie Robinson and Arthur Ashe, and even as having the potential to be as big an influence as Martin Luther King, others have been more circumspect and some have become critical of the way in which Woods has sought to distance himself from the politics of race. For example, in May 2000 the National Association for the Advancement of Colored People (NAACP) asked black athletes to boycott any events scheduled to take place in South Carolina which continued to fly the Confederate flag on its state capital building. Many black athletes heeded the call, including the New York Nicks basketball team and tennis player Serena Williams, but Tiger Woods, appearing to follow the earlier example of his role model Michael Jordan, responded by stating 'I'm a golfer. That's their deal, not mine' (Donegan 2002: 3).

It is understandable that for the CEO of 'Tiger Inc' it is important to remember that people of all political persuasions attend golf tournaments and buy golf equipment. But by explicitly distancing himself from the NAACP political stand supported by fellow black athletes Woods exposed himself to criticism for being unwilling to use his influence to support a legitimate political cause with which it might be expected that he would have some empathy. Although no reasons have been offered to explain Woods's reticence, with the exception of his father's remark that his son has a 'right not to take up every cause' and that 'Tiger ... does not want race to be an issue in his life' (Donegan 2002: 3), potential commercial risks associated with such a course of action may have entered the equation, as they seemed to have done with Jordan.

As sport stars the lives of Jordan and Woods have become increasingly closely intertwined with the corporate world and any progressive political potential they may have had has been compromised by their constitution as consumer culture icons and 'super-brands'. Through their elevation to the status of consumer culture role models they have come to symbolise 'America's radical racial transformation' (Cole and Andrews 2000: 121) and simultaneously they have served to deflect attention away from the 'new poverty', misery and social exclusion that remains the common experience of many African-Americans living in inner-city ghettos within a 'Dual America' (Castells 1998). Both Jordan and Woods exemplify the way in which black sporting figures have become marketable cultural figures and the wealth and celebrity status they have gained from playing sport and from taking advantage of endorsement opportunities that have been opened up by their sport stardom have contributed to the cult of the black athlete and an associated diffusion of anti-intellectual attitudes among young African-American males in particular (Hoberman 1997).

6

Cultures of Sport Stardom:
David Beckham and Anna Kournikova

The business of sport stardom

Professional sport, corporate sponsorship and television now constitute an indivisible trinity, in terms of economic rewards they form a golden triangle, from which each of the parties derives substantial benefits (Aris 1990). The political economy of professional sport is now heavily dependent on the continuing involvement of commercial corporations eager for their brands and products to be associated with sport events and sporting figures and television companies keen to broadcast matches and tournaments. As one observer has remarked, 'Sponsors and TV are the twin props of Sportsbiz' (Aris 1990: xi).

For their part commercial corporations have come to recognise that sport and sporting figures offer a rare, if not unique, quality of authenticity from which their brands can derive substantial benefit by association. Few, if any, other contemporary cultural forms can compare with sport which has surpassed even popular music 'as the most captivating medium most essential to being perceived as "young and alive"', so much so that it has 'completely permeated the logic of the marketplace in consumer goods' (Katz 1994: 25–26). There are very few forms of social life that can move relatively easily across cultural boundaries but sport is undoubtedly one of those forms, as commercial corporations keen to extend the global reach of their brands have been quick to recognise.[1]

From the 1980s sport events and sporting figures have been increasingly valued as the means through which all sorts of products and services, including those not related to sport at all could be marketed to consumers. Stadiums, scoreboards, the perimeter of the field of play, seating areas and executive boxes, jumbo-sized television screens, equipment, players' clothing, and match or event programmes have all been adorned with the marketing signs of commercial corporations that have recognised sport's unique status and appeal. For commercial corporations keen to enhance awareness of their products and brands sporting figures are attractive endorsers as they have unrivalled consumer recognition value. For example, David Beckham has been identified as 'the biggest thing in Britain ... [having] achieved, according to advertising experts, 100 per cent household recognition' (Northcroft 2003). Within the television industry sport programming also occupies a special place as it attracts and retains viewers more readily than other programme options.

In the past sport was a relatively inexpensive source of programming for television. In America it represented a reliable profit source for commercial television networks until the 1980s when the costs of broadcasting rights began to increase and advertising revenues, for a period at least, declined in relative terms. In the mid-1980s as cable television services came on stream and rights fees increased at an astronomical rate the major networks began to derive less direct financial benefit from sport coverage (Aris 1990). ABC lost money, NBC earned next to nothing and CBS earned only $10 million from sport broadcasting (Eastman and Meyer 1989). However, broadcasting 'ownership' of prestigious sporting events has provided American television networks with a means of differentiating themselves from their network and cable competitors and it continues to prove positive in respect of network image and promotion with both the public and advertisers (Eastman and Meyer 1989).

In Britain it took until the 1960s for sport to acquire an established position within television scheduling and major sport events were largely monopolised by the British Broadcasting Corporation (BBC) until relatively late in the century.[2] Although the development of Independent Television (ITV) in 1955 introduced a degree of competition and created the beginnings of a marketplace for televised sport events in Britain it was only towards the end of the 1980s with the growth of cable and satellite television in particular that the market began to open up. The first significant sign of a change occurred in 1988 when the cartel operated by the BBC and ITV was undone by the entry of British Satellite Broadcasting into negotiations with football authorities. Competition led to football increasing its television rights revenue from £3.1 million a year to £15 million a year (Aris 1990). In 1992 the emergence of Rupert Murdoch's BSkyB led to an even more competitive marketplace for sport broadcasting rights. Murdoch's view of sport's value to television was made clear in his address to the News Corp AGM in 1996 when he commented that sport 'absolutely overpowers film and all other forms of entertainment in drawing viewers to television' and that it was his intention to use 'sports as a battering ram and a lead offering in all ... [his] pay television operations' (cited in Cashmore 2000: 317).

Notwithstanding increases in the cost of broadcasting rights television sport continues to be cost effective when compared to other television programming forms and when consideration is given to audience viewing figures. However, not all sports have a universal appeal and some games clearly travel across cultural boundaries better than others. Events such as the Olympic Games administered by the IOC and the World Cup organised by FIFA have a global appeal and attract substantial revenue from commercial sponsors and broadcasting organisations. Other sports that have demonstrated a capacity to draw substantial global television audiences include athletics, golf, boxing, Formula One motor racing, tennis and association football. The latter, as Aris has observed, is a 'world passion' (1990: 75) and through the increased exposure that the development of global television broadcasting of high profile games and tournaments provides, prominent players have acquired global recognition and become international stars and cultural icons.

Pele: football's first global star

Television is a medium that offers captivating images of sportsmen and sportswomen in action, one that allows people viewing from their homes or in bars to appreciate the ability, agility, power, determination, commitment, emotion and aesthetic grace of participants in sport events. With the benefit of slow motion and replay technology allowing the viewer to see over and over again remarkable demonstrations of skill, appreciation of sporting events and performances is enhanced. Such developments have transformed television coverage of association football and the status of players. Consider the impact of television coverage of the 1970 World Cup final in Mexico. The introduction of colour and deployment of other technological innovations

> brought for the first time, the full spectacle to millions of television viewers in Europe and the Americas, with the game's first global superstar, Pele, at its epicentre. Constant television replays of the Brazilian triumph [4–1 over Italy] provide a crucial referent for the mythologizing of football's ultimate team. (Giulianotti 1999: 132)

Television coverage of the tournament elevated Pele to superstar status within football and turned him into a world figure, effectively into an international statesman who on many of his post-retirement trips around the world was treated in a manner comparable to many heads of state.

Television footage of his performances at the age of 30 in the 1970 World Cup have become part of football folklore, especially 'his outrageous dummy against Uruguay, his shot from the halfway line against Czechoslovakia, [and] his header which Banks saved so amazingly against England' (Mason 1995: 91). In the match against Czechoslovakia Pele attempted a chip shot from behind the halfway line which went over the Czechoslovakian goalkeeper Ivo Viktor's head and narrowly missed the goal. Pele's shot exemplified,

> daring skill, electric intelligence, and that greatest of human capacities – for new ideas flowing from one's discovery of changed circumstances (the keeper had left the goal line), ideas which compel you to depart … from accepted conventions, tactics, intended moves. (Keller 1993: 182)

Without doubt Pele was the first footballer to become a truly global figure, a player who transcended his sport. In his prime he was probably the highest paid sport figure in the world, his contract in 1960 with Santos the Brazilian club side is reported to have included '$27,000US to sign on, a $10,000 home for his parents, a Volkswagen and $150,000 a year win or lose, playing or not' (Mason 1995: 88). Before he was 20-years-old he was designated a 'national treasure' by the government of Brazil and in the course of his career he scored 1,281 goals in 1,363 matches played in 80 countries (Galeano 1998; BBCi 2002).

There are numerous signs of Pele's global popularity. In the 1970s a survey described Pele as 'the second-most recognised brand name in Europe after Coca-Cola' (Bellos 2002: 112). He was the first black figure to make the cover of *Life* magazine and in 1977 the United Nations held a reception to mark his support for UNICEF. In 1981 a poll of sportswriters organised by *L'Equipe* accorded him the status of 'sports champion of the century' (Mason 1995: 93). In 1999 a Reuters news agency poll designated him the 'greatest sports personality of the twentieth century' and in the same year the International Olympic Committee named him 'Athlete of the Century' even though he had never participated in the Olympics. In 2000 FIFA voted Pele joint Player of the Century with Diego Maradona (BBCi 2002).

Pele's playing career ended before the emergence of the new 'wired world' formed by the development of satellite television and the global economy, and before commercial sponsorship and an escalation in the cost of television broadcasting rights began to impact on the world of sport in general and football in particular. Although he was a great football player whose charm and 'awesome smile' were of potential commercial value, his career came before the 'internationalisation of the economy' and before satellite television opened up a global market for sport broadcasting and, in turn, a golden opportunity for high profile sporting figures to participate in commercial endorsement ventures. However, Pele did 'register his name as a trade mark', employ a manager and he 'advertised products – one of the few players to do so at that time' (Bellos 2002: 112). Although it was not really until the mid-1980s that the nature of sport representation began to change significantly and successful sporting figures started to benefit from lucrative endorsement opportunities, increasingly finding a place alongside figures from the worlds of film and popular music in a culture of stardom, Pele's status and continuing global appeal after his playing career ended enabled him to benefit from the new commercial opportunities that developed with the emergence of a 'wired world' (Halberstam 1991, 2001). Twenty-five years after retiring from the game Pele was reported to be earning in the region of £18 million a year from commercial endorsement contracts with *MasterCard, Coca-Cola, Nokia and Viagra* (Bellos 2002; Hattenstone 2003).

The sporting world David Beckham entered

David Beckham was born in 1975 in Leytonstone, London and made his league debut for Manchester United in 1995. The football world Beckham entered was one that had been transformed substantially over a number of years by a series of significant developments and events. Abolition of the maximum wage (1961), George Eastham's successful campaign against the retention and transfer system (1963), increasing television coverage of football matches beginning with a weekly highlights programme, *Match of the Day* on BBC (1964), and the English national side's success in the World Cup held in England (1966) and Manchester United's victory in the European Cup (1968) represented events that began to transform the cultural significance and market position of football and footballers in England. In addition a number of significant developments in the newspaper industry at the end of the 1960s – computerisation, colour printing and the 'tabloid revolution' – dramatically changed the character of sport reporting and the increased competition for readers between tabloid titles led to more column inches being devoted to sport as a whole and football in particular (Whannel 2001). In consequence high profile sporting figures became newsworthy both on and off the field of play.

Problems of crowd disorder, violence and incidences of hooliganism associated with football in the 1970s and 1980s led to increased match policing, the use of closed circuit television surveillance (CCTV), perimeter fencing and ultimately, after a number of tragic events, to the redesign of stadiums and the replacement of terraces by seats in the first two divisions of the English league and the Scottish Premier Division. To the list of earlier twentieth century major crowd disasters associated with football in Britain, 'Glasgow 1902 (25 killed, 517 injured) and Bolton 1946 (33 killed, 400 injured)', the 1980s had added Bradford 1985 (56 killed) and the Heysel Stadium in Brussels where, before the European Cup final between Juventus and Liverpool 39 people lost their lives and 454 were injured. Then in 1989 at Hillsborough before an FA Cup semi-final between Liverpool and Nottingham Forest, 96 people were killed as a consequence of crowd congestion made lethal by the presence of perimeter fencing that prevented those being crushed from escaping on to the pitch (Giulianotti 1999: 74–75).

Such events in the 1980s led to the 1990 Taylor Report and in due course to a conversion of the grounds of clubs in the higher divisions in England and Scotland to safer all-seater stadiums. The development of all-seater stadiums and associated initiatives, including increased surveillance, one manifestation of which has been ticket registration schemes, has produced a 'new politics of access to football' (Giulianotti 1999: 78–80). There have been a number of changes in the game at the higher level, including the composition and behaviour of crowds attending matches, the social standing and cultural significance of the sport, and its commercial appeal to television companies, advertisers and sponsors.

Since the 1960s 'football's political economy has undergone rapid modernization as its star players and clubs have been incorporated more deeply within the wider commodification of popular culture' (Giulianotti 1999: 88). A number of developments comparable to those that transformed the fortunes of the NFL and NBA in America, including merchandising initiatives, active pursuit of sponsorship deals, negotiation of lucrative television broadcast rights contracts and innovations in both the scheduling and coverage of events, along with increasing promotion and profiling of star players and the growing influence of agents, have been enthusiastically embraced by the football industry in Britain.

Furthermore, as recognition of the difficulty of cultivating international publics for American major league sports has increased (Leifer 1995), major American corporations with commercial interests in the sport industry, or those whose brands and/or products lend themselves to promotion through association with sport events and sporting figures, have sought to raise their profile in relation to association football, the sport that has maintained, if not enhanced, its global appeal and supremacy. For example, in 2004 Peter Hudson, Football Global Creative Director at *Nike* acknowledged the increased commercial significance of football for the company – 'The resources pouring into football are huge and we're now the second sport at *Nike*, which is incredible for an American athletics company' (Hudson 2004: 24).

In retrospect the NBA's Jordan years now appear as a passing golden age, an era when passionate advocates of basketball felt able to claim that it was 'on its way to dislodging soccer as the world game' (Katz 1994: 29). Basketball no longer represents any threat to football's global popularity, if it ever did. In a comparable manner the appeal of NFL, America's favourite television sport, remains largely confined to the heartland of America and its immediate cultural dominions. It is in this context and in relation to association football's global appeal and status as 'the world's premier sport' (Giulianotti 1999: xi) that the increasing commercial investment in the game of global corporations such as *McDonald's*, *Nike*, *Coca-Cola* and *Pepsi* needs to be set.

In the course of the 1990s *Nike* executives struggled with the fact that 'soccer was the most popular sport on earth' (Katz 1994: 203). The thinking within *Nike* was that the global marketing of products through the use of American cultural icons could take the company a long way in terms of carving out a share of the available market for sport goods, but to achieve staying power in markets beyond America and to compete more effectively with *adidas* it was necessary to connect with the 'soccer market' (Katz 1994). This led the company to raise its commercial profile in respect of the game in order to compete more directly with *adidas* the company that had effectively been monopolising the market.

In line with its policy of aiming to secure the leading players to promote its corporate brand *Nike* signed the Brazilian striker Ronaldo in 1996. Nike also signed a substantial contract – estimates vary between £100 million and £250 million – with the Brazilian Football Confederation 'making it both the supplier of sports kit and co-sponsor of the Brazilian team – the largest deal ever involving a national side' (Giulianotti 1999: 89; see also Bellos 2001). The company also entered football kit deals with a number of leading club sides including Arsenal and Manchester United. Advertising campaigns organised around international football tournaments served to further raise *Nike*'s profile with football fans. In the context of the 1998 World Cup in France, a *Nike* ad showed the Brazil international football squad playing in an airport to the samba rhythms of the Tamba Trio's version of Jorge Ben's 'Mas Que Nada'. Then in advance of the 2002 World Cup in Japan and South Korea, *Nike* employed Terry Gilliam to direct two celebrated advertisements 'The Secret Tournament' and 'The Rematch'. These two advertisements featured 24 of the world's best players organised into eight three-man teams:

Triple Espresso:	Totti, Nakata, Henry
The Untouchables:	Vieira, Scholes, Van Nistelrooy
Cerberus:	Wiltord, Thuram, Davids
Toros Locos:	Saviola, Luis Enrique, Ljungberg
Os Tornados:	Figo, Ronaldo, Roberto Carlos
Funk Soul Brothers:	Denilson, Seol, Ronaldinho
Equipo del Fuego:	Crespo, Lopez, Mendieta
Tutto Bene:	Rosicky, Cannavaro, Ferdinand

Nike Europe's Brand Communication Director, Stefan Olander, described the players who were involved in the advertisement as 'the personification of everything that Nike football stands for … They are creative, exciting and innovative when it comes to finding the single touch needed to score a goal and win a game. They also represent the spontaneity, joy and skill of the game' (Stubbs 2004). In the background of both advertisements there was a remix by Dutch dance outfit Junkie XL of Elvis Presley's 'A Little Less Conversation' which on the back of repeated ad exposure went to number 1 in the single's chart. Such imaginative football advertisements were in keeping with *Nike*'s exceptionally innovative advertising record and they served to dramatically raise *Nike*'s soccer profile.

The list of players involved in 'The Secret Tournament' and 'The Rematch' reflected Nike's growing influence within the football industry. The players included were those who were sponsored by *Nike* and who were using their products at the time, notable omissions included Zinedine Zidane and David Beckham, both of whom have long-standing contracts with *adidas*.

Agents for change

By the mid-1990s when David Beckham was making his Premier league debut for Manchester United, the cultural standing and economic fortunes of football in England had been radically transformed. From the mid-1970s agents had been handling the financial affairs of players, negotiating their contracts, overseeing and, not infrequently, initiating transfers, and by the time Beckham became a professional player agents had become an increasingly prominent feature of the football landscape.

Football agents have had a long history in the professional game. Agents have played a part in scouting and recruiting players on behalf of clubs since the late nineteenth century (Edwardes 1992; Giulianotti 1999). It is in respect of the representation of players' interests that the role of the agent has grown since the mid-1970s, in the first instance dealing with commercial ventures extraneous to the sport and subsequently, as the commercial and contractual relationships between clubs and players have become more complex and potentially lucrative, offering to players 'professional advice on contract and transfer negotiations' (Roderick 2001: 1). Agents are now key figures in professional sport as a whole and have acquired such an important influence that 'no top athlete would move without one. They are deal makers, financial advisers and father confessors all rolled into one ... [who] throw a protective cordon around the star' (Aris 1990: 48).

Credit for the rapid growth in influence of agents within the sport industry as a whole is generally given to Mark McCormack (1930–2003) who set up International Management Group (IMG) and has been described as the person who 'changed the face of professional sport' (Kelso 2003), 'the undisputed king of sports marketing' who was responsible for significantly increasing the amount of money that professional sportsmen and women can make from sport (Hodgetts 2002). In 1990 *Sports Illustrated* named McCormack as the 'Most Powerful Man in Sport'. The sports over which he exercised the most direct influence were golf and tennis. In 1960 he became the agent for Arnold Palmer and he and his organisation subsequently represented other leading golfers of the time, such as Gary Player and Jack Nicklaus, and later Tiger Woods. In tennis IMG's client list has included Pete Sampras, Andre Agassi, John McEnroe, Bjorn Borg and Venus and Serena Williams (Kelso 2003). Mark McCormack is widely credited with recognising 'the potential of sport as a corporate communications medium' and as having 'started the globalisation of sport and sports stars' (Hodgetts 2002).

From golf and tennis IMG diversified into a number of other sporting fields including football, athletics, rugby, cricket and motor racing. IMG's broadcast section, Trans World International (TWI), is the world's largest independent sport television production company. The IMG group also owns and represents a number of major sport events around the world (Hodgetts 2002). McCormack was undoubtedly a significant figure in the development of a celebrity endorsement culture in which sport stars now play a pivotal role, but other figures and other organisations have also played a considerable part in the establishment of 'the golden triangle' through which sport, television and commercial sponsorship have become interconnected mutually enriching elements (Aris 1990: 9).

In 1976 Donald Dell established ProServ an agency that sought to represent athletes across their entire career (Aris 1990). Initially it was tennis players, and in the first instance Arthur Ashe and Stan Smith, that Dell's fledgling organisation represented, but ProServ proceeded to act for a number of other sporting figures, as well as manage sport events and secure sponsorship and television deals. In the mid-1980s Dell's junior partner David Falk, who unlike Dell, was familiar with the world of basketball and conscious of the potential opened up by the new level of celebrity that was beginning to be acquired by NBA players, started representing Michael Jordan. Falk is credited with revolutionising the process of representing a player in a team game such as basketball, with 'creating the idea of the individual player as a commercial superstar' (Halberstam 2001: 139).[3]

Free agency and the Bosman case

While the representational skills of his agent undoubtedly contributed to Jordan's rapid rise to the status of a cultural icon, changes in labour laws which led to the introduction of 'free agency' in American sport, and which shifted power from owners to players, also played a very significant part. In 1975 basketball players took issue with the NBA's draft and reserve system and in the following year a judicial ruling pronounced the system of control exercised over players to be illegal. The advent of free agency led to a rapid rise in salaries and transformed the status of leading sporting figures who started to acquire a celebrity status comparable to popular entertainers as they appeared on talk shows, received large fees to endorse products on television and began to be 'better known for their salaries or simply for their "well-knownness" than for their athletic feats' (Rader 1983b: 353).

In European football what became known as 'the Bosman Case' had a comparable effect by ending the practice whereby a player could only move to another club with the agreement of both the purchasing club and the selling club, which held the player's registration and generally received a transfer fee, even if the player's contract had expired. The success of the case brought to the European Court of Justice in 1995 by the Belgian player Jean-Marc Bosman, notably that transfer regulations were in contravention of Article 48 of the Treaty of Rome which stipulated the right of all European Union workers to freedom of movement, meant that in future clubs had to sign players to longer and more lucrative contracts or risk them leaving on free transfers. The Bosman ruling increased player power within the game, providing those at the higher levels with greater control over their careers and an increased capacity to negotiate lucrative contracts. Out of contract players were able to demand higher wages and to move to clubs offering the best deals (Giulianotti 1999; Pearson 2004).

The Premier League and BSkyB

Alongside the significant events and developments identified above which have contributed to the transformation of economic conditions within football, as well as the game's cultural profile and significance, appropriate recognition needs to be given to the substantial effect the formation of the

Premier League and the establishment of Rupert Murdoch's BSkyB television network have had on the football industry and the status, profile and fortunes of leading players.

In 1991 the Football Association, demonstrating its long-standing antagonistic orientation to the Football League that dates back to the onset of professionalism within the game in the late nineteenth century, published its ideas on the future of football, which included a radical proposal for the teams in the First Division of the Football League to form a separate FA Premier League. In 1992 the clubs in the First Division of the 104-year-old Football League broke away to form a new Premier League. The effect of the change was to increase the power of the leading clubs and to give them more influence over decision-making processes, including one of enormous economic significance, notably the distribution of what were destined to become increasingly lucrative television broadcasting revenues.

The value of television rights to broadcast football matches increased significantly from 1988 after the BBC/ITV cartel was broken by the entry of British Satellite Broadcasting (BSB) into the television marketplace. The price of the four-year deal to broadcast 18 live matches, eventually won by ITV, increased by 350 per cent to £11 million a season. By 1992 when the broadcasting rights were due for renewal the Premier League had been established and BSB had merged with Sky to form BSkyB which identified the securing of the rights to broadcast live football as the catalyst for penetrating the broadcasting market and increasing subscribers for pay-TV (Szymanski and Kuypers 2000: 59).

The competition between ITV and BSkyB in 1992 led to a dramatic increase in the price of broadcasting rights for live football matches. The contract won by BSkyB provided exclusive rights to show 60 live matches at a cost (including BBC highlights fees) that represented a '1,800 per cent increase on the 1983–4 deal' (Szymanski and Kuypers 2000: 60). In 1997 BSkyB, with the BBC as its junior partner aiming to secure the highlights package, paid £743 million for the broadcasting rights for a period of four years (Giulianotti 1999). In the 1983/4 season, before the establishment of the Premier League and the increase in television broadcasting rights, each of the 92 league clubs received £28,261. By the 1997/8 season an average Premier League club was receiving almost £7 million (Szymanski and Kuypers 2000).

The contract for the period 2001–4 was negotiated under the shadow of European Union concern about the monopoly being exercised by BSkyB over transmission of live matches. The contract was won by BSkyB at a cost of £1.1 billion but this time the highlights package was awarded to ITV who offered £183 million for the rights. The 2004–7 live broadcasting rights contract for which BSkyB's bid was again the highest went for £1.024 billion but arrangements for the sale of the rights attracted criticism from the European Union whose Competition Commissioner Mario Monti declared that the new contract meant that 'BSkyB will have an even greater monopoly over live TV rights than was the case in the past' (Lyons 2003).

It is in this radically transformed environment, shaped by significant changes in the economic and cultural conditions of the industry, that Beckham's football career has developed and his cultural profile and commercial involvements have grown.

Beckham: footballer and consumer culture icon

For a sporting figure still in the prime of his career much has already been written about Beckham. There have been a number of autobiographical and biographical works (Beckham 2000; Burchill 2001; Kelly 2001; Beckham and Watt 2003). Academic treatise and papers have been written and the press have shown a near insatiable appetite for stories about Beckham, his life-style, his family and his affairs (Whannel 2001; Cashmore 2002). Television interviewers (e.g. Michael Parkinson) have welcomed Beckham on to their shows and comedians and impersonators (Ali G and Alistair McGowan) have identified David Beckham and his wife Victoria as popular subjects for humour. A Channel 4 television documentary 'Black Like Beckham' suggested that Beckham with his 'bling bling' taste in jewellery, clothes, beanie hats and liking for garage music had become black 'in all but the trifling detail of skin colour' and that he was 'the personification of multicultural Britain' (Midgley 2003). In America where English football has a very low profile David and Victoria Beckham were interviewed on ABC TV's *20/20 Primetime*, both participated in the *MTV Movie Awards* in Los Angeles in 2003 and the couple have been featured in *The New York Times* Style Section and *People* magazine. In addition David Beckham has appeared on the cover of *USA Today* with the by-line 'Face of an icon ... far more than a British soccer star' (Wapshott 2003).

In 2004 the female artist Sam Taylor Wood produced a 107 minute video portrait, entitled 'David', for the National Portrait Gallery which shows Beckham sleeping on a bed (Higgins 2004). Undoubtedly other cultural texts on Beckham will emerge in due course. There is the likelihood of Beckham taking a role in *Goal*, a $30 million US backed football film trilogy that has been described as an underdog story, 'Rocky meets 8 mile', that aims to promote 'the beautiful game' around the world (Irish Examiner. com 2003; Nottingham News 2004). And the tabloid press will ensure that Beckham's private life remains a public spectacle, as was the case in the spring of 2004 when they carried reports of extramarital affairs and details of mobile phone 'sex texting'.

Football autobiographies and biographies once represented a postscript to a playing career, but in Beckham's case they have publicised and promoted a career-in-progress. *My World* published barely five years after he secured a regular place in Manchester United's first team is in many ways a typical footballer's autobiography, save for the near 50 per cent of the book devoted to photographic material featuring 'Beckham the body' as active footballer, loving partner, caring father, passive fashion model and prospective gay icon. Some of the text and the images in the book have subsequently acquired an additional and unintended significance. For example, in a concluding passage which refers to his United contract running out in 2003, Beckham remarks that he is 'as dedicated to United now as I was when I first dreamt of playing for the first team', but he then adds prophetically that clubs sometimes sell their best players and that he hasn't ruled out going abroad (2000: 112–113).

Beckham is a cultural phenomenon quite unlike any other British footballer or indeed sporting figure, past or present. By virtue of his media and commercial profile he is probably better known around the world than any other figure in football, with the possible exceptions of respected former Brazil star Pele and the controversial Argentine international Maradona. Given Beckham's global sporting profile and popularity the other comparisons that might be made are with global sporting figures such as former basketball star Michael Jordan and golfer Tiger Woods.

In terms of status and place within his chosen sporting field Beckham is in a somewhat different category to both Jordan and Woods who have been widely acknowledged to be the best players in the history of their respective sports. Beckham is not the world's best footballer, although he is a highly motivated, skilful, very fit, exceptionally competitive and much admired player, who was voted into second place in polls conducted for World Footballer of the Year in 2000 and 2001. At Manchester United he won major honours, including six Premiership titles, two FA Cups, as well as the UEFA Champions League. In 2000 Beckham was appointed captain of the England team and in 2003 he joined arguably the world's premier football club, Real Madrid, becoming one of their 'galacticos', their galaxy of superstars, alongside Zidane, Figo, Ronaldo, Roberto Carlos and Raul. As Jorge Valdano the sporting director at Real Madrid declared on signing Beckham, 'He is a great professional, he loves football and he dedicates himself to his profession exclusively' (BBCi 2003).

Beckham's potential as a footballer was recognised at an early age by his father and was nurtured and systematically developed after he signed on as a schoolboy in May 1988 and then three years later as a trainee with Manchester United (Beckham and Watt 2003). In his first full season with Manchester United, 1995–6, the team won the Premiership. Beyond events taking place on the pitch the club was beginning to establish itself as an international brand. Beckham was one of a number of young outstanding players the club had nurtured from their youth academy through to the first team squad. But in due course Beckham's football reputation and cultural profile began to soar and as this occurred Manchester United the football club and global brand provided him 'with a platform, a stage and a theatre' (Cashmore 2002: 60).

In the opening weeks of the 1996–7 season in a match against Wimbledon at Selhurst Park at which BBC television cameras were present to record material for their Saturday night highlights programme *Match of the Day* Beckham inadvertently placed himself in the media spotlight. The game against Wimbledon was coming to a close when Beckham received a pass just inside his team's half and with Wimbledon goalkeeper Neil Sullivan some way off his goal line he chose ambitiously to take a shot. The chip shot sailed through the clear afternoon sky towards the Wimbledon goal and dropped over the retreating Sullivan's head into the net. When Pele had attempted to score in a broadly comparable situation in the 1970 World Cup match against Czechoslovakia he was the world's finest footballer and was coming towards the end of an illustrious career. Although it was audacious and astonishing Pele's attempt at goal from the half-way line was what football followers everywhere might, in retrospect, have regarded as precisely what one might expect from the world's greatest footballer, it was a moment that symbolised Pele's claim to be the best, that exemplified his originality, his authenticity.

What occurred towards the end of the match between Wimbledon and Manchester United on 17 August 1996 was not expected. David Beckham was 21 years of age, was at the beginning of his career and had just returned from a loan spell at Preston North End. As Beckham has acknowledged, the remarkable goal he scored that afternoon immediately captured the media's attention:

> I couldn't have known it then, but that moment was the start of it all: the attention, the press coverage, the fame, that whole side of what's happened to me since. It changed forever that afternoon in South London, with one swing of a new boot. (Beckham and Watt 2003: 94–95).

In analyses of sport stars there is always a risk that the very qualities that distinguish them from other prominent contemporary cultural figures may be marginalised, if not neglected altogether, as the focus falls on the social, cultural and economic processes that formed the conditions in which they acquired, or were accorded, star status. The particular sporting moments that exemplify special qualities, in respect of Beckham's phenomenal goal those qualities of 'daring skill [and] electric intelligence' attributed to Pele may not be inappropriate, are ultimately what establishes the player as a star performer. It is the capacity to demonstrate exceptional skills and abilities over and over again in highly competitive contexts, under pressure and against opposition, and their wider public dissemination through circuits of media representation and promotion that continually re-affirms star status. In Beckham's case it has been his ability to strike a dead ball, to cross with precision, to make long passes with unerring accuracy, to compete enthusiastically throughout the duration of a game, and to score important goals for his club and international team that have been distinguishing characteristics which press and television coverage have identified and embellished.

While it is true that to demonstrate athletic abilities and skills an audience is necessary and ultimately it is a combination of cultural intermediaries (sport reporters, commentators and analysts) and the spectators or viewing audience that 'confers greatness on a person' (Cashmore 2002: 41), the relational process through which special, frequently exceptional, qualities are ascribed to a player has to have at its foundation authentic attributes that are regularly, if not routinely, displayed in the course of matches. Indeed the relative exceptionality of such attributes must be regularly confirmed in performances for 'greatness' to be maintained. In short it is the actions, the moves, the performances given by players in the course of contests that constitute the foundations on which star status is ultimately predicated, although a number of other elements also play a part in the reproduction of the culture of stardom within which an individual such as Beckham has been accorded a prominent place.

The Beckham business: cultural and economic aspects

A red card incident in a game against Argentina in the 1998 World Cup, which England eventually lost, subsequently led to Beckham being the target of a vicious campaign of abuse. Accused of being responsible for England's defeat Beckham was subjected to trial by tabloid journalism and judged to be the most hated man in the country (Bose 2001). From the low point of the summer of 1998, when his sending-off 'provided a point of condensation for discourses of morality and fair play in sport, in which national pride became national shame' (Whannel 2001: 138), Beckham's career path was one of unbroken ascent until the spring of 2004. Successes on the field along with positive and newsworthy events outside football, including a high pro-file marriage to Victoria Adams and the subsequent birth of two children led to a proliferation of narratives of 'redemption and triumph' in the press (Whannel 2001: 138). Undoubtedly Beckham emerged stronger from the process of vilification to which he had been subjected in 1998 and in con-sequence was probably better prepared to cope with media revelations about his personal life in Madrid and media reaction to his relatively poor performance in the European Championships in Portugal in 2004.

The 1998/9 football season has been identified as a watershed in Beckham's career trajectory. Although media narratives were encouraging everybody 'not just football fans ... into loathing him' hostile crowd reac-tion gradually began to abate and within a few months 'the Beckham-taunting subsided [and a] grudging admiration took over' (Cashmore 2002: 29). The experience of the hostile reaction of fans and the derision of the media, which Beckham not only withstood but rose above to play a leading role in his club's treble-winning season, contributed to a much more deliberate process of image cultivation and management on Beckham's part (Cashmore 2002). When in 2004 a succession of lurid stories about relationships with other women emerged in the media a series of image-replenishing photo shoots were organised of the Beckhams seemingly happy together in the garden of their Hertfordshire home, on the ski slopes at Courchevel, and attending a private party at the Royal Albert Hall.

Beckham has been described as not only 'different from any other footballer' but also as different from 'any other athlete that's ever lived'

(Cashmore 2002: 165). While in commercial terms Beckham may trail behind American sport stars like Jordan and Woods his global profile is arguably comparable, indeed the American *Men's Journal* magazine had Beckham staring out from its front cover billed as 'The Most Famous Athlete in the World' (Wallace 2003). There are undoubtedly similarities between Beckham, Jordan and Woods in that as their reputation as sporting figures grew they became global celebrities, their fame extending well beyond their respective sporting fields, but there are also interesting differences. For example, Woods is a much valued, well known and popular figure but he has yet to command the same reverence and awe as Beckham who has been represented as a figure to worship (Cashmore 2002).

Inadvertently providing support for the hypothesis that 'football and religion are interrelated in complex ways' (Giulianotti 1999: 19) Beckham has been immortalised in a Buddhist temple, depicted as a modern-day religious icon, and portrayed as a Hindu god. The sculptor Thongruang Haemod produced a one foot high gold leaf statue of Beckham in official Manchester United kit. The statue stands alongside others at the foot of the main Buddha image in Bangkok's Pariwas temple, in a position normally reserved for minor deities. The local abbot has described football as being like a religion and the temple's senior monk has remarked that football has millions of followers and that it is important to 'share the feelings of millions of people who admire Beckham' (BBC News 2000a). The artist Sharon Lutchman has painted Beckham in a religious pose to reflect the fact that he has a comparable cultural status to figures in thirteenth- and fourteenth-century Italy, Russia, and Eastern Europe who would have been depicted as religious icons – 'I see David Beckham as a modern day religious icon – a person who appears as a god' (cited in Blenford 2003). In a comparable manner Beckham and his wife Victoria have been portrayed in a painting by Amrit and Rabindra Singh as the Hindu gods Shiva and Parvati. Beckham's quasi-religious iconic status is further exemplified by artist David Rayner's casting of the footballer in the image of Jesus Christ (Pierce 2003: 14). Rayner has been described as an artist who 'specialises in taking usually untouchable symbols of religious and secular heritage and turning them into images that are venerated in modern society' (Frame 2003). The fact that Rayner's simulacrum of Beckham made from Holy Communion wafers was displayed at the Selfridges department store in Manchester perfectly symbolises Beckham's consumer cultural iconic status and, in turn, serves as a reminder of the respects in which sport events and sporting figures may serve to 'heighten the sense of the sacred' (Featherstone 1991: 121).

Although Beckham is quite unlike any other athlete, in the sense that his celebrity status is possibly unique, there are grounds for comparison with the basketball star Michael Jordan. Both have acquired their sporting reputations and, initially at least, their social standing and cultural profile, from participation in competitive team sports. It was Jordan and his agent who first demonstrated that a star player in a team sport could acquire a comparable, if not greater, sporting and commercial profile to star players in such individual sports as tennis and golf (Halberstam 2001). The close articulation between Beckham's highly successful careers on and off the field of play might almost have been modelled on Jordan's example, in respect of which the adoption of the number 23 shirt by Beckham at Real Madrid, a number made famous by Jordan in his career with the Chicago Bulls, may constitute a form of symbolic confirmation (Bolton 2003; Couzens 2003).

Both Jordan and Beckham have contributed to the interpenetration of the worlds of sport and show business. Jordan's participation in the animated feature *Space Jam*, his cameo roles in a very successful series of *Nike* television advertising mini dramas, along with regular appearances in other advertising campaigns and appearances on TV talk shows have contributed to the dissolution of the boundary between sport, entertainment and show business. In a broadly comparable manner Beckham's much-publicised relationship with and subsequent marriage to Victoria Adams of the Spice Girls, his model looks and willingness to feature in fashion shoots and to appear on the cover of magazines such as GQ, *Face*, *Vogue*, *Marie Claire* and *Attitude*, his cameo roles in a series of *Pepsi* Football television advertising campaigns, as well as the confirmation of his status as a global cultural icon exemplified by the Asian comedy-drama film *Bend It Like Beckham* by Gurinder Chadha, have served to connect more closely together the worlds of sport and show business.

Scope for making comparisons between Jordan and Beckham increased in March 2004 when *adidas* announced an extension to Beckham's endorsement contract. The new deal ensured Beckham would continue to wear the *Predator* football boot made by *adidas* but also established that he would advise on the design of shoes and clothing for a personalised line of merchandising bearing a stylised graphic version of his trademark free kick which would constitute a distinctive personalised logo (Milligan 2004). *Nike* had produced a distinctive Jordan logo and benefited from his global appeal, one estimate being that he added '$3 billion to sales of National Basketball Association merchandise worldwide and $5.2 billion to Nike's top line' (O'Connor 2004). The expectation of *adidas* executives is that Beckham will have a comparable effect on their company's growth and global profile as Jordan and Woods have had on *Nike*'s fortunes. The contract with *adidas* runs until 2008 and confirms Beckham belongs at the top of what the marketing industry describes as 'the superbrand of athletes'. Emphasising Beckham's global appeal, Lauren Henderson of FutureBrand, an international branding consultancy, commented that 'He is in an elite that includes Tiger Woods and Michael Jordan ... Once you are at that level you can put your name to anything that is in keeping with your image' (quoted in Broadbent 2004).

Jordan has been described as 'famously secretive' about his private life, while Beckham has been portrayed as superficial or lacking in depth, as perhaps lacking a 'private self', as not amounting to anything more than what is 'served up on our TV screens and in print', and as someone who gives us

'only image' (Cashmore 2002: 44–45). Undoubtedly Beckham has given a good deal of thought to his image and understandably so because it has enormous personal and commercial significance. Two particular individuals and associated organisations have played a major role in securing lucrative football and commercial contracts and in managing Beckham's media image. Tony Stephens of SFX Sports Group (Europe) was Beckham's agent from 1995 until late in 2003. In his autobiography *My Side* Beckham describes Stephens as 'someone I know I can put absolute trust in, whatever the circumstances' (Beckham and Watt 2003: 253). Caroline McAteer of the Outside Organisation, Victoria Beckham's management company between 1997 and 2003, helped to shape David Beckham's media image, provided advice in areas not related to football, and by using her magazine and tabloid contacts ensured the Beckhams were frequently in the news.

But circumstances change and almost in parallel with Victoria Beckham's decision in 2003 to use Simon Fuller, who had masterminded the careers of the Spice Girls, as an adviser to resurrect her career, David Beckham after months of what were described as 'acrimonious negotiations' decided to leave SFX with whom he had been a client for ten years (Hughes 2003). Beckham announced that his business concerns would be handled in future by Footwork Productions, a company he set up in 1996, under the guidance of Terry Byrne a former England masseur and close friend (Beckham and Watt 2003; Hughes 2003). Responsibility for managing the Beckhams as a brand was given to Fuller's '19 Entertainment' company which Caroline McAteer, known as the 'Voice of the Beckhams' also joined on leaving the Outside Organisation (Campbell 2003; Timms 2003). Media reports in 2004 of a brief affair between Beckham and a former personal assistant who held a short-term contract with SFX in Madrid invited further speculation about the reasons Beckham parted company with the sports management group with which a new deal had been agreed a few months earlier.

Image rights

For high profile footballers 'image' constitutes a significant contractual issue. In the football industry merchandising represents a valuable income stream for leading clubs. When Eric Cantona was at Manchester United he contributed significantly to the sale of replica shirts and other merchandise (Bose 2001) and Beckham's SFX agents sought to obtain appropriate commercial recognition of their client's contribution to the club's multi-million pound merchandising operation in contract renewal talks held during the 2001/02 season (Draper 2002; Beckham and Watt 2003). The contract secured was reported to be worth £90,000 a week, a figure that included an estimated £20,000 for the use of Beckham's image (O'Connor 2003).

A key issue in discussions that took place in negotiations over Beckham's image rights was the relative enhancement values of the player's image and the club's brand. At the beginning of his career Beckham's image derived substantial enhancement from his membership of the Manchester United team, but as his profile grew and he became a global cultural icon the balance shifted and in many parts of the world, especially the Far East and the emerging football merchandising markets of Japan, China, Malaysia, Thailand and Indonesia it is the Manchester United brand that has benefited from association with Beckham who has become a brand in a manner that invites further comparison with Jordan.

In 2002 *Marks & Spencer* announced they were to produce a Beckham range of clothes for boys (Ananova 2002). The Beckham brand carries the logo 'DB 07' for which the switch in shirt number from 7 to 23 following the move in the late summer of 2003 to Real Madrid, coupled with subsequent 'infidelity stories', might not seem conducive to successful marketing, although it was reported that the range was still 'selling well' (Datson 2004). For *adidas* Beckham's move from Manchester to Madrid was especially welcome. The company had a longstanding kit sponsorship deal with the club, individual sponsorship contracts with Madrid players Zinedine Zidane and Raul, and a continuing commercially successful football boot deal with Beckham which was extended in 2004. And Beckham would no longer be seen bearing the 'swoosh' logo of their competitor *Nike* which in 2000 had negotiated the biggest football kit deal in the game's history with Manchester United.

The contract, which was to run from 2002, was reported to be worth £302.9 million over 13 years and effectively handed control of Manchester United's global replica kit and merchandising business to *Nike*. The fixed contract provided the club with at least £23 million each year whatever the sales figures, on condition that they finish in the top half of the Premiership or take part in European competition (Taylor 2000). While Beckham shirts had been United's biggest sellers, outsourcing the commercial and merchandising operation to *Nike* meant that the loss of the player would not have the same commercial significance for the club (O'Connor 2003; Syed 2003). Any direct commercial impact the transfer of Beckham to Madrid might have on Manchester United's replica shirt sales would be felt by *Nike*. Although no official statement on the commercial significance of the transfer was offered by *Nike* the corporation's view can perhaps be gauged from an interview given by Phil Knight the CEO in the period leading up to Beckham's move to Madrid. When asked what he felt about David Beckham, Phil Knight replied 'All I'll say is I wish we had him. I'll tell you that' (Hatfield 2003).

Research conducted by FutureBrand in the immediate period prior to Beckham's move revealed the extent of his following in Japan, China, Malaysia, Thailand and Indonesia. It indicated that almost whatever he endorsed would be enhanced in terms of sales figures or turnover. This served to confirm research already conducted by Castrol Asia Pacific which found that 'more than 80 per cent of consumers in Thailand, Vietnam and China said a link with the footballing superstar would be a positive reason to buy Castrol products' (Day 2002). The FutureBrand research suggested that around one-third of football fans outside the domestic market follow a specific team because of an affinity with a particular player, rather than from any sense of loyalty to a club (Fordyce 2003; Szep 2003). FutureBrand estimated that around 5 million of United's 16.6 million fans in Asia might follow Beckham and switch their allegiance to Real Madrid (O'Connor 2003).

The move to Madrid

The subject of Beckham's possible transfer from Manchester United became an increasing focus of press and media interest as signs of problems between the manager of the club, Sir Alex Ferguson, and the player grew from the 1999/2000 season onwards. A number of incidents have been reported as contributing towards the ending of Beckham's career with United but the most dramatic occurred in the 2002/03 season after a 0–2 defeat at home to Arsenal in an FA Cup fifth round tie. After the game there was a dressing room row in which Beckham was blamed for the defeat by Ferguson who in the course of a heated exchange of views kicked a boot in Beckham's direction causing a cut above his eye. The following day's newspapers had front page photographs of the eye wound and accounts of the 'dressing room flare up' (Roberts et al. 2003) and while Beckham subsequently issued a public statement suggesting that it had been an accident many observers of the sport identified it as a watershed moment that signified things would never be the same again between manager and player.

Beckham's move to Real Madrid in 2003 attracted a great deal of media interest. The media image Beckham took with him – good-looking, fashion conscious, constantly changing his hairstyle, devoted husband and father – had led the Spanish press to assume that his signing was primarily about generating shirt sales in emerging markets. As one of the journalists on the Spanish sports daily *As* observed 'We were expecting a clothes horse avoiding getting kicked, a pretty boy worried about his ponytail' (Lowe 2004a). But they witnessed a tireless player, one who in the words of a respected radio commentator 'battles, scraps, fights, works and runs … [and] defends with a warrior's spirit' (Lowe 2004a).

The Spanish sports paper *Marca* was won over by Beckham's performances and described the player as 'dynamic', and as 'touched by magic'. *El Mundo* described Beckham's debut in glowing terms, reporting that he 'fought, ran, sweated and didn't rest, playing as only he knows how' and *As* confirmed that Madrid supporters had accepted Beckham with surprising enthusiasm and remarked that 'Every time he runs on the pitch he looks to be the No. 1 galactico' (Smith 2003). Carlos Queiroz, his manager, commented that 'David gives us the intensity of English football' (Lowe 2004a) and Zinedine Zidane applauded Beckham's phenomenal work rate and described how his unwillingness to accept defeat transmitted itself to the rest of the team (Syed 2004). On the business front the fact that club and player coincidentally shared two common sponsors notably *Pepsi* and *adidas* offered a significant degree of commercial compatibility and provided a good foundation for reaching agreement in contract negotiations over image rights (O'Connor 2003). For the club it was Beckham's global popularity and merchandising potential, especially in the Far East, that was of most significant commercial value. Given the growing globalisation of the football market, the signing of arguably the world's most famous player represented a commercial coup which added substantially to Real Madrid's brand value.

From the moment Beckham's transfer was announced Real Madrid's commercial department was 'flooded with telephone calls from all over Asia and Europe' and the club's marketing personnel said they had never known such a response (Carlin 2003). On the very first day of sale in Madrid the complete stock of 8,000 'Beckham 23' shirts were sold out producing an immediate return of £400,000 for the club (Couzens 2003). Following Beckham's transfer kit suppliers *adidas* reported that world-wide demand for Real shirts was 350 per cent up on the previous year and that in the UK the shirt became the number one selling non-British club shirt. The addition of Beckham to Madrid's galacticos not only increased merchandise sales around the world, but meant that companies pursuing sponsorship deals with the club had to 'pay appreciably more for the privilege of basking in Real's spotlight with Beckham in the team' (Carlin 2003).

On being David Beckham: questions of identity and image

Beckham has been described as 'superficial', as offering 'only image' and as coming 'across as a bit phoney', in short as perfect for our image-fixated, depthless and superficial times (Cashmore 2002). Undoubtedly what the public know of Beckham is a product of circuits and relays of communication orchestrated by a number of parties – agents, publicists, legal representatives, public relations advisers, and management organisations acting on his behalf – and those working within advertising, marketing and the media.

Beckham is undoubtedly a celebrity. By definition the celebrity is a physically and socially remote figure, whose 'remoteness … is compensated for by the glut of mass-media information, including fanzines, press stories, TV documentaries, interviews, newsletters and biographies, which personalize the celebrity' (Rojek 2001: 52–53). What the public learn of Beckham largely takes the form of a series of images that are shaped by a variety of cultural intermediaries, but there are also public performances in matches which provide an authentic grounding for at least some of the images that are generated. It is appropriate and important to draw attention to the cultural intermediaries who are 'engaged in some way with making the public image of an athlete' (Cashmore 2002: 149–150), but it is also necessary to remember that the public image of sporting figures can not be divorced from the performances that constitute the basis of their reputation and status as stars.

But Beckham is not only a footballer, he is also the face of a number of marketing campaigns for major corporations around the world and he has become a globally recognised public figure, someone whose views, dress, life-style and conduct are subject to near continual media examination and comment. From directly and indirectly football-related advertising campaigns for *Pepsi* and *adidas*, to modelling *Police* designer eyewear, promoting *Castrol* engine oil, being presented as the face of *Meiji Sheiko* chocolate products in Japan and, with wife Victoria, extolling the virtues of the *Tokyo Beauty Centre*, Beckham's commercial endorsement portfolio has provided an income that exceeds what he receives from playing the game. While such commercial involvements mirror those of earlier generations of footballers who derived additional income from endorsing various products (Harding with Taylor 2003: 258–259) there is a difference in the scale of the income Beckham has been able to generate from such activities, which in turn is a reflection of the elevated cultural significance football has acquired, the transformed social status of footballers and, not least of all, the great value the corporate world now places on the capacity of high profile sporting figures to add an aura of authenticity to brands and products.

If Beckham's appearance in advertising campaigns follows a tradition within the game, his participation in photoshoots for a diverse range of magazines represents a significant, and potentially risky, departure, not least of all because it has amplified discussion of who he is, what he represents and what, if anything, he might stand for. Appearing in football-related advertising campaigns for *Pepsi* and *adidas* represents a continuation, an extension, of Beckham's image as a footballer. But fashion shoots that appeared in *Arena Homme Plus* (2000), *The Face* (2001) and GQ (2002) along with appearances on the front covers of the women's magazine *Marie Claire* – the first man to do so in its 14-year history – and the gay magazine *Attitude*, promoted discussion of Beckham's identity. Subsequently Beckham has been credited with being a 'gender pioneer', as representing something for 'every woman: father, husband, footballer, icon ... the ultimate hero' (Kelso 2002a) and as not simply avoiding 'negative qualities too often associated with famous footballers – drunkenness, violence, homophobia, sexism' (Lemos 2002) but as exemplifying a positive alternative. Confirmation of Beckham's wide-ranging appeal is provided by an observer of Real Madrid's trip to China in 2003,

> Beckham's multi-faceted persona ... has driven his celebrity into uncharted territory. Chinese women, unable to understand his words, discern his vulnerability from the body language and demure smile – and they are enchanted by it. Older women want to mother him; younger women want to marry him. Young male consumers ... aspire to his 'metrosexual' image – advertising-speak for the notion of an urban heterosexual male in touch with his feminine side. Meanwhile Beckham is already an icon in Beijing's fledgling gay community. And among the mainstream conservative majority, his monogamy and commitment to family are widely admired: all things to all men. (Syed 2003)

Carefully considered discussions with advisers would have taken place before Beckham agreed to participate in the production of media images that have helped to shape his multi-faceted persona. It would have been recognised that there are many commercial markets to cultivate and conquer and that a complex multi-faceted image would best maximise commercial potential.

One facet at least of Beckham's image as faithful and loving husband and proud and caring father who does not get drunk and is not disconcerted by the fact that he is a gay icon was called into question by reports of extra-marital affairs and phone sex. No longer can Beckham be regarded as sub-verting 'all football's conventions about masculinity, sex and carnality' (Cashmore 2002: 128). Beckham may be a product and a significant agent of a changing turn of the century masculinity exemplified by 'men's inter-est in fashion, style, narcissism and the possibility of being objectified ... nurtured by a decade of the style press (*Arena, GQ, FHM*)' (Whannel 2002: 212). But the notion that prior to media reports of infidelity and 'sex-texting' he could be regarded as subverting *all* of football's conventions about masculinity does not bear scrutiny, for the very way he plays the game, the competitiveness, energy, commitment and unrelenting enthusi-asm he shows in matches and the fierce team loyalty he displays, exempli-fies the very qualities of masculinity that are most central to football.

In the final instance it is Beckham's performances on the pitch that influ-ence how his image and narratives about him are read and received. Defeats for his club in 2004 in the Copa del Rey and Champions League and the loss of a substantial lead in La Liga, accompanied by a decline in his own form, exposed Beckham and his colleagues to criticism for their reported off the field lifestyles. As one 30 metre banner hung by disgruntled fans around the fencing to their training ground proclaimed 'For you lot whores and money; for us indignation and repression' (Scott and Talbot 2004). With the collapse of Real Madrid's form in 2004 and again in 2005 the Spanish press ceased to eulogise about Beckham's energy and dynamic runs. *Marca*, Spain's best-selling paper, described Beckham as a man who runs aimlessly, just like Forrest Gump, and speculation about his football future and the impact of stories about his private life on his 'brand health' intensified (Datson 2004; Lowe 2004b; Milligan 2004). While this speculation continued through the spring of 2004 news of a £40 million endorsement deal with *Gillette* to be 'the new face of the razor brand' suggested that Beckham's image had not been dam-aged by allegations of infidelity (Couzens 2004; Nugent 2004). But poor performances for England in the Euro 2004 tournament in Portugal, during which Beckham failed to score crucial penalties against France and Portugal, raised more concerns about his form, his priorities, and his future.

Model tennis careers from Billie-Jean King to Anna Kournikova

On the significance of appearance

Notwithstanding his successes on the football field, if David Beckham had not looked the part he would never have attracted the media interest that has made him a cultural icon, nor acquired the lucrative portfolio of endorsement contracts that has made him so wealthy. Without the degree of interest the media has shown in him Beckham would probably have become well known, but purely as a footballer, not as a 'global celebrity' (Cashmore 2002: 81). If Anna Kournikova, had not had the physical attributes to pass as a potential model and meet the requirements of tabloid editors eager to attract male readers, it is likely that the world would barely know of her, for her achievements as a tennis player were modest.

Kournikova is a remarkable phenomenon, as a tennis player she did not achieve any significant success in singles tournaments, although she recorded 16 Women's Tennis Association doubles titles and 2 Grand Slam doubles titles. However, her cultural profile and commercial success accorded her a prominent position within the women's game. To understand the Kournikova phenomenon consideration first has to be given to a number of broader features and concerns which women's tennis shares with other women's sports.

Analyses of sport and sporting celebrity have confirmed that the institution of sport remains patriarchal (Boslooper and Hayes 1973; Hargreaves 1994). Across the board, whether it is a question of participation, resources, rewards, or media coverage and representation, women have continued to be treated differently to men in the world of sport (Hargreaves 2000). Differences are particularly striking when consideration is given to sport stars and sporting celebrity.

Where are the great global female sport stars, the female sporting figures who would be instantly recognised anywhere in the world? Has there ever been a female player or athlete who has had anything like the global profile or impact on their sport and beyond that the likes of Pele, Ali, Jordan, Woods, or Beckham have had? There have been a great number of remarkable female athletes but their impact has tended to be relatively slight, limited in extent and duration, not because of any lack of ability or skill but predominantly because of the gendered character of modern sport. Media representations have tended to reproduce traditional sexual stereotypes and commercial interest in women's sport has tended to lag way behind men's sport. And where female sporting figures have succeeded in capturing the interest of the media it has frequently been their appearance or aspects of their life-style that have been accorded as much, if not more, attention as their sporting activity.

Sportswomen have had difficulty achieving enduring wide-ranging popularity. Relatively few women in sport have succeeded in reaching a sufficient level of popularity to stimulate commercial interest and generate endorsement portfolios. The American ice-skater Nancy Kerrigan constituted one exception, but her popularity, her fame and her commercial profile, were largely confined to the local American economic and cultural context and her appearance constituted a significant contributing factor:

> Had she been pear-shaped with carious teeth, scrubby hair, and pimples, only skating fans would have heard of her. Her athletic ability on the ice alone would have been quickly overlooked ... But the soft-focus treatment reserved

for Kerrigan, in spite of her failure to gain an Olympic gold medal, indicates that her physical appearance was uppermost in the minds of those who bombarded her with contracts. (Cashmore 2000: 178)

Seductive bodies

As the inter-relationship between sport, corporate sponsors and the media has grown the issue of appearance or the right 'look' has become more and more significant. Within our consumer society the appearance of the body – 'beautiful [and] openly sexual' – is accorded great significance and value (Featherstone 1982: 18). This is especially evident in representations of women in sport where emphasis tends to be placed on 'appearance (the athletic-looking body), fashion (the trendy-looking image) and physique (the sexy-looking shape); rather than on movement' (Hargreaves 1994: 160). The body of the female athlete or player, almost exclusively in what are deemed feminine appropriate sport, is an increasingly valuable marketable commodity in so far as sports events – matches and tournaments – provide an opportunity, through the presence of spectators but more importantly media coverage, for public display and promotion of brands and products, and not only in relation to sportswear and leisure wear but in respect of fashion more broadly as it seems 'increasingly to be taking its energy from sports' (Hargreaves 1994: 159).

In a detailed analysis of the conditions encountered by women and girls in sport Jennifer Hargreaves emphasises the close connections that exist between the growth in female sports and desirability of a more athletic and toned female form on the one hand and the commercialisation of the female body and sexuality on the other. For example, consider contemporary sportswear for women. The materials used and the designs employed in making sportswear for professional sportswomen are intended to enhance performance, but in the way they frame and selectively cover the body garments also reveal the body and highlight 'sexuality and eroticism' (Hargreaves 1994: 159). It is images of the sexualised bodies of well-known female sporting figures that predominate in magazine and press coverage of sport. The relative marginalisation of sport skills and performances and focus on the appearance or look of the sportswoman transforms 'athletes into objects of desire and envy, providing an unambiguous message that sportswomen are sexual women' (Hargreaves 1994: 162).

However, it should not be assumed that the sportswomen portrayed in the media are 'simply passive subjects', to the contrary there is increasing awareness of the commercial rewards that can be reaped from an accommodation to the 'imperatives of modern consumer culture' (Hargreaves 1994: 162). The employment of an agent and the cultivation of an image that may involve sportswomen exploiting their own sexuality can lead to increased media attention, corporations offering endorsement contracts and in due course to greater wealth.

The modern sport that most clearly exemplifies the features identified above is women's tennis. From its inception tennis was regarded as a 'feminine appropriate' sport. In comparison to other sports played by women it has acquired a high media profile and in consequence it has attracted corporate sponsors to events and tournaments and has provided leading players with a significant cultural profile and substantial endorsement opportunities.

Women's tennis: a brief history

Tennis was one of the first modern sports considered appropriate for women and upper- and middle-class women had access to it from its inception (Walker 1989). From the late nineteenth century tennis grew in popularity with women and while the initial response of the All England Club to the request for a 'ladies tournament' had been to reject the idea the first ladies championship was held in 1884 and was won by Maud Watson (Gillmeister 1998). However, to play tennis women had to bear the burden of an outfit that met the conventions of the time and preserved their modesty. It meant wearing a tightly laced corset and starched petticoats beneath long skirts that reached the ground with additional support from a girdle. A long-sleeved blouse, stiff collar, necktie or scarf, hat and boots served to further impede mobility and reduced the ladies game to what was described as baseline 'pat-ball'.

Charlotte 'Lottie' Dodd who at 15 years of age became in 1887 the youngest to win the Wimbledon championship was just one player who complained about the tennis outfit women were required to wear – 'how can they ever hope to play a sound game when their dresses impede the free movement of every limb? In many cases their breathing is rendered difficult' (cited in Gillmeister 1998: 204). Dodd proclaimed that it was male administrators and writers in journals such as *The Field* who prevented changes by regulating 'not only the length of the lady's racket, but also the length of her skirt' (Gillmeister 1998: 205).

Change was clearly on the agenda and long overdue as far as women players were concerned. In 1919 it duly arrived at Wimbledon in the form of a 20-year-old Frenchwoman, Suzanne Lenglen who had never before played on grass. Lenglen's tennis potential had been identified at an early age and her parents were determined to help her become a champion. It is reported that her father 'placed handkerchiefs in various corners of the court and ordered his prodigy to hit hundreds of balls at them' (Wertheim 2002: 20). At the age of 12 she was competing against adults at local tournaments in the south of France and she won the French Hard Court championship as a 14-year-old (Rader 1983b).

When she arrived at Wimbledon in 1919 Lenglen caused a sensation by forgoing the traditional style of clothing for a dress ending just below the knee with sleeves above the elbow which caused some women spectators to walk out in disgust (*Observer Sport Monthly* 2000).[4] Lenglen went on to win the Wimbledon ladies singles championship in 1919 and again in the following four years, winning the championship for a final time in 1925.

Conventional assumptions about female conduct were disrupted by her uninhibited and tempestuous behaviour, her quarrels with officials, the forcefulness of her game and the emphasis she placed upon winning. Delicacy and genteel behaviour was not what spectators witnessed and the power and competitiveness Lenglen demonstrated led to allegations about the nature of her private life.

Lenglen's emergence marked the moment at which tennis players began to acquire celebrity status. And because tennis was the first modern sport to become truly international Lenglen's celebrity status became internationally recognised. In 1926 at Cannes Lenglen met a rising star from America, Helen Wills, who would go on to dominate women's tennis through to the early 1930s. The match attracted great international interest and was a close contest, with Lenglen eventually winning 6–3, 8–6. Later that year Lenglen left the amateur game to join a professional tennis tour of the United States and Canada (Rader 1983b).

Acknowledged in England, France and America to be a star player, Lenglen became a 'household name' and was one of the first women in sport to be 'referred to in the press by her first name' (Walker 1989: 263). Her approach to the game, her mode of dress, style of play and behaviour implicitly called into question assumptions about women and women's tennis and the treatment of women in sport and in society as a whole. However, formality and pomposity and discrimination against women continued to be prominent features of the sport until the beginning of the 'open era' in the late 1960s. The acceptance of professionalism ended the 'shamateurism' that had plagued tennis and allowed players to be awarded prize money for competing in tournaments, but female players continued to fare less well than their male counterparts.

Discrimination and the transformation of women's tennis

When reference is made to the issue of discrimination in tennis it tends to evoke memories of the game before the advent of open tennis in 1968 and frequently leads on to a discussion of the campaign for equality of prize money between the women's and men's games. But as with other sports, for example baseball and golf, there has been another form of discrimination, one that has been somewhat less subject to analysis and discussion, that is virtually ignored in many historical surveys of the sport's development, namely discrimination on the grounds of race (Rader 1983b; Spencer 2001).

Tennis has justifiably been described as 'an overwhelmingly white middle-class sport' (Jacques 2003). Players and spectators tend to be middle class and predominantly white. In America tennis was a racially segregated sport until the 1950s. The US Lawn Tennis Association (USLTA) constituted the governing body for white Americans and the American Tennis Association (ATA) formed in 1916 promoted the playing of tennis in black communities (Spencer 2001). The ATA is the oldest black sport organisation and while it continues to promote tennis for black people it now welcomes members from all ethnic backgrounds (United States Tennis Association 2004a).

In the period following the end of the Second World War, a military conflict in which African-Americans served and died alongside whites, segregation became increasingly difficult to justify and in 1948 Dr Reginald Weir became the first black player to be allowed to compete in a USLTA tournament (Spencer 2001). Although it represented a breakthrough it did not have the impact Jackie Robinson had when he signed for the Brooklyn Dodgers and embarked on a career in major league baseball (Rader 1983b). When Robinson walked out to first base on 15 April 1947 in Brooklyn, New York to make his baseball debut 'the complexion of the game and the attitudes of Americans' changed (Lipsyte and Levine 1995: 162). In tennis the colour bar was not really broken until 1950 when Althea Gibson (1927–2003), a heroic figure, was permitted to enter the National Indoor singles tournament and became not only the first black person to be seeded, but reached the final of the tournament. Later that year she played in the USLTA National Clay Courts and then in August became the first black person to play in the USLTA National Championships, now the US Open (United States Tennis Association 2004b).

From three years of age Althea Gibson grew up in the ghettos of Harlem and it was there that a play street supervisor introduced her to 'paddle tennis' and recommended that she adopt tennis as her game. After showing considerable ability she received her first coaching at the Cosmopolitan Tennis Club in Harlem and in 1946 she reached the finals of the women's ATA championships where two black physicians, Dr Hubert Eaton and Dr Robert Johnson, recognised her potential and offered assistance and support. From 1947 Gibson recorded ten back-to-back ATA women's singles championships and demonstrated that she was the best woman player in black tennis. In 1951 she became the first black American to play at Wimbledon and in 1956 she succeeded in winning the French Championships, one of the four grand slam tournaments, becoming 'the first black to win … any major world's singles tennis championship'(Lumpkin 1982: 518).

In 1957 Gibson won the Wimbledon and US singles titles and successfully defended both the following year. As well as having an outstanding singles record Gibson was an excellent doubles player and held the women's doubles title at Wimbledon with three different partners in three consecutive years from 1956. As well as being ranked No.1 female player in the world she was also nominated Female Athlete of the Year for 1957 and 1958 (United States Tennis Association 2004b). Gibson's tennis success was of enormous significance as it demonstrated that African-Americans could reach the pinnacle of the sport. As the black historian Edwin B. Henderson commented, 'Althea wasn't playing for herself alone, but for all the brown-and-black skinned boys and girls who would follow her through the door' (1968: 268).

Since the late 1950s there have been very few high profile black players in tennis and racism has continued to surface as an issue within the game.

A black male tennis player did not reach the top of the game until 1968 when Arthur Ashe won the US Open some 15 days after winning the US amateur championship. On the very day he won the amateur title *The New York Times* reported that Washington DC country clubs were refusing to let teams 'compete in a league in which one team had a "Negro" player' (USTA.com 'Profile of Arthur Ashe'). In 1975 Arthur Ashe won the men's singles at Wimbledon and since then there has only been one other black male Grand Slam winner, Yannick Noah, who won the French Open in 1983. The most recent black male player to come close to winning a Grand Slam event was Malavai Washington who reached the singles final at Wimbledon in 1996 but lost in three sets.

In the 1970s Evonne Goolagong an Australian Aborigine had a series of successes in Grand Slam tournaments, winning a number of singles titles at the Australian and French Opens as well as at Wimbledon (Hargreaves 2000). In the 1970s and 1980s Lesley Allen ensured that African-American women retained some kind of profile at the higher level in the women's game by being ranked in the top 25. In 1988 Zina Garrison raised that profile by winning the Wimbledon women's mixed doubles title, a feat she repeated in 1990, when she also reached the women's singles final only to be defeated by Martina Navratilova. It is in this context that the emergence and subsequent record of success in Grand Slam events of the Williams sisters, Venus and Serena, assumes such significance.

The world of tennis that Anna Kournikova and the Williams sisters entered in the mid-1990s was one that had changed significantly as a consequence of the campaigning efforts of an earlier generation of women players, the most notable of whom was American tennis legend Billie-Jean King.

Billie-Jean King

King has been described as a heroic figure, someone who not only campaigned for equal treatment for female tennis players but also spoke to and for a generation of women who were striving to change attitudes, expose forms of discrimination to which they were routinely subject, and achieve equality with men. When King began to play tennis at major tournaments in the early 1960s the game remained a 'bastion of genteel sexism' (Rader 1984: 181). Between 1965 and 1968 King won three Wimbledon singles titles (1966, 1967 and 1968), US (1967) and Australian (1968) singles titles, and was ranked No. 1 in the world in 1966 (Lipsyte and Levine 1995: 284). King won three more Wimbledon singles titles (1972, 1973 and 1975) and three more US singles titles (1971, 1972 and 1974) in her career. However, notwithstanding her exceptional record as a player it is for leading a successful campaign to change the game and get a better deal for women players that she has been widely recognised as a heroic figure.

King challenged the way women were discriminated against, particularly in respect of the considerable inequality that existed in prize money awarded to male and female competitors at tournaments. Women were accorded secondary status as far as prize money was concerned from the very first Open tournament held at Wimbledon in 1968 and while the gap between the sums awarded to female and male winners at Wimbledon has been reduced steadily a difference has remained. Indeed in 2004 the gap increased marginally.

Year	Men's Singles Champion £	Ladies Singles Champion £
1968	2,000	750
1969	3,000	1,500
1971	3,750	1,800
1973	5,000	3,000
1975	10,000	7,000
1980	20,000	18,000
1990	230,000	207,000
1995	365,000	328,000
2000	477,500	430,000
2003	575,000	535,000
2004	602,500	560,500

Source: Wimbledon – The Official Website

As other tournaments emulated Wimbledon by admitting professional players they followed the precedent set in respect of a prize money ratio between men and women competitors. The assumption widely held by promoters and male players was that fans came to watch the men play. In some tournaments the prize money ratio between the men's and the women's events was even greater than at Wimbledon. When Margaret Court won the US Open in 1970 she received less than a third of the prize money that Ken Rosewall the men's champion received (Wertheim 2001). At the 1970 Pacific Southwest Championships held in Los Angeles Jack Kramer the promoter offered $12,500 for the winner of the men's singles tournament but only $1,500 for the winner of the women's singles tournament (Lumpkin 1982). In response to the growing disparity in prize money between the men's and the women's events a group of women players, led by King, threatened to boycott the tournament if the inequitable distribution of prize money remained. The promoter refused to concede any ground and in consequence nine leading players in the women's game signed contracts with the publisher of the *World Tennis* magazine to establish their own professional tennis circuit (Lumpkin 1982; Guttmann 1991; Lipsyte and Levine 1995; Wertheim 2001).

In 1970 the inaugural *Virginia Slims* of Houston tournament was established and in the following year it increased to a 19 city all-women professional tennis circuit. The *Virginia Slims* Circuit, underwritten and promoted by the Philip Morris Tobacco Company, offered a total purse of $309,100 (WTA Tour website; Wertheim 2002). The formation of the tennis circuit constituted a watershed moment for the women's game. In 1973 the Women's Tennis Association (WTA) was formed following a meeting in Wimbledon fortnight. The new tennis circuit and the new association allowed women players to make a credible threat to withdraw from the Wimbledon and American tournaments if more equitable prizes were not offered (Rader 1983b). The initial response of the USLTA was to threaten the players concerned that they would never be a part of the mainstream sport again, but the success of the new women's tour, which led to a lucrative television rights contract, forced the USLTA to drop their sanctions, merge their own tour with the new circuit and agree to equal prize money for men and women at the US Open (Guttmann 1991; Wertheim 2002).

In 1971 King became the first female athlete 'to earn $100,000 from prize money' and over the decade the gap in prize money between the men's and the women's game was steadily reduced as women began to receive a more equitable share of tournament purses (Lipsyte and Levine 1995: 286). The US Open offered equal prize money to men and women in 1973 but it took another 11 years before another Grand Slam tournament, the Australian Open, followed suit. For a brief period, between 1996 and 2000, the prize money for men's events was higher than that offered to women at the Australian Open, but by 2001 equal prize money had been restored. At the time of writing Wimbledon and the French Open are continuing to refuse to offer equal prize money for men's and women's events. The Wimbledon rationale for opposing equal prize money, articulated by Tim Phillips the All England chairman, is that 'women play shorter matches' (McVeigh 2003).

When Serena Williams met Venus Williams at Wimbledon in the women's singles final in 2003, for the first time in the championship's history the prize money on offer was the same as in the men's event. But this was not because the All England Club had finally recognised the validity of the long-running campaign women players had waged for equal prize money. The difference of £40,000 between the sums awarded to the champions in the men's and women's singles events, £575,000 and £535,000 respectively, was made up by *Berlei* bras who produce a Shock Absorber sports bra range that is endorsed by Anna Kournikova. Welcoming the news that the prize money in 2003 would be equalised, Larry Scott, chief executive of the WTA, commented that the WTA Tour was pleased that *Berlei* were investing in women's tennis and that it signified that the company appreciated the value and marketing power of the women's game (McVeigh 2003).

In the early 1970s King not only actively sought press coverage to promote women's tennis, she was also regarded as a 'catalyst for social change', a significant and influential figure who was an inspirational force in the passage of the 1972 Educational Amendments Act whose Title IX declared that 'no person on the basis of sex should be excluded from participation in any educational program or activity receiving financial assistance. (Lipsyte and Levine 1995: 289)

Title IX has helped considerably to raise the number of young women participating in sport in the USA. For example, in the ten-year period from 1970 it was estimated that the number of young women participating in high school sport rose from 294,000 to almost 2 million (Rader 1983b). However, King's inspirational influence was perhaps most dramatically exemplified by her participation in 1973 in what the media described as 'The Battle of the Sexes' (King with Deford 1982). As women campaigned to improve their status in the world of tennis in the early 1970s they were subject to the taunt that they were not as good as the men and were already being overpaid. Such criticisms were most powerfully articulated by a 55-year-old former Wimbledon triple champion Bobby Riggs (1918–95) who won the men's singles, men's doubles and mixed doubles tournaments in 1939. Riggs declared that even at his age he could beat the best players in the women's game and King took up the challenge.

The match between Riggs and King attracted great interest. King was offered over $100,000 for television rights and endorsements plus a further comparable sum if she won. At Houston Astrodome on 20 September 1973 before the largest ever crowd for a tennis match (30,492) King beat Riggs 6–4, 6–3, 6–3 by playing a classic serve and volley game (Rader 1983b; Guttmann 1991; Lipsyte and Levine 1995). Reflecting on the meaning and significance of the match for women and women's tennis King commented 'I knew it was about social change and I accepted the responsibility. I was scared to death I would lose and put us back a hundred years. I absolutely had to win' (Buckley 2003).

Women who are successful in professional sport, an institution that continues to be associated with masculinity and dominated by men, and who do not appear to actively promote their femininity or meet a sufficient number of the stereotypical criteria of femininity, may find themselves subject to rumours about their sexuality and be suspected of lesbianism.[5] Women's tennis has long been suspected of being a sport in which there is a high incidence of lesbianism (Mewshaw 1993). During the 1970s rumours were circulating about King's sexual orientation and there were stories about her husband's relationships with other women. King seemed to be especially close to Marilyn Barnett, officially her secretary/hairdresser and tour companion. In 1981, after their long relationship had come to an end, Barnett filed a palimony suit against King. Although she admitted the affair to the media King did not come out as a lesbian, she hid behind her marriage and claimed the relationship had been a 'mistake'. Despite her attempts to explain her conduct as out of character King lost virtually all of her endorsement contracts and on financial grounds was forced to postpone her planned retirement from tennis (glbtq website). It has been estimated that she lost in the region of '$1,500,000 … in sponsorship, advertising and endorsements during the three years following the revelation and millions of dollars after that in lost deals' (Hargreaves 2000: 147–8).

It was not until 1998 that King openly acknowledged her lesbianism, by which time Martina Navratilova had helped to change the way in which issues of gender and sexual preference were being addressed in the world of sport in general and tennis in particular. However, homophobia remains a prominent feature of sport and sponsors have remained very wary about associating their brands and products with gay personalities. In so far as this continues to be the case female sport performers who derive a significant part of their income from endorsements are likely to remain wary about openly expressing their sexual preferences if they are not heterosexual (Cashmore 2000).

Martina Navratilova

Martina Navratilova became a professional player in 1973 and in the same year toured the United States. In a tournament held in Ohio that year Navratilova was beaten by Chris Evert the American player who would become her main rival for much of her career (BBCi 2004). Then in 1975 she sought asylum in the USA and quickly acquired a green card and brief recognition in the press as 'the bisexual defector' (Lipsyte and Levine 1995: 341).

On court Navratilova quickly established herself as a leading player and in 1978 she defeated Chris Evert to win the Wimbledon singles title (a feat she repeated the following year) and went on to become No. 1 in the WTA's world ranking. From the early 1980s Navratilova dominated the women's game. She won six consecutive singles titles at Wimbledon between 1982 and 1987 and then in 1990 won the title for a record breaking ninth time. Her Wimbledon record of 20 Championship victories (9 singles and 11 doubles) equals that of Billie Jean King (6 singles and 14 doubles), but her singles record at Wimbledon and her overall Grand Slam record of 58 titles has justifiably led to her being regarded as the game's greatest female player (BBCi 2004; Donovan 2004).

Navratilova's success on court inevitably drew media interest and in consequence her private life and friendships were placed under the spotlight. Her lesbian sexuality and relationships were 'exposed to the glare of the media' (Hargreaves 1994: 170). One consequence of which was that although she is the best woman player of all time she lost lucrative endorsement opportunities because she was gay and ended up 'in the insulting position of having endorsement deals only for Yonex racquets, Avia shoes and Thorlo socks' (Mewshaw 1993: 144). Navratilova's openness about her sexual orientation earned respect, but undoubtedly led potential sponsors to avoid associating their products with her because of fears about possible consumer reaction. Unafraid to speak out on controversial matters Navratilova drew attention to the different treatment men and women sporting figures' sexual preferences and conduct were accorded in the media, by the commercial world and to a degree the public at large. Recalling her agent's comment that potential sponsors would become silent when he mentioned her name Navratilova acknowledged 'If I had been quiet about ... [being gay] I would have had ads. That's just fact' (Wertheim 2002: 135).

In 1991 Magic Johnson was forced to end his career with the Los Angeles Lakers and retire from the NBA because he had been diagnosed as HIV positive. The common response to Johnson's public statement was to praise his courage for speaking out. President George Bush moved quickly to appoint him to the National Commission on Aids and rather than being dropped by commercial corporations from sponsorship deals 'Pepsi and Converse All Star Basketball Shoes planned to feature Magic in public service announcements about safe sex' (Mewshaw 1993: 291). Reflecting on the reaction of the media and the corporate world in particular to Johnson's admission that he had become HIV positive through heterosexual activity, in his words because he had 'accommodated' so many women, Navratilova drew attention to the double standard that existed and remarked that if it had been her the response would have been that she 'had it coming'. Navratilova added that if it had been a heterosexual woman who had had as many partners, practised unsafe sex and in consequence become HIV positive 'they'd call her a whore and a slut and the corporations would drop her like a lead balloon' (Mewshaw 1993: 291).

Because she was so open about her lesbian sexuality Navratilova was effectively marginalised by commercial corporations interested in securing high profile and successful sporting figures to promote their brands and products. As she was setting new standards and winning nine Wimbledon singles titles she was 'largely shunned by sponsors' while lesser players such as Jennifer Capriati, Monica Seles and Gabriella Sabatini 'were paid millions to endorse cosmetics and clothes' (Mewshaw 1993: 292; see also Wertheim 2002: 135). However, Navratilova did acquire substantial wealth through tennis and during the course of her outstanding career she won over $20 million in prize money. But although she became a very wealthy woman she continued to demonstrate a commendable concern for the welfare of others by 'campaigning extensively for gay and lesbian rights, for animal welfare and for environmental causes' (Wertheim 2002: 133; BBCi 2004). By being open and outspoken about her sexuality Navratilova helped to bring about a degree of change in the way gay players are regarded in the women's game. For example, when Amelie Mauresmo 'came out' at the 1999 Australian Open her sponsors did not drop her, rather they applauded her courage (Wertheim 2002). Navratilova too has been a beneficiary of the cultural shift that she helped to bring about.

After retiring from the game in 1994 Navratilova pursued a number of interests, including obtaining a pilot's licence, writing novels, travelling and playing ice hockey in Aspen. By the winter of 2000 there were rumours that she planned to return to playing competitive tennis and in this period she was given her first contract to endorse a non-tennis related product. The motor vehicle company 'Subaru made her the centrepiece of a campaign that not only had a feminist bent but was unabashedly pitched to homosexuals'

(Wertheim 2002: 135). Then, shortly before she began playing again, an on-line clothing company, Lucy.com, offered her an endorsement contract, the company's CEO commenting that 'Anyone who would say having Martina is bad for your brand name because she is gay is insane' (Wertheim 2002: 135).

Martina Navratilova had a long and remarkably successful career during the course of which she developed from a powerful but 'chunky' young woman to a lean and muscular player whose athleticism and stamina set new standards of fitness and power for women's tennis. The standards set by Navratilova have been raised by a later generation of players that includes the Williams sisters, Venus and Serena, who have brought greater power, increased athleticism and speed to the women's game. But women's tennis is not simply about power and performance it is also about appearance, as the career trajectory of the Russian player Anna Kournikova confirmed.

Anna Kournikova

On her entry to the professional tennis circuit at 15 years of age in 1996 Kournikova made a big impact by reaching the fourth round of the US Open, her first Grand Slam tournament. The following year on her debut at Wimbledon she reached the semi-finals and it seemed as though a successful tennis career was beckoning. However, even in the early stages of her career it was not only her performances on the tennis court that were gaining her attention, she was also attracting the interest of the media, and press photographers in particular, for her looks. The long blonde hair, pale complexion and attractively athletic figure that tennis clothing served both to enhance and display, ensured that Kournikova would feature significantly in press coverage of any major tournament in which she was involved.

While attractiveness has undoubtedly served Beckham well in securing sponsorships and other lucrative commercial deals outside of football, it nevertheless remains the case that the sponsorship deals and media coverage he has received follow from a consistent record of outstanding performance within his chosen sporting field. With Kournikova sponsorships and other lucrative commercial opportunities have arisen not from a consistent record of successful performances on the tennis court, but as a consequence of an image of sexual attractiveness and an associated media profile.

Kournikova serves as an ideal example of the way in which the

> The careers of female athletes are influenced not only by the sports they play, but also by the images they portray ... whereas for men athletic ability is the main determinant of earning ability, for most female performers the additional dimension of sexual attractiveness is what secures sponsorship and media coverage. (Hargreaves 1994: 206)

Eroticization of the female sporting body

If proof is needed of the significance accorded to heterosexual attractiveness in women's sport and associated media representations and marketing campaigns Kournikova's career provides it. The observation that sportswear 'enhances sexuality' and 'highlights … eroticism' and that the bodies of female sporting subjects are sexualised in media coverage, especially in magazine and press photography, was confirmed every time a tournament featuring Kournikova was covered by the media (Hargreaves 1994: 159, 162).

If a sport involving women is not attracting the degree of attention that those charged with its government and administration consider possible and desirable, calls are likely to be made for changes. For example, in 2004 Sepp Blatter the president of FIFA spoke to reporters about the future of women's football and remarked 'let's get women to play in different and more feminine garb than the men'. When asked to clarify whether he meant short skirts he replied 'No, but in tighter shorts for example. In volleyball women wear different clothes from the men'. And just to make sure his implicit promotion of aesthetics and sexuality over technical ability was not missed he concluded by stating that 'Beautiful women play football nowadays, excuse me for saying so' (Anderson 2004).

Blatter's reference to volleyball is not without significance, in 1999 the Federation Internationale de Volleyball (FIVB) ruled that the waistband on the bottoms worn by women beach volleyball players should be no more than five centimetres from the top of the leg. Add the cropped tops that are also a requirement and women competitors are playing in what are best described as bikinis. As the promotions manager of *Speedo*, the sponsor of two leading United Kingdom players, remarked on the specification of a maximum size for women volleyball player's clothing, 'yes, it was entirely to give the sport more sex appeal' (Millar 2000). The England netball team has also come under comparable pressure to wear a more 'attractive' strip, or as the All England Netball Association's marketing manager ruefully remarked, to play 'the angle of sexuality' (Millar 2000). The Sports Sponsorship Advisory Service funded by Sport England effectively endorsed the exploitation of the 'sex appeal' of female athletes by offering the suggestion that Kournikova's 'success' might be regarded as a model for all those involved in less popular sports. The head of the organisation, Simon Scott, argued that low-profile sports might '"sex-up" their activities in the hope of grabbing more of the sponsorship pie' (BBC News 2000b).

Uncovering Kournikova

From her first appearance at a major tennis tournament it has been largely from the angle of sexuality that the media have approached Kournikova and during the course of her subsequent career, both on and off court, magazine, press and television coverage and a multiplicity of internet sites, have not deviated from that orientation. And as her tennis career developed Kournikova actively exploited her sexual appeal to attract the media and increase commercial interest. Kournikova has appeared on numerous magazine covers, including men's magazines such as *Esquire, GQ, FHM,* and *Maxim,* women's magazines like *Vogue, Cosmopolitan* and *OK!*, sport publications such as *Sports Illustrated, Sports Illustrated for Women, Women's Sport & Fitness, Women in Sport* and *Total Sport*, as well as specialist tennis publications like *The Tennis Magazine, Tennis World* and *Ace*. She also featured on the cover of the 'Celebrity 100' edition of *Forbes* magazine.

Kournikova joined the WTA Tour in 1995 and in 1997 became only the second woman to reach the Wimbledon singles semi-final on her debut, the first being Chris Evert. In 1998 *People* magazine listed her as one of the '50 Most Beautiful People in the World' and in 1999 Kournikova won her first Grand Slam doubles title and ended the year ranked as the world's No. 1 doubles player. In the following year she reached 8th place in the singles rankings and appeared on the cover of *Sports Illustrated*, but by the middle of the year her ranking had fallen to 17th. Her prize money from tennis during her career was modest. For example in 1999 she made £467,000 from performances on the court, whereas from endorsement deals she was reputed to have earned over £7 million (BBC News 2000b). Her annual endorsement income in this period came from a number of sources including, calendars, magazine shoots and related activities (£1 million), *Yonex* the tennis racket manufacturer (£1 million), *adidas* (£2 million) and *Berlei* the underwear manufacturer (£3 million) (Burkeman 2000).

Kournikova's celebrity status made her popular with promoters of tennis tournaments who used her rather than more successful players to attract spectators. For example, in 2000 The *Ericsson* Open in Florida invited the public to 'Come See Anna's Serves and Curves' (Wertheim 2002: 100). At Wimbledon that year Kournikova was not ranked in the top 16 and her form going into the tournament was not good. However, the tabloid press made Kournikova the focus of their coverage, included photographs of her in seductive poses and placed emphasis in their reporting on her 'supermodel physique' (Harris and Clayton 2002). Billboards across London displayed her image promoting *Berlei* sports bras with the caption 'Only the balls should bounce' and when finally she appeared at Wimbledon, on Centre Court playing the 10th seed Sandrine Testud, she was subjected to the scrutiny of 36 photographers whose lenses never strayed far from her body. During the year she earned $640,459 from playing tournaments but her endorsement income was estimated to have risen to over $10 million with the addition of a contract from *Omega* watches (Wertheim 2002).

Sexuality and the promotion of women's tennis

Undoubtedly Kournikova has been a major beneficiary of the commercialisation of women's tennis and of the way in which the game seems to have embraced the idea of playing on the sexual attractiveness of its players. As Jim Fuhse, the director of player promotions and special projects of the WTA tour, has commented 'We're never going to stop selling sex ... If anything I'd like to see us be *more* risqué and take more chances. Look, if a player doesn't sell tickets because of her tennis, she has to do something else to contribute' (cited in Wertheim 2002: 154).

Research on the ways in which the female sporting body is objectified in media representations has revealed the growing popularity of the 'sports photography ... shot of the sportswoman which has an erotic quality' (Hargreaves 1994: 164). Some images of female athletes resemble 'those of women in soft-core pornography, where the camera lingers on the signifiers of sexuality' (1994: 164). The representation of women's tennis from the mid-1990s provides further confirmation of these research findings. The prominence in tennis coverage of the seductive figure of Kournikova personifies the trend towards 'flesh peddling', as do press 'photo calls' at which players pose for photographers away from the court. Photographs of female players in swimsuits or bikinis, or on catwalks modelling fashionable clothing have become an increasing part of the marketing of women's tennis and the promotion of its celebrity figures.

The inaugural Collin's Cup tournament held in Dublin in 2002 provides one example of the trend. Women's tennis equivalent to golf's Solheim Cup pitted Europe's leading female tennis players against the best women players from the United States.[6] But the event did not simply involve playing tennis, billed as 'The Trilogy' it had at its centre the women's tennis tournament but there were also two other elements, a fashion event and a music event. The fashion show held in the Royal Society Show Grounds before the tennis tournament featured a number of leading supermodels and female tennis players, including Anna Kournikova, Daniela Hantuchova, Barbara Schett, Jelena Dokic, and Lindsay Davenport. Reflecting on the show one observer remarked that it was 'the event that Anna Kournikova was created for as tennis and the catwalk [came] together' (Harman 2002), another observer searching to find the right words to describe what took place made reference to 'an evening of fusion' – 'Fashion and sport, glamour and sport, sex and sport, that sort of thing' (Barnes 2002). A further example of this trend was provided by Serena Williams posing for *Sports Illustrated's* 2003 annual swimsuit edition (Anonymous 2003c). As one analyst has remarked 'the unremorseful emphasis on good backsides as well as good backhands has done wonders for women's tennis, cementing its status as the world's most popular and financially successful women's sport' (Wertheim 2002: 153).

The way in which the women's game has been developing led French tennis player Nathalie Tauziat (2000) to voice criticisms of the increasing importance accorded to 'aesthetics and charisma' in contrast to sporting performance and sporting ability, particularly in the marketing of tennis and the organisation and promotion of tournaments. Tauziat suffered during the course of her career for having a reputation for being disinclined to go out of her way to please tournament organisers and sponsors. This was advanced as an explanation of the disparity between Tauziat's world ranking of 10 throughout 1999 and her WTA and tournament organisers 'Commitment List' placing of 15th. By way of contrast, Kournikova, less successful in tournaments, was 12 on the world ranking and yet placed at 6 on the 'Commitment List'. The list has served as a mechanism for committing 20 high profile players to a certain number of tennis tournaments during the year. If they play all the events to which they have committed themselves at the beginning of the year they qualify for an end of year bonus calculated according to their position on the list. Tauziat, who reached the Wimbledon final in 1998, was entitled to a $15,000 end of year bonus, while Kournikova would have received $100,000 if she had played in all the tournaments to which she had given a commitment at the beginning of the year (Henderson 2000).

The rankings reached by the WTA and tournament organisers at their meeting held at the US Open tournament each year did not reflect, in Tauziat's view, the form or tournament performance of players but rather their box office appeal, their ability to increase ticket sales. Tauziat's fears that women's tennis was determined to promote itself as a glamorous sport and was too ready to accept the idea that tennis was just another part of the entertainment business had been heightened by the appointment in 1998 by the WTA of film producer Arnon Milchan, whose films appropriately include *Pretty Woman*, as international television rights and marketing partner. Milchan agreed to provide $120 million in a nine-year deal for the world-wide television rights to the WTA Tour and on reaching an agreement he set out to conclude sponsorship deals for the tour with a number of companies.

In 1995 the tour did not have a sponsor. In 1996 and for a part of 1997 *Corel* sponsored the tour and provided $4 million a year. On becoming an interested party in women's tennis in 1998 Milchan began to invite prominent Hollywood figures to Grand Slam tournaments and in turn invited leading players in the women's game to prestigious international film festivals. Arnold Schwarzenegger accompanied Milchan to the French Open and Sean Connery was his guest at Wimbledon. While the Cannes Film Festival was being held Milchan invited Serena Williams and Iva Majoli to a function with celebrities from the film world. By 2004 the WTA Tour had 'partnerships' with a number of commercial sponsors, including *Porsche, Whirlpool Europe, Dubai Duty Free, Lotto Sport Italia, Eurosport, Regency Enterprises, Luxilon Sports, Waterford Crystal, Saddlebrook Resort, Tretorn* and *Tennis Warehouse* (WTA Tour website).

It has been suggested that for Milchan 'women's tennis is just another movie' and that ensuring prominent figures from the world of film are seen in the stands watching high profile tournament matches adds to the spectacle (Wolverton 1998). It is a viewpoint that has received endorsement from the WTA Tour's CEO who has acknowledged that there are parallels between Hollywood film stars and attractive tennis players and that women's tennis is 'in the entertainment business' (Wertheim 2002: 154). While Nathalie Tauziat expressed concern about the possibility that tennis was being demeaned by association with the entertainment business and the emphasis being placed upon the sexual attractiveness of leading players,

Billie-Jean King, when asked what she thought about Milchan's approach, replied that 'You've got to give people a spectacle' and that 'Sex is a part of it. I mean, if someone is really good looking … They're going to get more. What I don't want is it to always be just the cute woman' (Scotti 1998). In 1998 King was able to add, 'Take Kournikova. She would not be getting all this attention if she didn't play great tennis' (Scotti 1998). The passage of time would cast doubt on the validity of King's claim.

adidas and athletic performance

In 1995 when she joined the women's professional tennis circuit Kournikova was ranked 281. From 1996 to 2000 her overall singles ranking steadily improved year by year, 57 (1996), 32 (1997), 13 (1998), 12 (1999), and 8 (2000). From 2001 it has been a different story, one of a slide down the rankings to 74 (2001), followed by improvement to 35 (2002), then injury and poor form leading to a ranking of 305 (2003) and subsequent reports of retirement from competitive tennis (source WTA Tour website). In 2002 one of her main sponsors, *adidas*, expressed concern about her sliding form and indicated that she must improve if she wished to retain her existing lucrative endorsement contract with them. Herbert Hainer the Chief Executive of *adidas* is on record stating, 'More sporting success is vital if she is to be taken seriously as an athlete … She will have to train harder and then attack to hopefully win her first tournament' (cited in Fordyce 2002). As another observer of the sport recognised, *adidas* had clearly reached the point where they wanted to see some return on their outlay, they wanted to see Kournikova playing well and winning a tournament and sales of product lines she has been associated with increasing across the globe (White 2002).

Kournikova has been described as the 'world's most photographed/downloaded/Internet-searched woman' (Wertheim 2002: 100). She is always in the news, whether, as in 2003, it is for being identified as the number one searched athlete on the internet for the second consecutive year, or for being beaten into second place behind Barbara Schett in a poll conducted by *Ace Tennis* magazine to find the most attractive female tennis player.[7] She is almost certainly 'the most photographed brand model in world sport' (White 2002) and in so far as that is the case she has continued to represent potential commercial value and to attract sponsors. But her commercial value and attractiveness is not what it once was for those companies who are associated with her that have a direct stake in the sport goods and sportswear industry, those whose brand image is closely articulated with sport.

The risk for *adidas* and *Yonex* has been that Kournikova's lack of success on court may reflect badly on their respective brands and products. In 2004 *Yonex* continued to feature Kournikova on their UK corporate website, although she was merely one of 11 tennis players profiled. There were five other female players, Martina Hingis, Monica Seles, Magdalena Maleeva, Elena Dementieva and Daja Bedanova and Australian Lleyton Hewitt was being promoted as the key player. In contrast on the *adidas* websites in 2004, including their Russian website, there was no trace of Kournikova. The signature women's athlete was Belgian tennis star Justin Henin-Hardenne who reached the final at Wimbledon in 2001, as well as the semi-final stages in 2002 and 2003, won the French and US Opens in 2003 and was rewarded by being ranked No. 1 in the world, and was the winner of the Australian Open in 2004 (WTA Tour website).

In 2004 Kournikova's career seemed to be over, although she was still listed on the WTA website. In 2003 her tennis career was in freefall as she sought to cope with continuing poor form and a recurring back injury and it was no surprise to find that *adidas* was in effect quietly distancing itself from her. Kournikova represented the very antithesis of the 2004 *adidas* advertising campaign 'Impossible is nothing' which featured one of the stars of women's boxing, Laila Ali, the daughter of Muhammad Ali. The *adidas* campaign presented to the viewer a message that had affinities with *Nike's* 'Just Do It' promotional message, but it had at its centre a powerful young female athlete and a positive message for women in boxing, indeed in sport as a whole.

The *adidas* campaign stated boldly that 'Impossible is not a declaration it is a dare. Impossible is potential. Impossible is temporary. Impossible is nothing'. Sadly for Kournikova by 2004, as far as tennis was concerned, potential had disappeared, loss of form seemed permanent and winning anything appeared impossible. The authenticity Kournikova may once have had as a prospect, as a young player with potential, seemed to have gone and all that appeared to remain was the possibility of further endorsement and marketing opportunities that involved her cashing-in on her looks and sexual appeal.[8] In her critical book on women's tennis Tauziat (2000) presciently cautioned that if Kournikova achieved tennis results to match her looks then she might become the most popular player in history, but if she were to fail the system might well crush her.

Although for sporting females it remains the case that sexual attractiveness plays a significant part in the securing of media coverage and commercial sponsorships and that marketing their bodies has become part of the sport business, a level of athletic ability and performance, if only as promise or yet-to-be realised potential, is also necessary as the Kournikova case ultimately confirms. Reflecting in 2002 on Kournikova's deteriorating form it was noted by sport journalists that despite having a ranking outside of the top 30 she was the second highest earner in the game, behind Venus Williams the No. 1 player at the time. As a member of the International Tennis Writer's Association observed of Kournikova, 'She is one of the people who transcend the sport. People who know nothing about tennis know her name. She's one of the most famous people on the planet, and that's got to be good for the game. Let's face it, we're all in showbiz' (Kelso 2002b). It was this attributed rather than achievement-based celebrity status, her being known for being well known, that constituted, albeit for a relatively brief time, Kournikova's value to the game of tennis.

The Williams sisters

In stark contrast to Kournikova the fame and celebrity status enjoyed by Venus and Serena Williams is achievement based, it derives from 'perceived accomplishments ... in open competition' (Rojek 2001: 18). From humble roots playing on neighbourhood courts in Compton, a rough suburb of Los Angeles (California, USA) and coached by their father Richard, the son of a sharecropper, who had had no formal tennis training, Venus and Serena Williams quickly demonstrated their tennis potential. In 1993 the family moved to Florida where the tennis education of the two young girls continued to be closely supervised by their father, a pattern that appears to be a feature of women's tennis.[9]

It is reported that Richard Williams, having identified tennis as offering a potential route out of the ghetto for his daughters, set out to provide them with the physical attributes, tennis ability and mental aptitude that would give them an opportunity of making it as professional tennis players. In 1991, the year that Mewshaw was doing his research for *Ladies of the Court*, Venus Williams was 11-years-old and her sister Serena was 10. Although the sisters were not on the circuit, not even the junior tennis circuit because their father had determined to keep them well away from what he described as a 'freak show' (Wertheim 2002: 73), Venus had already made an impression by being in *Sports Illustrated* and on the front page of *The New York Times*.

The impression that emerges from Mewshaw's account of women's tennis in the early 1990s is that Richard Williams was carefully and calculatingly 'building a market for his [elder] daughter', even going to the trouble of distributing a promotional 'booklet about his daughter to potential sponsors' while all the time claiming to be fending off what he described as agents 'hustling' his family (1993: 206, 208). One incredulous agent, who asked not to be identified because he had hopes of representing Venus, remarked that nobody was hustling the family, that nobody was rushing to sign her up because there were difficulties. Requested to elaborate he stated:

> It's not just that she's too young. She's black. Okay, it's sad, it's sickening, but face it, tennis doesn't have a great track record with black players. Zina Garrison had to reach the Wimbledon finals before she got a clothing contract. So do you really believe sponsors or agents are falling over each other to pay millions to a little black girl who's never played anyplace outside of Southern California? (quoted in Mewshaw 1993: 207)

The tennis world the Williams sisters entered as professionals in 1994 (Venus) and 1995 (Serena) was one in which African-American players remained a rarity. On her professional debut Venus Williams lost in a second round match to the world's second-ranked player. But at one stage she was leading 6–2, 3–1 and the overall quality of her performance indicated a player of rare ability and power. Reporters were quick to acknowledge the potential Venus displayed and declared that 'tennis had a brilliant new talent ... who could well be sports' next Tiger Woods' (Price 1997). Responding to the positive media interest that followed Venus's professional debut Richard Williams provocatively announced that she was not the best player in the family and that the younger Serena 'was every bit as athletic as Venus ... [but] she was meaner' (Wertheim 2002: 73).

Richard Williams was not the regular tennis father. To begin with he was black, he held strong views on tennis, and he continually insisted that tennis would not be all that mattered for his daughters. Indeed Venus was withdrawn from junior tennis by her father when she was 11 in order that she could concentrate .on her school education. Richard Williams confidently predicted that his two daughters would come to dominate the game. But because they had not featured on the junior tennis circuit when they turned professional and started playing competitive tournaments they were effectively outsiders. Two tall, physically strong African-American women who did not conform to the white, middle-class deferential tennis stereotype, who were cool, confident and very competitive, as well as being exceptionally talented, and of whom much had already been written and a great deal more expected when they got on court, were not warmly welcomed by the other players on the circuit.

It was precisely in anticipation of the indifference, resentment, hostility and mockery their daughters might be faced with when they entered such a socially exclusive sport as tennis, a sport, much like golf, 'whose gated boundaries have been defined by race and class' (Phillips 2002), that Oracene and Richard Williams sought to provide both Venus and Serena with a resilient self-confidence. The preparation was not wasted. In 1997 Venus Williams played in the US Open, the event being staged for the first time at the new Arthur Ashe Stadium. Venus became the tournament's first unseeded women's finalist in the open era. But throughout the tournament there was an undercurrent of resentment and criticism being expressed towards the Williams family. It was reported that other competitors complained about Venus's 'arrogance, her unfriendly demeanour, her trash-talking' (Price 1997) and in response her mother complained about the tour being racist. In the semi-final her opponent, Irina Spirlea, is alleged to have deliberately collided with Venus and after the event explained to reporters that 'it happened because "she thinks she's the f---ing Venus Williams"' (Price 1997). The press conference after the final deteriorated into a stand-off between Venus Williams and white journalists pushing her to respond to her father's remarks prior to the final that players had been heard using the word 'nigger'.

Venus and Serena Williams are exceptional, they are different from other women players on the circuit in that they 'expect to dominate ... have little use for tennis's politesse and stand on ceremony for no one'

(Wertheim 2002: 74). Their carefully nurtured self-confidence has sometimes been interpreted as arrogance and they have been criticised by John McEnroe for lacking humility (Keating 2000). But, if they were male and white then, perhaps 'we would applaud their "intensity", "their competitive streak", their "ferocity". Because they are women, black women no less, they are "catty", and they are "trash-talkers"' (Wertheim 2002: 74). Notwithstanding their record of success in Grand Slam singles and doubles tournaments and their commercial success in being awarded lucrative endorsement contracts, the sisters have had to endure a great deal of criticism, the antipathy and sometimes hostility of spectators, as well as barbed comments from other players.

Authentic achievements against the odds

It was the younger sister Serena who first achieved a Grand Slam breakthrough by winning the US Open at Flushing Meadow in 1999. It might be assumed that an American doing well on home soil would have been warmly welcomed by a patriotic crowd, but it was reported that during an early round match Spanish opponent and former Wimbledon champion Conchita Martinez was loudly cheered while Serena Williams was booed (Phillips 2002). In the following year Venus Williams won Wimbledon, becoming only the second African-American to win the title, the US Open, and an Olympic gold medal in both the singles and doubles (with Serena).

The Williams sisters began to be credited with changing the face of tennis, with transforming its image, and with opening the game up to a wider public. Following Venus's successes USTA data suggested more 'minorities' were taking tennis up, polls suggested that over twice as many African-Americans (11 per cent) considered themselves to be 'avid tennis fans' as whites (4.7 per cent), and those running the Arthur Ashe Tennis Academy in Washington identified the successes of the Williams sisters as the catalyst for changing the way in which African-Americans regarded tennis (Wertheim 2002).

In 2001 Venus Williams held on to her Wimbledon and US Open titles. In defeating Serena Williams in the US Open final the Williams sisters made another entry in the record books by becoming the first sisters to meet in a Grand Slam final since 1884 when Maud Watson defeated Lilian Watson at Wimbledon (WTATour.com). The year 2002 witnessed a continuing rapid development in Serena Williams's game. After being forced to withdraw from the Australian Open at the beginning of the year through injury Serena triumphed in three successive Grand Slam tournaments, the French Open, Wimbledon and the US Open. Only six other women in the history of the game have achieved three successive Grand Slam tournament victories. What was also remarkable was that the final opponent in each Grand Slam event was her sister Venus. At the end of the year Serena and Venus were ranked respectively 1 and 2 in the women's game. Reflecting on their father Richard Williams's sometimes erratic, irrational and disturbing conduct, an investigative reporter comments,

Question his methods, question his behaviour, and question his sanity, but the man has done – twice! – what countless tennis parents before him have not been able to do: nurture a prodigiously talented, well-adjusted champion, without making sacrifices at the altar of junior tennis. In short he has done right by Venus and Serena. Virtually everything he prophesized for his daughters has come to pass. (Wertheim 2002: 78)

At the beginning of 2003, Serena Williams reached another milestone by winning the Australian Open, her fourth successive Grand Slam title. Once again Venus was her opponent. Serena became only the fifth woman in the history of the game to hold all four titles at once, the others being Maureen Connelly, Margaret Court, Martina Navratilova and Steffi Graf. The Williams sisters also won the doubles event to record their sixth Grand Slam doubles title. Later in the year Serena won Wimbledon, again defeating Venus in the final, a success which meant that she had won five of the previous six Grand Slam tournaments (WTATour.com).

Such outstanding playing success inevitably brought the Williams sisters substantial rewards in prize money and lucrative commercial endorsement contracts. After her Grand Slam and Olympic successes in 2000 Venus Williams was awarded a $40 million contract with sportswear company *Reebok* with whom it is documented that she has had a sponsorship agreement since she was 11 (www.venuswilliams.com). Then in 2002, the year in which Venus and Serena had become the first siblings to occupy the top two positions in world tennis rankings – at mid-year Venus occupied the top position but at year end it was Serena – Venus passed the $10 million mark in career prize money. Serena's career prize money total was more than $9 million. Between them Venus and Serena Williams have at least ten endorsement and partnership commercial involvements. Both sisters have associations with *McDonald's, Avon Products Inc., Wilson Racquet Sports*, and *Wrigley's Doublemint*. Venus has a contract with *Reebok* and a partnership with *Wilsons Leather* for whom she designs leather and suede apparel. In addition Venus established an interior design company *V Starr Interiors* that specialises in residential design. Serena received a lucrative contract, reported to be worth £30 million, from *Nike* towards the end of 2003 (Flatman 2004) and she holds another personal endorsement contract with *Close-Up* (www.serenawilliams.com). Their websites enjoy the benefits of *Tennis Photo Library* and they receive support from the *WTA Tour*.

Between them the Williams sisters have collected numerous awards. These include *WTA Tour* Player of the Year and *ESPY* awards for 'Best Female Athlete' and 'Best Female Tennis Player' for Venus in 2000 and 2002 respectively and for Serena in 2002 and 2003 respectively.[10] In 2003 Venus was ranked No. 4 and Serena was ranked No. 1 in a poll of 60 marketers, sponsorship consultants and media organisations that produced a 'Top 10 Most-Marketable Female Athletes' listing. Both sisters were listed in 2000 in *Forbes Magazine* 'Power 100 in Fame and Fortune', Venus being listed at 62 and Serena at 68. Only five female athletes made the list and all were tennis players, the others being Martina Hingis (51), Anna Kournikova (58) and Monica Seles (66). The ranking of individuals is a composite of a number of attributes, including earnings, number of website hits, press clips and frequency of television coverage. Venus and Serena Williams maintained a place on the *Forbes* 'Power 100' from 2000 through to 2003, as did Anna Kournikova and Martina Hingis and a significant number of high profile male sporting figures, including Michael Jordan and Tiger Woods.

Over the period 2000–34 Michael Jordan's rankings were 5, 6, 9, 13 and 7 respectively. Tiger Woods was ranked 7, 2, 2, 3 and 2 respectively. In contrast Anna Kournikova was ranked 58, 54, 67, 70 and 82, Venus Williams 62, 57, 60, 65 and 77 and Serena Williams 68, 71, 72, 60 and 63. In 2003 David Beckham was listed for the first time at 56 but in 2004 was ranked at 22 (www.forbes.com). Few female sporting figures appear on the Forbes list. There were no more than five listed in any one year between 2000 and 2003 and, with the exception of golfer Annika Sorenstam in 2003, all were tennis players. In contrast a large number of male sporting figures from a variety of sports fields made the list in each of the years in question.

The Williams sisters made a significant impact on the world of tennis in the early years of the current century and they have been rewarded with lucrative commercial contracts and a significant level of media attention. An early sign of their rising celebrity status came with their inclusion in an episode of *The Simpsons* animated television show (2001). The celebrity status of the sisters has been further confirmed by their appearances on Oprah Winfrey's NBC talk show (2002) and David Letterman's CBS Late Show (2003), as well as by their co-presentation of an award at the MTV Video Music Awards (2003). Venus Williams has developed her interests in fashion and interior design and Serena Williams has pursued her interests in fashion and clothes design and has made cameo appearances in music videos, television dramas, and a film, 'Beauty Shop', starring Queen Latifah (WTATour.com).

Both Venus and Serena Williams sustained injuries in 2003 that kept them away from the tennis circuit for several months and this contributed to their mid-year 2004 WTA rankings of 8 and 10 respectively. Predictably, given the range of their interests beyond tennis, there has been media speculation about how long they will continue to play the game. What is beyond question is that their on court performances have added a new dimension to women's tennis and that their pride in their heritage and racial identity and the way they have conducted themselves when faced with the antipathy of white middle-class tennis crowds has elevated them to the status of role models within the black community (Spencer 2001; Jacques 2003).

Tennis has been described by Billie-Jean King as '*the* sport for females' (1982: 188). The cultural profile of women's tennis is certainly higher than any other women's sport and this is reflected in the celebrity status and commercial value accorded to prominent and successful female tennis players. As Serena Williams is reported to have remarked, 'Women's tennis is where it's at' (cited in Wertheim 2002: 6). It is the one women's sport that has consistently attracted a relatively significant degree of media interest and coverage and that has continually produced players who have been accorded celebrity status, players who have transcended their sport and become known even to those who have little if any interest in tennis. However, to date, even the heroic, highly successful and celebrity figures from the world of women's tennis have been unable to match the global cultural appeal and commercial success enjoyed by the likes of Michael Jordan, Tiger Woods and David Beckham.

Notes

1 As one International Sports and Leisure group executive charged with the responsibility of overseeing the marketing package for the 1988 Olympics is reputed to have commented,

> There are ... only four things that travel across borders: sport, music, violence and sex. And it's difficult to find sponsors for violence and sex'. (cited in Aris 1990: 169)

2 Until 1982 there were only three television channels in Britain, (BBC 1, BBC 2 and ITV) and the emergence in that year of Channel 4 was merely a modest expansion, initially representing a commercial equivalent to the minority status BBC 2 channel established in 1964. With BBC and ITV exercising a monopoly over the broadcasting of major sport events, to have any sport profile Channel 4 had to resort to the broadcasting of what were regarded as minority sports in Britain – swimming, cycling, road-running, Australian rules football, American baseball and Japanese sumo wrestling (Aris 1990).

3 In 1992 Falk left the ProServ agency to set up Falk Associates Management Enterprises and Jordan duly followed him (http://sikanwang.hypermart.net/michael_jordan.html)

4 Suzanne Lenglen is frequently identified as the first figure to have broken tennis dress conventions at a major tournament. However, the Californian player May Sutton, who became the first American to win a singles championship at Wimbledon in 1905, has been credited with not only signalling a transition in the nature and style of women's tennis – 'strong forehands, an overhead, mannish serve, and great footwork' – but also with pioneering 'women's emancipation from medieval sports attire' by wearing 'shorter skirts, fewer petticoats, rolled up sleeves and avoidance of high collared shirtwaists' (Lumpkin 1982: 513).

5 The awareness on the part of women tennis players of this state of affairs is illustrated by Chris Evert's recollection in 1994 of how she sought to present herself:

> 'I went out of my way to appear feminine ... I didn't really want to be considered a woman athlete the way that women athletes were in those days, because they were masculine and that was a bad word, twenty to twenty-five years ago. You know, masculinity for a woman meant muscles and strength and that just wasn't feminine and I was afraid of it'. (Lipsyte and Levine 1995: 344)

6 The Solheim Cup was established in 1990 by Karsten and Louise Solheim. It is an international golf competition for women, played biennially, and featuring the top European-born players from the Evian Ladies European Tour and the top US-born players from the Ladies Professional Golf Association. The format is similar to the Ryder Cup (http://www.solheimcup.com/)

7 See two website articles, 'Anna's the best on net' at http://www.askmen.co.uk/toys/entertainment/54b_gossip.html and 'Schett beats Kournikova in best-looking poll' at http://www.ananova.com/news/story/sm_326264.html?menu=

8 The most telling example being Kournikova's acceptance in 2003 to become a tourism ambassador for a Thai resort known for its sex industry. See 'Anna Kournikova to be ambassador for "sex industry" resort', http://www.ananova.com/news/story/sm_809105.html

9 The role of fathers in the tennis careers of their daughters raises interesting and controversial issues. In his study of the women's tennis tour in the early 1990s Michael Mewshaw identified a significant number of leading female players who were coached by their fathers. Consider the following; Monica Seles's father, 'never a player himself', taught his daughter using instructional manuals (1993: 34–5); Jennifer Capriati was not only coached by her father, her career was orchestrated by him (1993: 29, 51); and Mary Pierce was instructed by a self-taught father-coach who also insisted on acting as her manager. Pierce's father has been described as the 'Tennis Father from Hell' (1993: 222). On a number of occasions Pierce suffered 'aggravation from her father' who would throw objects at her and after she lost in one tournament actually hit her across the face (1993: 61, 167, 172–173, 222). Andrea Jaeger was also coached by her father, 'a former, boxer, bricklayer, and barkeeper' (1993: 158–159). From the age of 13 Kathy Rinaldi was coached by her father, a trained dentist who 'had no background in tennis' (1993: 71).

Steffi Graf, winner of 22 Grand Slam titles, although not coached by her father, was said to be held on a tight rein by him. Peter Graf is described as 'one of dozens of fathers on the circuit who badgered their children to achieve what they could never have hoped to accomplish' (Mewshaw 1993: 58).

10 *ESPY* awards were established in 1993 by *ESPN* for 'Excellence in Sports Performance'. Over his career Michael Jordan received four awards for Best NBA Player (1993; 1997–9), an award for Best Male Athlete (1993), and was voted Male Athlete of the Decade for the 1990s. During his career Tiger Woods has received 15 ESPY awards, including three 'Best Male Sportsman' awards (2000–2).

7

Concluding Remarks: Sport Stars, Authenticity and Charisma

On the consequences of the transformation of sport

The development of modern sport from the late nineteenth century has been shaped by increasing professionalism, steadily rising media coverage, and growing commercial sponsorship. The impact of these inter-related processes of transformation has provoked debate and led to concern being expressed about a possible degeneration of sport (Lasch 1991). Critics have lamented the loss of what has been described as a 'play spirit' (Huizinga 1949), have identified 'over-seriousness' and the prominence of a 'spectator-orientation' as detrimental to sport (Hoch 1972; Rader 1984) and have argued that as sporting figures have been accorded increasing media publicity and have become celebrity figures there is a growing risk that they are 'no longer playing ... "for the sake of the game"' (Inglis 1977: 155). Undoubtedly sport has been radically transformed by the impact of professionalism, the media (especially television coverage), associated forms of commercialisation and the growth of sponsorship. But have such changes been entirely to the detriment of sport?

As sport events and competitions have become increasingly commercialised sport and business have grown ever closer, leading one observer to refer to 'sportsbiz' (Aris 1990). Sport competitions and tournaments are now not only sport events they are also commercial events, involving sponsors and agents working with clubs, teams and athletes. And in so far as they generally receive extensive press and television coverage they are also media events. Increasing commercialisation and an associated growth in media coverage have changed the culture and the economy of sport. They have affected the organisation, scheduling and awareness of sport events, people's relationship to and experience of competitions, tournaments, matches, teams and players. And they have transformed the terms on which professionals *play* sports and have raised the social status and cultural profile of professional sportsmen and sportswomen to such an extent that leading figures have become stars and celebrities on a par with figures from the wider world of entertainment. A significant consequence of such developments is that sport has become more spectacular, an outcome that for some critics signifies degeneration (Hoch 1972; Rader 1984; Lasch 1991).

Modern professional sport is routinely played in front of spectators, but rather than compromising or corrupting sporting values, the presence of knowledgeable and enthusiastic spectators who are able to appreciate and enjoy the skills and abilities on display effectively constitutes a collective endorsement and celebration of sport's values. Comparably robust responses can be made about criticisms that increasing commercialization and television coverage, along with a growth in promotional and marketing strategies have led to a 'contamination of standards' (Lasch 1991). Without doubt more attention is now directed towards the marketing and promotion of sport events and organisations do attempt to increase spectator numbers by offering pre-match entertainment and numerous other inducements, including 'broadcasting recorded cavalry charges … and surrounding the spectator with cheerleaders, usherettes and ball girls' (Lasch 1991: 106). In a comparable manner, in their pursuit of appropriate audiences for sport events, for which they have purchased broadcasting rights for substantial sums of money, television companies have had an impact on the sporting calendar and a degree of influence on rule changes introduced by sport governing bodies.

But increases in the marketing, promotion and sponsorship of events, the provision of pre-match or pre-tournament entertainment, and the influence of television have not taken place in a vacuum, they have been paralleled by other important changes in professional sport, including continuing rising levels of fitness, improvements in technique, associated increases in skill and enhanced performances from sportsmen and sportswomen, whose rewards from professionalised play have grown commensurately. The increasing interest of the television industry in sport has led to significant changes, including not only a reorganization of the scheduling of events but also associated innovations in where and even how sports are played. For example, numerous tennis tournaments are now played on artificial surfaces, some of these are indoors permitting play in all weathers, and such events are quite different from the game played on grass. But such innovations, along with rule changes directly affecting match play (e.g. tie breaks), have not in practice proven detrimental to tennis, rather they have contributed to the game's continuing development, constituting a challenge to players to adapt their techniques and playing styles to different surfaces, conditions and circumstances.

The idea that increasing television coverage and an associated greater promotion of professional sport have led to 'dilution', to a less knowledgeable audience for sport events is contentious (Lasch 1991). The audience for many professional sport events has grown, as has the level of understanding of sport, in substantial part because of the various ways in which the medium of television allows for the multiplicity of actions involved in sport events – movements, patterns of play and sublime moments of skill – to be viewed and re-viewed, analysed and appreciated. If commentators sometimes offer what an ardent and knowledgeable sport fan might regard as 'an interminable stream of tutelage in the basics of the game' (Lasch 1991: 106), for the uninitiated the very same commentary may represent helpful clarification that serves to increase interest and understanding, thereby adding to the game's potential fan base. Even for the sporting cognoscenti the medium of television, with its array of cameras, video replay and slow motion technologies, and expert analysis, may make possible a greater appreciation of the athletic skill, ability, and technique on display in sport performances than would otherwise be the case.

Notwithstanding the significance of the processes of transformation to which it has been subject, professional sport has retained its distinctiveness. From its inception modern professional sport has involved display, performance and an element of ceremony and as it has developed it undoubtedly has become more of a spectacle. But does this signify a trivialisation of sport? Undoubtedly the conventions associated with modern sport have been affected by changes, but it would be wrong to assume that increasing professionalism, media coverage and commercialism have been completely detrimental to the meaning of sport. Indeed, while such developments have radically transformed modern sport they have contributed significantly to improvements in standards of play and levels of fitness, in the technical and aesthetic aspects of performances, as well as in respect of the social status, cultural profile and rewards of athletes. Professional sport events are spectacles, at their best they are truly impressive public displays of ability, skill, power, athleticism, competitiveness, courage and commitment. They constitute exhilarating collective aesthetic and emotional experiences which few, if any other, cultural events can equal (Inglis 1977; Cashmore 2000). Professional sports are richly appreciated and passionately enjoyed directly by masses of spectators at events and in a mediated form by the growing number of television viewers around the world drawn to the attractions of sport coverage.

However, as sport has become more of a business, rivalry between sport teams and sporting organizations has been taking place not only on the field of play but also in the marketplace, where sport clubs increasingly compete for market share (Rader 1984). There are a number of legitimate concerns that arise in this context. These include the consequences for open competition of an increasingly close connection in some sports between playing success and commercial standing (Deloitte and Touche sport 2004). Professional sport has become increasingly subject to the logic of commodity production and now occupies a prominent place in a consumer society. With growing commercialism, exemplified by the increasing prominence of sponsorship, merchandising and rising rewards for leading sportsmen and sportswomen, athletes *may* be more inclined to place their own interests and rewards above local, regional, or team loyalty. And as with growing media coverage, marketing and associated promotional initiatives sport has become more of a spectacle, leading players, able with the help of agents to negotiate lucrative sporting and commercial endorsement contracts, have become celebrity figures. In such transformed circumstances it has become more common to regard leading sporting figures as stars or celebrities, rather than as local or national heroes representing a particular community, class, or race (Rader 1984; Lasch 1991).

On the authenticity of the sport star

Although it has been exposed to significant economic and cultural transformations, more than any other form of public life, sport retains a substantial degree of authenticity. In an age dominated by image and artifice sport, while not unaffected, has retained its verisimilitude and continued to possess credibility. In a world where the inauthentic, 'the fake, the virtual, the spun and the mass produced', increasingly predominates, the appeal of sport has grown (Boyle 2003: 4). The actions of athletes and players witnessed live in stadiums or represented through the complex circuits of TV production (selection of images, framing, editing, commentary, close-ups, replays, analysis and interviews) continue to be regarded as genuine and trustworthy and retain their authenticity. The actions that occur may have been planned and practised, but the moves are authentic, they take place in the face of uncontrollable conditions, against competitors and opponents employing their own game-play strategy. Although media pundits and journalists may attempt to anticipate, in effect script, for spectators and viewers the way a sport event may evolve, it will simultaneously be recognised that the event will take its own unpredictable and authentic course. The actions performed by players in any one instant are a product of the contingent character of the pattern of play, of the unpredictable outcomes of a complex combination of moves in the game up to that moment in time. Such actions and their outcomes are necessarily uncertain, the final result ultimately unknowable.

Sport is intriguingly indeterminate. Its courses of action, associated patterns of play and consequent outcomes have an authenticity, a demonstrably genuine quality that few, if any, forms of social and cultural life can now equal. It is sport's unrivalled quality of authenticity that contributes significantly to its popular cultural appeal. Ultimately it is through the exceptional quality of their performances, and media coverage of the same, that individual athletes or players generally become widely known and acquire star status, although there are significant exceptions, as the example of Anna Kournikova demonstrates. In addition to their popularity, their being well known, it is the perceived authenticity of the sport star's ability demonstrated in performance that is recognised to be of unique commercial value by corporate clients and sponsors seeking to promote their products in an increasingly competitive marketplace.

It is to authenticity that corporations aspire as they seek to differentiate themselves from competitors and promote their brands (Grant 2000). As cultivating authenticity has become more and more vital for brand promotion corporations have turned increasingly to sport stars for endorsement. It is not only the wide-ranging popular cultural appeal of sport stars that attracts corporations, but also what their popularity is based on, notably the authenticity of their exceptional performances in competitive settings, rooted in a continually developing tradition of professional sport that is truly global in extent and capable of transcending differences of age, class, gender and race. The qualities associated with exceptional sporting performance, notably ability, skill, technique, speed, power, grace, motivation, commitment, courage, co-operation, competitiveness, pleasure, emotion, discipline, determination, fairness and success are witnessed, are displayed live in public, in front of spectators and in a mediated form on television. It is the authenticity of such human qualities displayed by the sport star, sustained and repeated, in competition, under pressure, against opposition and in public with which corporations implicitly seek to associate their brands when they offer endorsement contracts to leading sporting figures. In a consumer society, where 'so much of what is served up to us is fake', brand endorsement by sport stars provides an invaluable, arguably unrivalled, aura of authenticity (Boyle 2003: 59).

Endorsements by sport stars accord brands a valuable degree of authenticity by association, which is why in 2001 American corporations were willing to allocate $897 million to finance them (Milligan 2004). The qualities and characteristics displayed by sport stars are in tune with an individualising modern sensibility that is preoccupied with consumer culture and life politics and seeking authenticity (Lowenthal 1961). For example, it has been said of David Beckham that he is a 'perfect symbol of our times' and that his 'dedication, style and down-to-earth honesty accord perfectly with people's desire for authenticity, spectacle and a figure they can relate to and understand' (Milligan 2004: 63).

Authenticity, charisma and discipline

The authenticity of sporting figures like Michael Jordan, Tiger Woods and David Beckham ultimately derives from the quality of their playing performances, from their records of success in competition. In turn, the perceived authenticity of sporting performance contributes to the charisma of sport stars, to their being revered as holders of 'specific gifts of the body and spirit', qualities that are understandably considered 'not accessible to everybody' (Weber 1970: 245). Such charisma is unstable, fragile and vulnerable because it is perpetually bound up with the quality of sporting performance, with the holder, the sport star, continually proving him/herself by demonstrating in their chosen sporting field an ability to 'perform miracles' (Weber 1970: 249). The imperative to which the sport star has to continually respond to maintain their authenticity was neatly encapsulated by Nike's 'Just do it' marketing slogan and adidas's later 'Impossible is nothing' advertising campaign. By demonstrating sublime moments of skill and 'doing it' over and over again and showing the impossible is nothing by achieving it, sport stars confirm the authenticity of their exceptional status, their significant difference, if not their uniqueness.[1]

As modern professional sport has developed the importance of individual action has not diminished, it has grown, as has the value of charismatic star players. Modern sport organisations continually search for potential stars, for players with charisma, those with an apparent ability to rewrite the record books and set new standards by doing the unheard-of. The identification of Michael Jordan's potential and his surprisingly rapid adaptation to the NBA in his rookie year with the Chicago Bulls, sustained demonstration of exceptional ability, unique energy level, and career record represents one example. But modern professional sport is also an institution that imposes rational discipline on its subjects, an institution in which relentless competition and demands for improvements in performance standards require athletes to participate conscientiously in scientifically based methodical training programmes, rigorously follow exercise and dietary regimes, and adopt an appropriate life-style.

However, in sport, discipline and charisma are not incompatible. It is precisely by embracing rational discipline, by being consistently methodical in training and preparation and cultivating a style of life conducive to optimal athletic performance, that the charismatic sport star is able to maintain 'alertness and ... superiority' and to extend 'his [her] sphere of domination' (Weber 1970: 253–254), as the careers of highly successful sporting figures like Michael Jordan and Martina Navratilova demonstrate. Where discipline is lacking, where athletes fail to consistently and methodically train and prepare correctly, and/or have a life-style that is inappropriate, performance and reputation eventually suffer, as in different ways the career paths of soccer players George Best and Paul Gascoigne, and tennis player Anna Kournikova confirm.

Authenticity is a vulnerable quality. It is predicated on trust in the genuineness of the qualities and/or performances of individuals that have been witnessed and is undermined by doubt and suspicion. For example, the authenticity of the rematch between Muhammad Ali and Sonny Liston for the World Heavyweight boxing title in 1965 became a matter of considerable debate after Liston was knocked out by one punch in the first round and accusations were made that the bout had been fixed by 'the Muslims' or 'the Mafia', in other words that Liston had dived (Tosches 2000). Trust generally only becomes an issue in discussion of sport and the performances of sporting figures when authenticity is in doubt, when there are suspicions about what occurred, about what led to a particular performance or outcome. It is fears about an erosion of trust in the authenticity of sport and the performances of sporting figures that has led governing bodies in a variety of sporting fields to express concern about and introduce measures to counter the threats posed by corruption, match-fixing and the use of performance-enhancing drugs (Hoberman 1992; Marcotti 2004).

But the authenticity of sport is not only called into question by allegations of corruption and match-fixing and suspicions about the use of performance-enhancing drugs, it is also vulnerable by virtue of the increasingly close relationship that now exists between sport and commerce. There is a risk of commercialisation, exemplified by the increasing intrusion of the commodity form, undermining the authenticity of sport (Goldman and Papson 1998). The loyalties of sportsmen and sportswomen to their respective sports and the teams with which they are associated can be affected by commercial involvements as the conflict between the US Olympic Committee and *Nike* contracted members of the USA basketball team at the Barcelona Games in 1992 demonstrated (Katz 1994; see Chapter 5).

Another example of the threat close commercial relationships may pose to sport's authenticity is provided by reports that circulated in the wake of events surrounding the World Cup Final in 1998 between France, sponsored by *adidas*, and Brazil who were sponsored by *Nike*. Ronaldo, who had twice been voted FIFA player of the year, was not on the initial team list submitted before the match, but did appear on a second list handed in shortly before kick-off. Brazil, or 'team *Nike*' as they sometimes have been described, lost 0–3 to France and Ronaldo's performance was described as 'slow and apathetic, his posture downcast' (Bellos 2002: 318). The official explanation given by the Brazilian Football Confederation (CBF) for Ronaldo initially being left out of the starting line-up was that he had had a convulsive fit in his sleep. Other explanations offered have been that Ronaldo's fit may have been caused by pain-killing drugs administered to the player by the team doctor, or that pressure on the player from the media, sponsor, and the CBF led to an acute panic and/or stress attack (Yallop 1999).

Ronaldo's very late inclusion (less than 40 minutes before kick-off) has licensed all manner of speculation about the role a lucrative sponsorship deal with *Nike* might have played in leading CBF president Ricardo Teixeira to decree that the player, who was at 'the fulcrum of their huge advertising campaign', should play (Yallop 1999: 308; Bellos 2002: 319). Speculation was further fuelled by subsequent revelation of details of the contract between *Nike* and the CBF, notably that there were clauses stipulating that five friendly matches a year had to be played against opponents acceptable to the company, that at least eight acknowledged regular first team players must participate and, if selected, that Ronaldo must play for the full 90 minutes. However, a Brazilian Congressional Commission of Inquiry investigated the *Nike*-CBF contract and other associated matters and concluded that no evidence could be found to support the contention that Ronaldo had been chosen to play in the final because of pressure from *Nike*. Nevertheless, concerns about the broader impact of increasing commercialisation on football in Brazil have endured (Bellos 2002).

The merest suspicion that commercial pressure may be being exercised to influence purely sporting decisions is potentially damaging to sport's authenticity. It is also potentially damaging to the interests of commercial corporations in so far as the value of sport star endorsers to the commercial world rests on their retaining their authenticity as outstanding performers whose primary preoccupation is the achievement of sporting success. If commercial pressures and contractual agreements are considered to be affecting sporting decisions and performances then doubts may begin to surface about the sport star's priorities, commitment, motivation, will to win and credibility. This is especially the case when there is evidence of a sporting figure experiencing a decline in form or there is a period of below par performance. An appreciation of this risk, of the vulnerability of the authenticity of the sport star, was demonstrated in a series of *Nike* advertisements featuring Tiger Woods that appeared during a period in 2003 when he was having a run of poor form and the media was discussing his choice of equipment and his decision to discard his *Nike* driver and return to a 975D Titleist club. The *Nike* advertisements categorically affirmed that Woods was free to play with whatever equipment he chose, that he was not a '"Nike" athlete' and that he would do whatever it takes to win 'including switching equipment' (see Chapter 5). The campaign signified that endorsement contracts would not interfere with the sporting decisions Woods would make and sought to re-affirm his authenticity by showing him categorically stating that golfing success was his priority. Simultaneously the campaign served to promote, once more, the *Nike* brand as making an empowering stand for 'sport for its own sake' (Goldman and Papson 1998: 176).

The achievements of high profile professional sporting figures possess a quality that is increasingly rare in a world made cynical by the proliferation of image, spin and artificiality, their reality is indisputable, save for those infrequent instances in which suspicions of corruption or of the use of performance-enhancing drugs may cast doubt on the authenticity of events and outcomes. Professional sporting performances are subject to measurement and adjudication. Standards reached and results achieved are carefully monitored and recorded by governing bodies. Press reports and television coverage provide additional cultural records of sport performances. The medium of television not only offers a visual report and archive of sport events and performances, it also intensifies the intrinsically dramatic character of professional sport, embellishes its status as spectacle and contributes to the elevation of sport stars to the status of global cultural icons.

Sport, television and the corporate world have become increasingly interconnected (Aris 1990). Within contemporary sport it has meant that playing success, cultural profile and financial standing have become increasingly closely articulated (Whannel 2002). The new cultural economy of professional sport has had a dramatic impact on the fame and fortune of leading professional sportsmen and, to a lesser extent, sportswomen. As the revenue from gate receipts, television coverage, sponsorship, and merchandising sales has increased, agents acting for athletes and players have negotiated contracts offering significantly increased financial rewards for their clients for playing sport. The growth of media interest, rising levels of commercial sponsorship and the increasing employment of leading sporting figures to endorse products and brands has not only served to further transform economic fortunes but has significantly raised the cultural profile and visibility of sport stars. The market does now intrude into 'every corner of the sporting scene' (Lasch 1991: 117) and the scale and extent of media coverage, especially in respect of television, has raised the cultural profile of sporting figures, made them more self-conscious and turned them into celebrities and cultural icons (Inglis 1977). But if professional sport has become 'the playground of corporate capitalism' (Whannel 2002: 215) its cultural significance and value extend beyond the commodity form and the market.

There is more to sport, the features that first attracted and have held the interest of the media and the corporate world endure, notably the excitement and emotion aroused by the uncertainty of sporting encounters, the capacity for performances of exceptional quality, the prospect of new standards being set as players and teams break records, and the pleasure derived, and frequently collectively shared, from feeling, whether as a spectator or a viewer, in some sense a part, as a witness, of an event or an achievement that has a unique place in cultural life.

Sport is truly global in scope, as is its unique appeal, which overrides differences of age, class, gender and race. Professionalism, television coverage, commercial sponsorship and endorsement arrangements have contributed to the global popularity of sport stars and to the elevation of a few to the status of global cultural icons. By virtue of the manner in which they play their sport, the outstanding ability, inventiveness, power, technique and success they demonstrate, leading sportsmen and sportswomen possess an unrivalled capacity to emotionally lift and inspire spectators and viewers. It is in an ability to frequently transcend expectations by producing moments of sublime skill and athleticism while overcoming determined opposition that the authenticity of the sport star ultimately resides and it is this increasingly rare quality that makes sport stars uniquely valuable to commercial corporations concerned to raise the profile and status of their brands through the creation of a close association with the status and popular appeal of sporting prowess and success.

Note

1 The football star Thierry Henry who plays for Arsenal and France provides an appropriate example. A very modest person off the field of play, an individual who values his privacy, Henry is truly charismatic on the pitch, a player whose power and explosive acceleration, outstanding technical ability, exceptional vision and all-round contribution during matches has made him a talismanic figure, one whose ability to perform the extraordinary has excited and enthralled fans around the world. As is the case with other high profile sporting figures Henry has endorsement contracts with a number of companies including *Nike, Pro Evolution Soccer, Renault* and *Pepsi*. The term 'va-va-voom' used by Henry in car advertisements for *Renault* was included in the *Oxford Concise English Dictionary* (11th edition) to describe 'the quality of being exciting, vigorous or sexually attractive'. Henry was also a key figure in the establishment in 2005 of the 'Stand Up Speak Up' campaign to combat racism in football (www.standupspeakup.com).

References

Adams, R. L. A. (1995) 'Golf', in K. B. Raitz (ed.) *The Theater of Sport*, Baltimore, ML, Johns Hopkins University Press.

Ananova (2002) 'Beckham to fashion new Marks & Spencer range for boys', http://www. ananova.com/business/story/sm_526716.html

Anderson, A. (2004) 'Women's short shrift to Blatter kit idea', sport.telegraph 17 January, http://www.telegraph.co.uk/sport/main.jhtml?xml=/sport/2004/01/17/sfnwom17.xml

Andrews, D. L. (1998) 'Excavating Michael Jordan: notes on a critical pedagogy of sporting representation', in G. Rail (ed.) *Sport and Postmodern Times*, New York, State University of New York Press, pp. 185–219.

Andrews, D. L. (1996a) 'The fact(s) of Michael Jordan's blackness: excavating a floating racial signifier', *Sociology of Sport Journal*, Vol. 13, pp. 125–158.

Andrews, D. L. (1996b) 'Deconstructing Michael Jordan: reconstructing postindustrial America', *Sociology of Sport Journal*, Vol. 13, pp. 315–318.

Andrews, D. L., Carrington, B., Jackson, S. J. and Mazur, Z. (1996) 'Jordanscapes: a preliminary analysis of a global popular', *Sociology of Sport Journal*, Vol. 13, pp. 428–457.

Andrews, D. L. and Jackson, S. J. (eds) (2001) *Sport Stars: The Cultural Politics of Sporting Celebrity*, London, Routledge.

Anonymous (2003a) 'Super Bowl ads at $70k a second', *The Times*, 25 January, p. 52.

Anonymous (2003b) 'Tiger Woods goes back to Nike driver', http://www.golftoday.co.uk/ news/yeartodate/news03/woods60.html

Anonymous (2003c) 'Tennis ace aims for cover prize', *The Times*, 20 February, p. 6.

Aris, S. (1990) *Sportsbiz: Inside the Sports Business*, London, Hutchinson.

Armstrong, E. G. (2001) 'Michael Jordan and his uniform number', in D. L. Andrews (ed.) *Michael Jordan, Inc.: Corporate Sport, Media Culture and Late Modern America*, New York, State University of New York Press.

Armstrong, E. G. (1996) 'The commodified 23, or, Michael Jordan as text', *Sociology of Sport Journal*, Vol. 13, pp. 325–343.

Ayres, C. (2003) 'Basketball prodigy aged 3 signed up by sportswear firm', *The Times*, Saturday 1 June, p. 17.

Baerwald, T. J. (1995) 'Basketball', in K. B. Raitz (ed.) *The Theater of Sport*, Baltimore, ML, Johns Hopkins University Press.

Bailey, P. (1978) *Leisure and Class in Victorian England: Rational Recreation and the Contest for Control 1830–1885*, London, Routledge.

Barnes, S. (2002) 'Sex sells, but is sport flirting with danger?', *The Times*, 6 December, p. 46.

Baudrillard, J. (1983) *Simulations*, New York, Semiotexte.

Baudrillard, J. (1981) *For a Critique of the Political Economy of the Sign*, St. Louis, MO, Telos Press.

Bauman, Z. (1987) *Legislators and Interpreters: On Modernity, Post-modernity and Intellectuals*, Cambridge, Polity.

BBCi (2002) 'Pele: footballing legend', http://www.bbc.co.uk/dna/h2g2/A757451

BBCi (2003) 'Real joy at Beckham deal', http://news.bbc.co.uk/sport1/hi/football/ 2999310.stm

BBCi (2004) 'Martina Navratilova: tennis player', http://www.bbc.co.uk/dna/h2g2/A594434

BBC News (2000a) 'Beckham meets Buddha', 16 May, http://news.bbc.co.uk/1/hi/world/ asia-pacific/742997.stm

BBC News (2000b) 'Anna: tennis's one love', 26 June, http://news.bbc.co.uk/1/hi/uk/802861.stm

Beckham, D. (2000) *My World*, London, Hodder & Stoughton.

Beckham, D. and Watt, T. (2003) *David Beckham: My Side*, London, Collins Willow.

Bellah, R. N., Madsen, R., Sullivan, W. M., Swidler, A. and Tipton, S. M. (1996) *Habits of the Heart: Individualism and Commitment in American Life*, London, University of California Press.

Bellamy, Jr. R. V. (1998) 'The evolving television sport marketplace', in L. A. Wenner (ed.) *Media Sport*, London, Routledge.

Bellamy, Jr. R. V. (1989) 'Professional sports organizations: media strategies', in L. A. Wenner (ed.) *Media, Sports and Society*, London, Sage.

Bellos, A. (2002) *Futebol: The Brazilian Way of Life*, London, Bloomsbury.

Bellos, A. (2001) 'How Nike bought Brazil', The *Guardian*, 9 July, http://media.guardian. co.uk/marketingandpr/story/0,7494,518919,00.html

Best, G. with Collins, R. (2002) *Blessed: The Autobiography*, London, Ebury Press.

Billings, A. C. (2000) 'In search of women athletes: ESPN's list of the top 100 athletes of the century', *Journal of Sport & Social Issues*, Vol. 24, No. 4, pp. 415–421.

Birley, D. (1995) *Land of Sport and Glory: Sport and British Society, 1887–1910*, Manchester, Manchester University Press.

Blenford, A. (2003) 'Unveiling St. David, a true icon of football', *Evening Standard*, 28 January, p. 19.

Bolton, S. (2003) 'The number 23', *Guardian Unlimited*, http://www.guardian.co.uk/netnotes/ article/0,6729,990894,00.html

Boorstin, D. J. (1963) *The Image, or What Happened to the American Dream*, Harmondsworth, Penguin Books.

Bose, M. (2001) *Manchester Unlimited: The Rise and Rise of the World's Premier Football Club*, London, Texere.

Boslooper, T. and Hayes, M. (1973) *The Femininity Game*, New York, Skein & Day.

Bouchier, N. B. and Findling, J. E. (1983) 'Little Miss Poker Face', in R. B. Browne and M. W. Fishwick (eds) *The Hero in Transition*, Bowling Green, OH, Bowling Green University Popular Press.

Bourdieu, P. (1984) *Distinction: A Social Critique of the Judgement of Taste*, London, Routledge & Kegan Paul.

Bowden, M. (1995) 'Soccer', in K. B. Raitz (ed.) *The Theater of Sport*, Baltimore, ML, Johns Hopkins University Press.

Boyle, D. (2003) *Authenticity: Brands, Fakes, Spin and the Lust for Real Life*, London, Flamingo.

Broadbent, R. (2004) 'Stars go global in a galaxy of their own', *The Times*, 4 March, p. 3.

Brown, S. (2001) 'The Tiger economy', http://news.bbc.co.uk/sport1/hi/golf/1644880.stm

Browning, R. (1955) *A History of Golf*, New York, Dutton.

Buckley, W. (2003) 'Hustler Riggs took chances with women', The *Observer*, 6 July, http://sport.guardian.co.uk/print/0%2C3858%2C4706602-108598%2C00.html

Burchill, J. (2001) *Burchill on Beckham*, London, Yellow Jersey.

Burkeman, O. (2000) 'Something about Anna', The *Guardian*, 23 June, http://www.guardian. co.uk/print/0,3858,4032766-103680,00.html

Campbell, D. (2002) 'UNITED (versus Liverpool) NATIONS', The *Observer Sport Monthly*, No. 21, January, pp. 44–47.

Campbell, D. (2003) 'Battle for the Beckhams', The *Observer*, 20 July, http://media.guardian. co.uk/marketingandpr/story/0,7494,1001763,00.html

Captain, G. (1991) 'Enter ladies and gentlemen of color: gender, sport and the ideal of African-American manhood and womanhood during the late nineteenth and early twentieth centuries', *Journal of Sport History*, Vol. 18, No. 1, pp. 81–102.

Carlin, J. (2003) 'The Real dealer', *Guardian Unlimited*, 22 June, http://observer.guardian.co.uk/ sport/story/0,6903,982602,00.html

Cashmore, E. (2002) *Beckham*, Cambridge, Polity.

Cashmore, E. (2000) *Making Sense of Sports*, third edition, London, Routledge.

Castells, M. (1998) *End of Millennium*, Vol. III of *The Information Age: Economy, Society and Culture*, Oxford, Blackwell.

Castells, M. (1996) *The Rise of the Network Society*, Vol. I of *The Information Age: Economy, Society and Culture*, Oxford, Blackwell.

Castoriadis, C. (1997) 'Culture in a democratic society', in D. A. Curtis (ed.) *The Castoriadis Reader*, Oxford, Blackwell.

Chandband, I. (2004) 'Much Adu about the minor who'll be a major sensation', The *Evening Standard*, 29 March, p. 56.

Chaudhary, V. (2003) 'Tiger's tip: just do it: throw them away', The *Guardian*, 30 July, p. 1.

Coakley, J. (2001) *Sport in Society: Issues and Controversies*, seventh edition, London, McGraw-Hill International.

Cole, C. L. and Andrews, D. L. (2001) 'America's new son: Tiger Woods and America's multi-culturalism' [revised and updated version of 2000 article], in D. L. Andrews and S. J. Jackson (eds) *Sport Stars: The Cultural Politics of Sporting Celebrity*, London, Routledge.

Cole, C. L. and Andrews, D. L. (2000) 'America's new son: Tiger Woods and America's multi-culturalism', *Cultural Studies: A Research Annual*, Vol. 5, pp. 109–124.

Collins, T. (1998) *Rugby's Great Split: Class, Culture and the Origin of Rugby League Football*, London, Frank Cass.

Couzens, G. (2004) 'Beckham brand unharmed by scandal', *MediaGuardian*, 27 April, http://media.guardian.co.uk/advertising/story/0,7492,1203921,00.html

Couzens, G. (2003) 'Why did Beckham choose number 23?', The *Scotsman*, 8 July, http://news.scotsman.com/topics.cfm?id=740502003&tid=298

Crowley, M. (1999) 'Hot air: the case against Michael Jordan', http://www.bostonphoenix.com/archive/features/99/01/21/MICHAEL_JORDAN.html pp. 1–7.

Danzig, A. and Brandewein, P. (eds) (1948) *Sports Golden Age: A Close-Up of the Fabulous Twenties*, New York, Harper & Bros.

Datson, T. (2004) 'Infidelity stories may hit Beckham's brand affairs', *Reuters Business News*, 6 April, http://uk.biz.yahoo.com/040406/80/eqg5r.html

Davies, D. (2003a) 'Woods in hard drive back to the future', The *Guardian*, 30 July, p. 25.

Davies, D. (2003b) 'Has the Swoosh taken the woosh out of Tiger?', The *Guardian*, 8 April, p. 27.

Davies, D. (2001) 'Just your regular kind of millionaire', The *Guardian*, 16 June, http://www.guardian.co.uk

Day, J. (2002) 'Beckham swaps baby oil for engine oil in BP sponsorship deal', *Marketing and PR News*, 30 April, http://media.guardian.co.uk/marketingandpr/story/0,7494,707296,00.html

Debord, G. (1973) *Society of the Spectacle*, Detroit, Black and Red.

Deloitte and Touche Sport (2004) *The Deloitte Football Rich List: The Money League of the World's Top 20 Clubs*, www.footballfinance.co.uk

Denzin, N. K. (1996) 'More rare air: Michael Jordan on Michael Jordan', *Sociology of Sport Journal*, Vol. 13, pp. 319–24.

Donegan, L. (2002) 'Old father shrine', The *Observer Sport Monthly*, 7 April, pp. 1–8, http://observer.guardian.co.uk/osm/story/0,6903,678180,00.html

Donovan, M. (2004) 'Greatest champions: Martina Navratilova', http://www.wimbledon.org/en_GB/news/features/history/champions_navratilova.html

Draper, R. (2002) 'United's money men may insist Beckham has to go', *ESPN Soccernet*, 6 January, http://www.soccernet.com/england/news/2002/0106/20020106mufcbeckham.html

Du Gay, P. and Pryke, M. (2002) 'Cultural economy: an introduction', in P. du Gay and M. Pryke (eds) *Cultural Economy*, London, Sage.

Dunning, E. and Sheard, K. (1979) *Barbarians, Gentlemen and Players: A Sociological Study of the Development of Rugby Football*, Oxford, Martin Robertson.

Dyer, R. (1992) *Stars*, London, British Film Institute.

Eastman, S. T. and Billings, A. C. (2000) 'Sportscasting and sports reporting: the power of gender bias', *Journal of Sport & Social Issues*, Vol. 24, No. 2, pp. 192–213.

Eastman, S. T. and Meyer, T. P. (1989) 'Sports programming: scheduling, costs, and competition', in L. A. Wenner (ed.) *Media, Sports, & Society*, London, Sage.

Eco, U. (1987) 'Sports chatter', in *Travels in Hyperreality*, London, Picador.

Edwardes, C. (1992) 'The new football mania', in I. Hamilton (ed.) *The Faber Book of Soccer*, London, Faber and Faber.

Elias, N. (1986) 'The genesis of sport as a sociological problem', in N. Elias and E. Dunning (eds) *Quest for Excitement: Sport and Leisure in the Civilizing Process*, Oxford, Blackwell.

Engel, M. (2003) 'Jordan walks on air for the last time', The *Guardian*, 16 April, p. 25.

Enrico, D. (1997) 'For Nike, Tiger Woods ads are stroke of luck', *USA Today*, 8 September, p. 8B.

Featherstone, M. (1991) *Consumer Culture and Postmodernism*, London, Sage.

Featherstone, M. (1982) 'The body in consumer culture', *Theory, Culture & Society*, Vol. 1, No. 2, pp. 18–33.

Flatman, B. (2004) 'Return service', *The Sunday Times*, 21 March, p. 19.

Ford, J. (1977) *This Sporting Land*, London, New English Library.

Fordyce, T. (2003) 'Beckham's true worth', *BBC Sport*, 5 June, http://news.bbc.co.uk/sport2/hi/football/teams/m/man_utd/2965336.stm

Fordyce, T. (2002) 'Kournikova's crisis deepens', *BBC Sport*, 3 April, http://news.bbc.co.uk/sport1/hi/tennis/1908492.stm

Foucault, M. (1979) *The History of Sexuality Volume 1: An Introduction*, London, Allen Lane.

Frame, D. (2003) 'Holy unexpected image of Beckham', *Manchester News*, 31 March, http://www.manchesteronline.co.uk/news/stories/Detail_LinkStory=55098.html

Fresco, A. (2003) 'Beckham upbraids airline for role in ad', *The Times*, 29 May, p. 15.

Galeano, E. (1998) *Football in Sun and Shadow*, London, Fourth Estate.

Gamson, J. (1992) 'The assembly line of greatness: celebrity in twentieth century America', *Critical Studies in Mass Communication*, Vol. 9, pp. 1–24.

Giddens, A. (1990a) *The Consequences of Modernity*, Cambridge, Polity.

Giddens, A. (1990b) 'Gazza's goal slump', *The Times Higher Education Supplement*, No. 946, 21 December, p. 11.

Gillmeister, H. (1998) *Tennis: A Cultural History*, London, Leicester University Press.

Gitlin, T. (1998) 'The culture of celebrity', *Dissent*, Summer, pp. 81–83.

Giulianotti, R. (1999) *Football: A Sociology of the Global Game*, Cambridge, Polity.

glbtq website 'King, Billie-Jean (b. 1943)', http://www.glbtq.com/arts/king_bj.html

Goldman, R. and Papson, S. (1998) *Nike Culture*, London, Sage.

Grant, J. (2000) *The New Marketing Manifesto: The 12 Rules for Building Successful Brands in the 21st Century*, London, Texere.

Greene, B. (1996) *Rebound: The Odyssey of Michael Jordan*, London, Penguin.

Guttmann, A. (1991) *Women's Sports: A History*, New York, Columbia University Press.

Guttmann, A. (1978) *From Ritual to Record: The Nature of Modern Sports*, New York, Columbia University Press.

Halberstam, D. (2001) *Playing For Keeps: Michael Jordan and the World He Made*, London, Yellow Jersey Press.

Halberstam, D. (1991) 'A hero for the wired world', *Sports Illustrated*, 23 December, pp. 76–81.

Hamilton, I. (1993) 'Gazza Agonistes', *Granta* 45, pp. 9–125.

Hannigan, D. (2004) 'Bigger then Pele?', *The Sunday Times*, 28 March, p. 19.

Hannigan, D. (2003) 'Much ado about Freddy, the boy wonder', *The Sunday Times*, 1 June, p. 10.

Harding, J. with Taylor, G. (2003) *Living to Play: From Soccer Slaves to Soccerati – A Social History of the Professionals*, London, Robson Books.

Hargreaves, John (1986) *Sport, Power and Culture: A Social and Historical Analysis of Popular Sports in Britain*, Cambridge, Polity Press.

Hargreaves, Jennifer (2000) *Heroines of Sport: The Politics of Difference and Identity*, London, Routledge.

Hargreaves, Jennifer (1994) *Sporting Females: Critical Issues in the History and Sociology of Women's Sports*, London, Routledge.

Harman, N. (2002) 'Kournikova set to reign at last ... after a fashion', *The Times*, 4 December, p. 44.

Harris, J. and Clayton, B. (2002) 'Femininity, masculinity, physicality and the English tabloid press', *International Review for the Sociology of Sport*, Vol. 37, Nos. 3–4, pp. 397–413.

Harris, B. (2000) 'Woods gets industry attention with ball switch to Nike', http://www.tigertales.com/tiger/ball0608.html

Harvey, D. (1989) *The Condition of Postmodernity: An Enquiry into the Origins of Cultural Change*, Oxford, Blackwell.

Hatfield, S. (2003) 'What makes Nike's advertising tick', The *Guardian*, 17 June, http://www.guardian.co.uk/business/story/0,3604,978807,00.html

Hattenstone, S. (2003) 'And God Created Pele', The *Guardian*, 30 June, http://www.guardian.co.uk/g2/story/0%2C3604%2C987611%2C00.html

Henderson, E. B., with the editors of *Sport* magazine (1968) *The Black Athlete: Emergence and Arrival*, New York, International Library of Negro Life and History Series Publishers Company Inc.

Henderson, J. (2000) 'Sex and the singles women', The *Observer Sport Monthly*, 4 June, http://observer.guardian.co.uk/osm/story/0,6903,328382,00.html

Higgins, C. (2004) 'In bed with Beckham: video portrait captures star asleep', The *Guardian*, 27 April, p. 1.

Hoberman, J. (1997) *Darwin's Athletes: How Sport Has Damaged Black America and Preserved the Myth of Race*, New York, Houghton Mifflin Company.

Hoberman, J. (1992) *Mortal Engines: The Science of Performance and the Dehumanization of Sport*, New York, Free Press.

Hoch, P. (1972) *Rip Off the Big Game: The Exploitation of Sports by The Power Elite*, New York, Anchor Doubleday.

Hodgetts, R. (2002) 'Sport's global godfather', *BBC Sport Online*, 1 November, http://news.bbc.co.uk/sport1/hi/front_page/2367813.stm

Holt, R. (1999) 'Champions, heroes and celebrities: sporting greatness and the British public', Introduction to *The Book of British Sporting Heroes*, compiled by James Huntington-Whiteley, London, National Portrait Gallery Publications.

Holt, R. (1996) 'Cricket and Englishness: the batsman as hero', in R. Holt and J. A. Mangan (eds) *European Heroes: Myth, Identity, Sport*, London, Frank Cass.

Holt, R. (1989) *Sport and the British: A Modern History*, Oxford, Oxford University Press.

Holt, R. and Mangan, J. A. (eds) (1996) *European Heroes: Myth, Identity, Sport*, London, Frank Cass.

Hopcraft, A. (1971) *The Football Man: People and Passions in Soccer*, Harmondsworth, Penguin.

Horne, J. and Manzenreiter, W. (2002) 'The World Cup and television football', in J. Horne and W. Manzenreiter (eds) *Japan, Korea and the 2002 World Cup*, London, Routledge.

Horne, J., Tomlinson, A. and Whannel, G. (1999) *Understanding Sport: An Introduction to the Sociological and Cultural Analysis of Sport*, London, E. & F. N. Spon.

Houlihan, B. (2003) 'Sport and globalisation', in B. Houlihan (ed.) *Sport and Society: A Student Introduction*, London, Sage.

Hudson, P. (2004) 'Talking a good game', an interview with Simon Talbot, *FourFourTwo*, No. 116, April, p. 24.

Hughes, M. (2003) 'Beckham pays £2m to part from agents', The *Scotsman*, 11 December, http://sport.scotsman.com/topics.cfm?tid=298&id=1356582003.

Huizinga, J. (1949) *Homo Ludens: A Study of the Play Element in Culture*, London, Routledge & Kegan Paul.

Huntington-Whiteley, J. (1999) *The Book of British Sporting Heroes*, London, National Portrait Gallery Publications.

Inglis, F. (1977) *The Name of the Game: Sport and Society*, London, Heinemann.

Irish Examiner.com (2003) 'Beckham said to be close to film deal', 19 September, http://www.examiner.ie/breaking/2003/09/19/story114090.html

Jacques, M. (2003) 'Tennis is racist: it's about time we did something about it', *Guardian Unlimited*, 25 June, http://sport.guardian.co.uk/wimbledon2003/story/0,,984568,00.html

James, C. L. R. (1969) *Beyond A Boundary*, London, Stanley Paul.

Kane, M. (1971) 'An assessment of black is best', *Sports Illustrated*, 18 January.

Katz, D. (1994) *Just Do It: The Nike Spirit in the Corporate World*, Holbrook, MA, Adams Publishing.

Keating, F. (2000) 'Short work and some humility from the sisters without mercy', The *Guardian*, 29 June, http://www.guardian.co.uk/print/0,3858,4034883-103688.html

Keller, H. (1993) 'The Brazilians 1970, in I. Hamilton (ed.) *The Faber Book of Soccer*, London, Faber and Faber.

Kellner, D. (1996) 'Sports, media culture, and race: some reflections on Michael Jordan', *Sociology of Sport Journal*, Vol. 13, pp. 458–467.

Kelly, F. (2001) *David Beckham: Portrait of a Superstar*, London, Scholastic.

Kelso, P. (2003) 'Sport's promoter McCormack dies', *The Guardian*, 17 May, http://sport.guardian.co.uk/print/0,3858,4671001-108678,00.html.

Kelso, P. (2002a) 'Beckham scores a first with Marie Claire', The *Guardian*, 24 April, http://media.guardian.co.uk/news/story/0,7541,689629,00.html

Kelso, P. (2002b) 'Fame, set and match', The *Guardian*, 1 July, http://media.guardian.co.uk/mediaguardian/story/0%2C7558%2C746928%2C00.html

Kennedy, E. (2001) 'She wants to be a sledgehammer? Tennis femininities on British television', *Journal of Sport & Social Issues*, Vol. 25, No. 1, pp. 56–72.

King, B. J. with Deford, F. (1982) *The Autobiography of Billie-Jean King*, London, Granada.

Kirsch, G. B. (1999) 'The Americanization of golf: 1888–1914', in Science and Golf III: Proceedings of the 1998 World Scientific Congress of Golf, Champaign, IL, pp. 330–336.

Klein, N. (2001) *No Logo*, Flamingo, London.

Kuper, S. (2003) *Ajax, the Dutch, the War: Football in Europe During the Second World War*, London, Orion.

LaFeber, W. (2002) *Michael Jordan and the New Global Capitalism*, New York and London: Norton.

Lanfranchi, P. and Wahl, A. (1996) 'The immigrant as hero: Kopa, Mekloufi and French football' in R. Holt, J. A. Mangan and P. Lanfranchi (eds) *European Heroes: Myth, Identity, Sport*, London, Frank Cass.

Lasch, C. (1991) *The Culture of Narcissism: American Life in an Age of Diminishing Expectations*, London, W. W. Norton & Company.

Lash, S. and Urry, J. (1994) *Economies of Signs and Space*, London, Sage.

Leifer, E. M. (1995) *Making the Majors: The Transformation of Team Sports in America*, London, Harvard University Press.

Leighton, T. (2003) 'End of WUSA the end of women's football?', *footballculture.net*, http://www.footballculture.net/players/feat_wusa.html.

Lemos, G. (2002) 'David Beckham – S/he-ro', http://www.footballculture.net/players/profile_beckham.html

Levine, P. (1985) *A .G. Spalding and the Rise of Baseball: The Promise of American Sport*, Oxford, Oxford University Press.

Lipsyte, R. (1975) *SportsWorld: An American Dreamland*, New York, Quadrangle/The New York Times Book Co.

Lipsyte, R. and Levine, P. (1995) *Idols of the Game: A Sporting History of the American Century*, Atlanta, GA, Turner Publishing.

Lowe, S. (2004a) 'Beckham's Real test of character', *sport.telegraph*, 3 February, http://www.telegraph.co.uk/sport/main.jhtml?xml=/sport/2004/02/03/sfnbek03.xml&sSheet=/portal/20

Lowe, S. (2004b) 'Run, Forrest, run! Crisis time in Madrid', *Guardian Unlimited*, 13 April, http://guardian.co.uk/continental/story/0,8018,1190718,00.html

Lowenthal, L. (1961) *Literature, Popular Culture, and Society*, Englewood Cliffs, NJ, Prentice Hall.

Lowerson, J. (1989) 'Golf', in T. Mason (ed.) *Sport in Britain: A Social History*, Cambridge University Press, Cambridge.

Lumpkin, A. (1982) 'The contributions of women to the history of competitive tennis in the United States in the twentieth century', in R. Howell (ed.) *Her Story in Sport: A Historical Anthology of Women in Sport*, West Point, NY, Leisure Press.

Lumpkin, A. and Williams, L. D. (1991) 'An analysis of *Sports Illustrated* feature articles, 1954–1987', *Sociology of Sport Journal*, Vol. 8, pp. 16–32.

Lyons, W. (2003) 'EU concern over BSkyB's Premier deal', The *Scotsman*, 2 October, http://business.scotsman.com/topics.cfm?tid=280&id=1088342003

Malcolmson, R. (1973) *Popular Recreations in English Society 1700–1850*, Cambridge, Cambridge University Press.

Mandell, R. D. (1984) *Sport: A Cultural History*, New York, Columbia University Press.

Manzenreiter, W. and Horne, J. (2002) 'Global governance in world sport and the 2002 World Cup Korea/Japan', in J. Horne and W. Manzenreiter (eds) *Japan, Korea and the 2002 World Cup*, Routledge, London.

Marcotti, G. (2004) 'Lack of trust blights game', *The Times, The Game* section, 26 April, p. 21.

Marshall, D. W. and Cook, G. (1992) 'The corporate (sports) sponsor', *International Journal of Advertising*, Vol. 10, No. 1, pp. 307–324.

Mason, T. (1996) '"Our Stephen and our Harold": Edwardian footballers as local heroes', in R. Holt, J. A. Mangan and P. Lanfranchi (eds) *European Heroes: Myth, Identity, Sport*, London, Frank Cass.

Mason, T. (1995) *Passion of the People? Football in South America*, London, Verso.

Mason, T. (1993) 'All the winners and the half times ...', The *Sports Historian*, No. 13, pp. 3–13.

Mason, T. (ed.) (1989) *Sport in Britain: A Social History*, Cambridge University Press, Cambridge.

McChesney, R. W. (1989) 'Media made sport: a history of sports coverage in the USA', in L. Wenner (ed.) *Media Sports and Society*, London, Sage.

McDaniels, P. (2000) *Uneven Lies: The Heroic Story of African-Americans in Golf*, The American Golfer Inc.

McDonald, M. G. (1996) 'Michael Jordan's family values: marketing, meaning and post-Regan America', *Sociology of Sport Journal*, Vol. 13, pp. 344–365.

McDonald, M. G. and Andrews, D. L. (2001) 'Michael Jordan: corporate sport and postmodern celebrityhood', in D. L. Andrews and S. J. Jackson (eds) *Sport Stars: The Cultural Politics of Sporting Celebrity*, London, Routledge.

McEnroe, J. and Kaplan, J. (2002) *Serious: The Autobiography*, London, Little Brown.

McIlvanney, H. (1992) 'The World Cup Final, 1966', in I. Hamilton (ed.) *The Faber Book of Soccer*, London, Faber and Faber.

McKinstry, L. (2002) *Jack and Bobby: A Story of Brothers in Conflict*, London, Collins Willow.

McLuhan, M. (1973) *Understanding Media*, London, Abacus.

McVeigh, K. (2003) 'On equal terms: for one year only', The *Scotsman*, 4 July, http://sport.scotsman.com/tennis.cfm?id=727542003

Mewshaw, M. (1993) *Ladies of the Court: Grace and Disgrace on the Women's Tennis Tour*, London, Little Brown and Company.

Miciak, A. R. and Shanklin, W. L. (1994) 'Choosing celebrity endorsers', *Marketing Management*, Vol. 3, No. 3, pp. 51–59.

Midgley, C. (2003) 'Young, gifted and ... black?', *The Times*, 27 March, p. 11.

Millar, B. (2000) 'Factor phwoar', *Observer Sport Monthly*, 3 December, http://observer.guardian.co.uk/osm/story/0,6903,404503,00.html

Milligan, A. (2004) *Brand It Like Beckham: The Story of How Brand Beckham was Built*, London, Cyanbooks.

Monaco, J. (1978) *Celebrity: The Media as Image Makers*, New York, Delta.

Morin, E. (1960) *The Stars*, New York, Grove Press.

Negus, K. (2002) 'Identities and industries: the cultural formation of aesthetic economies', in P. du Gay and M. Pryke (eds) *Cultural Economy*, London, Sage.

Neilson, B. J. (1995) 'Baseball', in K. B. Raitz (ed.) *The Theater of Sport*, Baltimore, ML, Johns Hopkins University Press.

Nicholson, G. (1992) 'George Eastham', in I. Hamilton (ed.) *The Faber Book of Soccer*, London, Faber and Faber.

Nixon, S. (2003) *Advertising Cultures: Gender, Commerce, Creativity*, London, Sage.

Northcroft, J. (2003) 'All the right moves', *The Sunday Times*, 15 June, p. 17.

Nottingham News (2004) 'Beckham movie debut', 13 February, http://www.touchnottingham.com/newspub/story.cfm?ID=1088

Nugent, H. (2004) 'David Beckham nets the best deal a man can get', *The Times*, 28 May, p. 3.

Observer Sport Monthly (2000) 'The 10 greatest tennis matches', 2 July, http://observer.guardian.co.uk/osm/story/0,6903,337031,00.html

O'Connor, A. (2004) 'A brand new ball game for Beckham', *The Times*, 4 March, p. 3.

O'Connor, A. (2003) 'Is Beckham a pawn in the game?', *The Times*, T2, 12 June, pp. 4–5.

Oriard, M. (1993) *Reading Football: How the Popular Press Created an American Spectacle*, London, The University of North Carolina Press.

Orwell, G. (1992 [1945]) 'The sporting spirit', in I. Hamilton (ed.) *The Faber Book of Soccer*, London, Faber and Faber.

Owen, D. (2001) *The Chosen One: Tiger Woods and the Dilemma of Greatness*, London, Simon & Schuster.

Parry, R. L. and Lewis, L. (2003) 'Love affair beginning to wane as icon becomes too big in Japan', *The Times*, 18 June, p. 38.

Patton, P. (1986) 'The selling of Michael Jordan', *New York Times Magazine*, 9 November, pp. 48–58.

Pearson, G. (2004) 'The Bosman Case, EU law and the transfer system', Fact Sheet One, Football Industry Group, University of Liverpool, http://www.liv.ac.uk/footballindustry/ bosman.html

Phillips, C. (2002) 'Ignored, resented, jeered and mocked: a youngest sister moves coolly to greatness', The *Guardian*, 21 December, http://sport.guardian.co.uk/tennis/comment/ 0,10070,864094,00.html

Pierce, A. (2003) 'People', *The Times*, 1 April, p. 14.

Pope, S. W. (1997) *Patriotic Games: Sporting Traditions in the American Imagination*, New York, Oxford University Press.

Porter, D. L. (1983) 'America's greatest sports figures', in R. B. Browne and M. W. Fishwick (eds) *The Hero in Transition*, Bowling Green, OH, Bowling Green University Popular Press.

Postman, N. (1985) *Amusing Ourselves to Death: Public Discourse in the Age of Show Business*, Harmondsworth, Penguin Books.

Price, S. L. (1997) 'Venus envy', *Sports Illustrated*, 15 September, http://sportsillustrated.cnn. com/siforwomen/2000/sportswoman/venus_envy/

Rader, B. G. (1984) *In Its Own Image: How Television Has Transformed Sports*, London, The Free Press.

Rader, B. G. (1983a) 'Compensatory sport heroes: Ruth, Grange and Dempsey', *Journal of Popular Culture*, Vol. 16, No. 4, pp. 11–22.

Rader, B. G. (1983b) *American Sports: From the Age of Folk Games to the Age of Spectators*, London, Prentice-Hall.

Raitz, K. B. (1995) *The Theater of Sport*, Baltimore, ML, Johns Hopkins University Press.

Ratnesar, R. (2000) 'Changing stripes', *Time*, 14 August, pp. 48–52.

Real, M. R. (1989) 'Super bowl football versus world cup soccer: a cultural-structural comparison' in Wenner, L. A. (ed.) *Media, Sports and Society*, London, Sage.

Real, M. R. (1975) 'Super bowl: mythic spectacle', *Journal Of Communications*, Vol. 25, No. 1, pp. 31–43.

Rein, I., Kotler, P. and Stoller, M. (1997) *High Visibility: The Making and Marketing of Professionals into Celebrities*, Chicago, NTC Business Books.

Remnick, D. (2000) *King of the World: Muhammad Ali and the Rise of an American Hero*, London, Picador.

Roberts, B., Byrne, P. and Mcgurran, A. (2003) 'Truth about dressing room flare-up', *Daily Mirror*, 18 February.

Roderick, M. (2001) 'The role of agents in professional football', *Singer and Friedlander Football Review 2000–01 Season*, http://www.le.ac.uk/crss/sf-review/00-01/01article3.html

Rojek, C. (2001) *Celebrity*, London, Reaktion Books.

Rooney, J. F. and Davidson, A. B. (1995) 'Football', in K. B. Raitz (ed.) *The Theater of Sport*, Baltimore, ML, Johns Hopkins University Press.

Rosaforte, T. (2001) *Tiger Woods: The Championship Years*, London, Headline.

Rubenstein, L. (1997) 'Casting a vote for sportsman of the century', *GolfWeb Library*, article posted 1/3/97, http://services.golfweb.com/library/lorne/lorne970102.html

Ruschetti, P., Bleuler, R. and Fischer, D. (2003) 'FIFA marketing', http://www.fifa.com/en/ display/article,70669.html

Ryan, B. (1995) 'Tennis', in K. B. Raitz (ed.) *The Theater of Sport*, Baltimore, ML, Johns Hopkins University Press.

Scott, M. and Talbot, S. (2004) 'Beckham camp cool on Chelsea', The *Guardian*, 20 April, p. 32.

Scotti, C. (1998) 'Billie-Jean King: "You've got to give people a spectacle"', *BusinessWeek*, August, http://yahoo.businessweek.com/1998/33/b3591099.htm

Sinnette, C. H. (1998) *Forbidden Fairways: African-Americans and the Game of Golf*, Chelsea, Michigan, Sleeping Bear Press.

Smart, B. (1992) *Modern Conditions, Postmodern Controversies*, London, Routledge.

Smith, G. (1996) 'The chosen one', *Sports Illustrated*, Vol. 85, pp. 28–52.

Smith, S. (2003) 'What they said about … David Beckham', The *Guardian*, 2 September, http://www.guardian.co.uk/editor/story/0,12900,1033661,00.html

Smith, S. (1994) *The Jordan Rules*, New York, Pocket Books.

Spencer, N. E. (2001) 'From "child's play" to "party crasher": Venus Williams, racism and professional women's tennis', in D. L. Andrews and S. J. Jackson (eds) *Sport Stars: The Cultural Politics of Sporting Celebrity*, London, Routledge.

St. John, L. (2001) 'Belles of the ball', *The Sunday Times Magazine*, 4 February, pp. 16–23.

Stevens, M. (2000) 'Is race why first US pro has been nearly forgotten?', *Florida Golf News*, May, http://www.floridagolfmagazine.com/teetimespast/may2000.html

Stodghill, R. and Grover, R. (1997) 'Tiger, Inc.', *Business Week*, Issue 3524, pp. 32–36.

Strasser, J. B. and Becklund, L. (1993) *Swoosh: The Unauthorized Story of Nike and the Men Who Played There*, New York, HarperBusiness.

Stubbs, P. (ed.) (2004) 'Gilliam's 2002 Nike ad', *Dreams*, http://www.smart.co.uk/dreams/tgnike.htm

Sugden, J. and Tomlinson, A. (1998) *FIFA and the Contest for World Football: Who Rules the Peoples' Game?* Cambridge, Polity Press.

Syed, M. (2004) 'Time to admit that Beckham is one of the Real greats', *The Times*, 16 March, p. 42.

Syed, M. (2003) 'Beckham explores new frontiers of fame', *The Times*, 1 August, pp. 44–45.

Szep, J. (2003) 'Beckham brings Asian treasure', *xtramsn sport*, 14 June, http://www.xtramsn.com/sport/0,,3951-2448817,00.html

Szymanski, S. and Kuypers, T. (2000) *Winners and Losers: The Business Strategy of Football*, Harmondsworth, Penguin.

Tarshis, B. (1972) 'The harlem boys of summer', *Saturday Review*, 30 September.

Tauziat, N. (2000) *Les Dessous du Tennis Feminin*, Paris, Editions Plon.

Taylor, D. (2000) 'United put finishing touches to £300m kit deal', The *Guardian*, 4 November, http://football.guardian.co.uk/print/0,3858,4086036-103,00.html

Timms, D. (2003) 'Fuller scores Beckham brand deal', The Guardian, 24 July, http://media.guardian.co.uk/print/0,3858,4718729-105237,00.html

Tosches, N. (2000) *The Devil and Sonny Liston*, Boston, Little Brown & Co.

United States Tennis Association (2004a) 'American Tennis association maintains its vitality', http://www.usta.com/misc_pages/custom.sps?iType=1927&icustompageid=5785

United States Tennis Association (2004b) 'Althea Gibson', http://www.usta.com/misc_pages/custom.sps?iType=1927&icustompageid=5792

Vande Berg, L. R. (1998) 'The sports hero meets mediated celebrityhood', in L. A. Wenner (ed.) *MediaSport*, London, Routledge.

Walker, A. (1970) *Stardom: The Hollywood Phenomenon*, New York, Stein and Day.

Walker, H. (1989) 'Lawn tennis', in T. Mason (ed.) *Sport in Britain: A Social History*, Cambridge University Press, Cambridge.

Wallace, S. (2003) 'Beckham obsession irks United', *Sport.telegraph*, 23 July, http://www.sport.telegraph.co.uk/sport/main.jhtml?xml=/sport/2003/07/23/sfnman23.xml

Walvin, J. (1994) *The People's Game*, revised edition, Edinburgh, Mainstream.

Wapshott, N. (2003) 'OK, he plays soccer … what does she do?', *The Times*, 4 June, pp. 6–7.

Weber, M. (1970) *From Max Weber: Essays in Sociology*, London, Routledge & Kegan Paul.

Wenner, L. A. (ed.) (1998) *MediaSport*, London, Routledge.

Wenner, L. A. (ed.) (1989) *Media, Sports and Society*, London, Sage.

Wertheim, L. J. (2002) *Venus Envy: Power Games, Teenage Vixens, and Million-Dollar Egos on the Women's Tennis Tour*, New York, Perennial.

Whannel, G. (2002) *Media Sport Stars: Masculinities and Moralities*, London, Routledge.

Whannel, G. (2001) 'Punishment, redemption and celebration in the popular press: the case of David Beckham', in D. L. Andrews and S. J. Jackson (eds) *Sport Stars: The Cultural Politics of Sporting Celebrity*, London, Routledge.

Whannel, G. (1992) *Fields in Vision: Television Sport and Cultural Transformation*, London, Routledge.

Whannel, G. (1983) *Blowing the Whistle: The Politics of Sport*, London, Pluto.

White, J. (2002) 'Kournikova's sponsors finally discover that beauty will only ever be skin deep', The *Guardian*, 4 April, http://sport.guardian.co.uk/columnists/story/0,10260,678430,00.html

Whiting, R. (1989) *You've Gotta Have Wa: When Two Cultures Collide on the Baseball Diamond*, London, Collier-Macmillan.

Whitson, D. (1998) 'Circuits of promotion: media, marketing and the globalization of sport', in Wenner, L. A. (ed.) *MediaSport*, London, Routledge.

Williams, J. (1994) 'The local and the global in English soccer and the rise of satellite television', *Sociology of Sport Journal*, Vol. 11, pp. 376–397.

Wimbledon Official Website 'The championships: prize money, 1968–2004', http://year-round.wimbledon.org/en_GB/about/championships/prize_moneyhistory.html

Wolverton, B. (1998) 'Women's tennis: volley of the dolls', *BusinessWeek*, August, http://yahoo.businessweek.com/1998/33/b3591097.htm

WTA Tour.com 'The WTA Tour Story', http://www.wtatour.com/thewtatour/stories/toustory.asp

Yallop, D. (1999) *How They Stole the Game*, London, Poetic Publishing.

Yesalis, C. E. and Cowart, V. E. (1998) *The Steroids Game: An Expert's Inside Look at Anabolic Steroid Use in Sports*, Champaign, IL, Human Kinetics.

Index